THE GREAT IRISH FAMINE

EDITED BY
CATHAL PÓIRTÉIR

THE THOMAS DAVIS LECTURE SERIES
General Editor: Michael Littleton

Published in association with
RADIO TELEFÍS ÉIREANN

MERCIER PRESS

MERCIER PRESS
PO Box 5, 5 French Church Street, Cork
16 Hume Street, Dublin 2

A CIP is available for this book from the British Library

ISBN 1 85635 111 4

10 9 8 7 6 5 4 3

Acknowledgement

The editor and publisher would like to thank Carcanet Press Ltd. and W.W. Norton and Company, Inc. for permission to reproduce excerpts from *Outside History: Selected Poems 1980-1990* by Eavan Boland, Copyright © 1990 by Eavan Boland.

Printed in Ireland by Colour Books Ltd.

CONTENTS

THE CONTRIBUTORS

Cathal Póirtéir is a graduate of University College Dublin. He is a Senior Radio Producer in RTÉ where he works on current affairs and features programmes. His forthcoming publications on the Famine include *Famine Echoes* (Gill and Macmillan), a radio folk history of the Famine, *Gnéithe den Ghorta* (Coiscéim), a series of lectures for Raidio na Gaeltachta; and *Glórtha ón Ghorta* (Coiscéim), the Irish language folklore of the famine.

Kevin Whelan is the Bicentennial Research Fellow at the Royal Irish Academy in Dublin. He has written extensively on eighteenth- and early nineteenth-century Ireland, emphasising the interplay between environment, economy, society and culture. He has recently co-edited *The United Irishmen: Radicalism, Rebellion and Revolution* (Lilliput Press, 1993). His collected essays will be published by Field Day in conjunction with Notre Dame Press.

S. J. Connolly is Reader in History at the University of Ulster at Coleraine. He has written *Priests and People in Pre-Famine Ireland 1780–1845* (Dublin, 1982), *Religion and Society in Nineteenth-Century Ireland* (Dundalk, 1985), and *Religion, Law and Power: The Making of Protestant Ireland 1660–1760* (Oxford, 1992). He is currently editing the *Oxford Companion to Irish History*.

David Dickson is Senior Lecturer in the Department of Modern History, and Fellow of Trinity College Dublin. Recent publications include *The United Irishmen: Radicalism, Republicanism, Rebellion* (co-edited with Kevin Whelan and Dáire Keogh).

E. Margaret Crawford is a Senior Research Officer at Queen's University Belfast. She edited *Famine – the Irish Experience, 900–1900* and has written numerous articles on medical and dietary aspects of the Great Famine.

Larry Geary is a history graduate of UCC. He has worked in Irish, British and Australian universities, and is currently a Wellcome Research Fellow in the History of Medicine at the Royal College of Surgeons in Ireland, where he is writing a history of medical charities and the poor law medical service in Ireland.

Christine Kinealy is a graduate of Trinity College Dublin. She is a Fellow of the University of Liverpool and lectures in Irish and British history. Her re-assessment of the famine, *This Great Calamity. The Irish Famine 1845–52* was published by Gill and Macmillan in November 1994 .

Peter Gray was born in Belfast in 1965 and educated there and at Cambridge University. He completed his doctoral thesis, on the politics of land during the Great Famine, in 1992. He is currently a British Academy post-doctoral fellow at Downing College, Cambridge.

Mary E. Daly is Associate Professor of Modern Irish History at University College Dublin and co-editor of the journal *Irish Economic and Social History*. Her publications include *The Famine in Ireland* (Dublin, 1986) and *Industrial Development and Irish National Identity 1922–39* (Dublin, 1992). She is currently finishing a history of the Department of the Environment.

Irene Whelan was educated at University College Galway and the University of Wisconsin–Madison, from which she holds M.A. and Ph.D. degrees. She received the Newcombe Fellowship from the Woodrow Wilson Foundation for her doctoral work on Irish evangelicalism in the late eighteenth and early nineteenth centuries and she is currently employed as an assistant professor of history at Manhattanville College in Purchase, New York.

James S. Donnelly, Jr, is the author of *Landlord and Tenant in Nineteenth-Century Ireland* (1973), *The Land of the People of Nineteenth-Century Cork* (1975), and the new chapters on the Great Famine in Volume V, Part I, of *A New History of Ireland*

(1989). With Samuel Clark, he is the co-editor of *Irish Peasants* (1983). He is currently writing a book on Knock Shrine and the cult of Mary in modern Irish Catholicism. A past President of the American Conference for Irish Studies, he is Professor of History at the University of Wisconsin–Madison.

David Fitzpatrick is Associate Professor of Modern History at Trinity College, Dublin. His Book *Oceans of Consolation: Personal Accounts of Irish Migration to Australia* was published in 1995.

Patrick Hickey, C.C, is curate in the parish of Drimoleague/ Drinagh, Co. Cork. He is a graduate of St Patrick's College, Maynooth, Salamanca and University College Cork. His thesis was 'A Study of four peninsular parishes in west Cork, 1796–1855', M.A., UCC, (1980). He has contributed to P. Flanagan and C.G. Buttimer, *Cork, History and Society,* (Dublin), 1993.

Tim P. O'Neill is a lecturer in Modern Irish History in University College Dublin. The author of many articles on nineteenth-century poverty and public health, he was born in County Offaly and is married with four children.

Margaret Kelleher lectures in English in Mater Dei Institute of Education, Dublin. She has written a number of articles on Irish and Bengali Famine literature; her comparative study of representations of women in Famine literature, *The Feminization of Famine,* is forthcoming.

Cormac Ó Gráda teaches economics and economic history at University College Dublin. His latest books are *Ireland: A New Economic History 1780–1939* (Oxford University Press, 1994) and *An Drochsaol: Béaloideas agus Amhráin* (Coiscéim, 1994).

INTRODUCTION

CATHAL PÓIRTÉIR

THIS THOMAS DAVIS LECTURE SERIES is to mark the arrival of the potato blight in Ireland in 1845 and the Great Famine which followed.

One hundred and fifty years ago, in the late summer of 1845, the fungus *phytopthora infestans* struck Ireland for the first time causing potato blight. Repeated failures of the potato crop led to the deaths of one million people in the next five years and two million more fled the country in the ten years following the first blight. It was a watershed in Irish history and the last major European famine.

The nutritious potato had been the mainstay of the agricultural labourers and cottier class and dominated the diets of at least one-third of the population. When the blight hit the first year it was a disaster for those who depended on it. When the blight returned in the following years it meant death for many of those who were already living precariously at subsistence level, and emigration for those who had the resources to flee disease, death and poverty.

The British government was faced with a disaster on a massive scale. Although famines had occurred many times in Ireland, the unforeseen nature of the potato blight and its duration posed a huge challenge to the administration in Ireland and its political masters in London.

When the previously unknown fungus struck in 1845 the view of the government and those influential on its policies was to be important to the way in which it dealt with the famine in the neighbouring island. The social, economic and religious doctrines of the age all had their role to play in the way the government reacted to the catastrophe.

Many of the changes brought about or hastened by famine deaths and emigration were consistent with what many theorists saw as being beneficial for the economic development of Ireland in the long term. The pattern of development which had seen the move to dependency on the potato for cottiers and landless Irish labourers changed. Many of the reforms led to more short-term hardship and evictions and emigration increased as land reforms and social change gathered pace. The radical reforms that might have lessened the impact of the blight, had they occurred before the 1840s, were now on the agenda of both government and tenant-right agitator alike. The landlord was no longer propped up by a social order based largely on the poor and potato dependent labourer. After the Famine three million of the labourers, cottiers, and small holders were literally dead or gone.

With the benefit of hindsight and the perspective of a developed twentieth century country much of the dogma which dictated government policy and the implementation of relief schemes appear hard-hearted, to say the least. To gain an understanding of the circumstances which led to the Great Famine and the attempts made to deal with it, we must take into account the many and varied elements which helped to create the Ireland of the period and the thinking of that time, both in Ireland and Britain. In attempting to do this we should look at the history of famine in Ireland prior to the Great Famine and the way in which Irish agriculture evolved in the period leading up to it. Today we have many difficulties in trying to imagine and understand much of what happened during that period: a huge population dependent on the potato, an unknown disease striking at the heart of its diet, unprecedented levels of death and the great speed of emigration. We find many of the theories of the political economists of the time uncaring, the administration of relief far from adequate and the mass evictions and emigration hard to accept. Many of our difficulties in relating to these and other facets of the Great Famine are because of our perspective at the tail end of the twentieth century. Many of our judgements are made with the benefit of hindsight and we must remember that the cause of the blight was unknown at the time it first struck, that medical science was not as developed as it is today and that to find explanations for much of what happened we must take a broad view of the circumstances prevailing at the time.

In trying to achieve a balanced overview of the Great Famine we have called on contributors from many disciplines and they deal with the subject from a variety of viewpoints. Each contributor brings his or her own expertise to bear on a specific strand of the history of the Famine. The historians, economists, geographers and others in this series of lectures are actively involved in research, must of which challenges, updates or complements other work on the Great Famine published over the last century and a half. Their contributions vary in the sources they call on, the facts they present and the way in which they interpret them. While their analysis and conclusions may differ in emphasis or in substance, it is hoped that such a wide-ranging examination of the Famine and the context in which these essays place it, will be of value to the general reader in trying to get a fuller and clearer picture of what happened and why it happened.

Dr Kevin Whelan examines the massive changes in the Irish agricultural community in the periods before and after the Famine. He highlights the role of the potato in the evolution of the cottier system and the way in which it deformed the class structure of a rapidly expanding population. The economic development which the potato aided saw a huge movement of population from east to west with new communities growing up in previously little populated areas. Among the changes outlined are the onslaught on the rundale and clachan systems and consequent changes in cultural moulds including the devastation of the Irish language communities. Dr Whelan also outlines some of the changes in Irish landlordism and landscape policy, encouraged and welcomed by the United Kingdom government.

Dr Seán J. Connolly provides an overview of Irish politics during the period. He highlights the dislocation between the six-year holocaust of crop failure, disease and death and the political movements for Repeal, the Young Irelanders and the Tenant League. He also analyses the

11

structure of the political system which was largely the preserve of wealthy landowners and their sons and how it failed to produce an adequate response to the disaster of famine.

Dr David Dickson reminds us of Ireland's other Great Famine of 1740–1741 which has often been overshadowed by the Famine of the 1840s. He compares and contrasts the duration, severity and geographical spread of the famines and also reflects on the reasons for the two disasters and the types of society in which they happened.

Dr E. Margaret Crawford takes a detailed look at the diet of the famine period and how the unique dependence of at least one-third of the people on the potato had developed from the beginning of the eighteenth century when the two main sources of food had been pastoral products and grain. She also examined the role and nutritional value of other food sources, including relief foods, during the Famine and the way in which nutritional deficiency diseases increased in the absence of the potato.

Dr Laurence M. Geary turns his attention to the other diseases which claimed so many lives during this and other famines. Although fever had no respect for social classes, it tended to begin among the poor and spread upwards, the contagiousness striking both towns and country areas. Typhus fever, relapsing fever, typhoid, dysentery, diarrhoea and smallpox are examined along with their relationship to famine and the social conditions associated with it. The links between poverty, malnutrition and disease are analysed and the dangers of badly chosen or badly cooked food highlighted.

Dr Peter Gray unravels the complex issue of how ideology motivated and influenced British government policy. He links government thinking to public opinion and sites it within the intellectual context of Britain at the time. The role of classical economic orthodoxy and variants of it are examined along with Providentialism and the Christian political economics of the period. The political context for the world view of government is explained and it is demonstrated how this resulted in a dogmatism based on false premises which contributed to the deaths of thousands in the famine conditions of Ireland in the 1840s.

The pivotal role of the Poor Law in Ireland is examined by Dr Christine Kinealy. The origins of the system are reviewed along with its transformation into the main method of relief during the Great Famine. The differences between the Irish Poor Law and the English Poor Law are highlighted as are the modifications to it which were carried out in response to the Famine. One of the most important decisions was to make the Poor Law responsible for the provision of all relief after August 1847 and the transfer of the financial burden from central to local resources. Other changes included allowing outdoor relief and the introduction of the controversial Quarter Acre or Gregory Clause with the subsequent rise in evictions. The view of the Poor Law as a tool to transform the Irish economy is shown to have taken priority over the immediate needs of the distressed poor. Our attention is also drawn to the experience on the ground where the realities of distress led to official policy being ignored by many in their response to the suffering community around them.

Professor Mary Daly focuses on the operations of Famine relief between 1845–47 when a series of special government programmes were put in place to deal with the crisis. She recalls that neither famine nor government relief schemes were new and points to the inadequacy of government efforts to relieve hunger after 1847 when the government wrongly declared the Famine over. How it dealt with the operations of famine relief in the first three years, while inadequate, was nevertheless a major effort in dealing with an unprecedented disaster, despite the fact that they regarded Irish society as a whole, and the landlord class in particular, as being to blame for rampant population growth, sub-division of holdings and dependence on the potato which they regarded as a morally inferior food. When those views combined with a *laissez faire* economics reading of the famine as the will of God, and a way to remedy many of Ireland's social ills was an appealing choice for the British government of the time. It is argued that if blame is to be attached that it should have a much wider catchment and include landlords, land agents, farmers, clergy and Irish politicians.

Dr Irene Whelan puts the stigma of souperism in context with a detailed look at the wider context of Protestant evangelism in Britain and Ireland before and during the Famine period and how it became linked with the distribution of relief in certain places.

Professor James S. Donnolly, Jr examines the mass evictions of the Famine period and contends that what happened during and as a result of the clearances had the look of genocide to a great many Irish contemporaries as well as to nationalist propagandists after the Great Famine. While he maintains that genocide was not in fact committed, he challenges the revisionist historiography of the Famine, in which Mitchel and other nationalist propagandists are dismissed as the creators of a baseless myth of genocide.

Dr David Fitzpatrick reminds us that getting out of famine-stricken Ireland was a matter of life or death for many of those who emigrated and that the unprecedented scale of emigration, two million in ten years, undermined the gradations and hierarchies of Irish society. The contradictory evidence about the social class of the emigrants is reviewed along with the reasons for the redirection of most of the emigration from Britain to the United States. The Famine exodus resulted in a startling redistribution of the surviving Irish population and continuing depopulation played a major part in the evolving social structures in Ireland and left an ambiguous legacy in the memory of expatriate survivors, caught between resentment at their exile and the eagerness with which so many of them grasped the chance of a new and better life.

Many of the main elements in the discussions on the operations of relief schemes, how the Poor Law worked, attitudes of officialdom and clergy on the ground are discussed in Patrick Hickey's paper on the Great Famine in the Skibbereen Union. This focus on one particular geographical area allows us the opportunity to examine to what extent many of the general observations made about the

14

extent of the disaster and the attempts to alleviate it can be upheld, or otherwise, in a detailed local study. Perhaps it is appropriate that an area which attracted so much outside attention during the Famine, should be the area to be included in a detailed local study one hundred and fifty years later.

Dr Tim P. O'Neill examines the persistence of famine in Ireland after the Great Famine and shows that starvation still threatened in the west of Ireland into the twentieth century, even after the foundation of the Irish Free State. The sensitivity of both British and Irish governments to the word 'famine' is demonstrated. He maintains that if famine is defined as an extreme scarcity of food in a district, then there were many minor famines in late nineteenth century Ireland but if widespread death from starvation is the defining factor that there were few, if any, famines in Ireland after the Great Famine. We are left in no doubt about the recurring food shortages and extreme hardship in many remote areas in the west, with the loss of crops between 1859 and 1864 being the most serious minor famine after the 1840s. It is pointed out that fewer deaths occurred because relief agencies were more sensitive to the threat of death, there was less eviction, and cheap alternative food and credit in new shops were available. The better-known minor famine of 1879–80 is also examined along with the contemporary interest in it, the role of private charities and government thinking and policy of the time.

The lectures by Cathal Póirtéir and Dr Margaret Kelleher investigate the way in which famine has been dealt with in memory and imagination. Cathal Póirtéir examines the folklore of the Famine and the possibilities of using the oral tradition as an additional historical source and as a means of understanding the impact of the Famine on the minds of the generations who came directly afterwards. Many of the images available in the folk tradition play their role in the literature of the Famine which Margaret Kelleher examines in detail. The difficulties of finding the language to describe the horrors of famine are discussed along with a review of the poetry and prose of the Famine period and later

15

interpretations of the disaster in Irish Literature. The combinations of fact and fiction, the individual perspectives of the writers and the critical and public reactions to their various works are drawn together in this essay.

Professor Cormac Ó Gráda centres his thoughts on the Great Famine and today's famines and suggests that the generous response of the Irish public to Third World famines may not be directly linked to the history or memory of famine in Ireland, as is often claimed. Rather he links the giving of aid to the Third World to the Irish tradition of overseas missionary activity and raises the possibility that Irish people have distanced themselves from what happened in Ireland in the 1840s while responding to similar disasters elsewhere. The similarities and differences between the circumstances of the Great Famine and modern famines in other countries are also examined. The philosophical contexts, the proportions of the disasters, the infrastructures and levels of general poverty in the regions are compared and contrasted with the Irish experience in the 1840s. We are left in no doubt that ideology and attitudes to relief and poverty can still exacerbate food shortages and that class prejudice has played its part in dictating how some administrations viewed and dealt with famine up to the present day.

I hope that this series of Thomas Davis Lectures will help towards a better understanding of the Great Irish Famine of the 1840s and place it in a context which will make its interpretation and analysis a continuing matter of interest for researchers and the general reader alike.

Finally I would like to thank all the contributors for their willingness to take part in the project and for their forbearance and courtesy in my dealings with them. I hope they will feel that their work has been treated with due care and attention despite the sometimes harsh deadlines dictated by broadcasters and publishers. Gabhaim buíochas ar leith le Cormac Ó Gráda a spreag agus a chomhairligh mé go minic ón uair a rith sé liom an chéad uair go mba chóir dom tabhairt faoin tionscnamh seo. Bhí sé fial lena shaineolas agus lena chuid ama, mar is dual dó. My particular thanks to

Michael Littleton of RTÉ, the General Editor of the Thomas Davis Lectures, and Mary Feehan of Mercier Press for their encouragement and willingness to share their experience with me.

CATHAL PÓIRTÉIR

PRE AND POST-FAMINE LANDSCAPE CHANGE

KEVIN WHELAN

IT IS NOT A SIMPLE task to endeavour to recover in any meaningful way the buried experience of the Famine, or to imaginatively reappropriate the consciousness or culture of pre-Famine Ireland, on the eve of its extinction. It is difficult to grasp at an individual level the implications of a tragedy which wiped out one million people in half a decade, as if the modern population of Dublin was to be obliterated before the end of the 1990s. It is also difficult to empathise with the scale of the poverty. In seemingly prosperous Kilkenny in 1835, a German visitor noted with fascinated disgust how a local mother had picked up gooseberry skins which a fellow traveller had spat out of the stagecoach, carefully placing them in the mouth of her child. In Limerick city in 1844, a labourer named John Cherry told a local doctor that 'the people are so poor that they are ready to eat one another'.

To understand the build-up to the Famine, it is necessary to begin with the inevitable potato. While the potato began its Irish career as a garden crop of the gentry, it quickly jumped the garden wall and was given the freedom of the fields. By the late seventeenth century, it had become a widespread field crop especially in Munster, although it was a supplementary rather than a principal food source (the main diet still revolved around butter, milk and grain products). But in the first two decades of the eighteenth century, it became a base food of the Munster poor, especially in winter.

The relatively rapid expansion of the economy between 1760 and 1815 saw the potato pushing out of Munster, forcing the oatmeal-eating zone to retract towards the northwest, and beginning to make inroads into the more varied diet zone of south Leinster. By 1800, it had become a staple food all the year round for the cottier and small farm class, and there was an accelerating tendency towards monoculture. In the difficult year of 1822, distress was concentrated west of a line from Sligo to Cork: the oatmeal zone, for example, in Donegal, was not affected in any serious way.

The potato's spread was also pivotal to the evolution of the cottier system, which delivered an extremely cheap and very disciplined workforce to the farmer, but at the cost of depressed living standards (essentially a potato wage) for the labourer. Thus the potato figured prominently in the paradox of a rapidly expanding agrarian economy, co-existing with decreasing living standards for a proliferating social base. The potato facilitated economic expansion while deforming the class structure. In a pre-mechanised production system, Irish tillage expanded its output by expanding its labour force – achieved by the proliferation of cottiers, who were essentially paid a minimum 'potato wage'. This was a barrier to innovation (in that low-cost labour made capital-intensive methods undesirable) and a way of disciplining a captive labour force by limiting its independence. It also favoured the farmer in that the high manure residue from the previous year's potato crop made for increased tillage yields (as did the prevalent spade as opposed to horse cultivation techniques). Therefore, expansion of tillage led to an inexorable expansion of the potato acreage, and a concomitant expansion of the cottier class. By 1841, there were over half a million cottiers, with one and three-quarter of a million dependents. The principal beneficiary of this system was the English consumer. The Corn Laws saw the percentage of British corn imports rise from 16% in the 1790s to 80% by the 1830s. This cheap food was made available by the rapid expansion of Irish imports, based on the cottier system and the potato.

The potato had a number of advantages which made it an attractive proposition in Irish circumstances. It was well adapted to a wet, sunless climate and to sour acidic soils, especially when it had a long growing season in a temperate climate: the potato's principal enemy was frost more than rain. Unlike grain, the potato required no processing to make

it edible; this meant that its producers retained direct control
over their means of subsistence;

Grá mo chróí na preataí
Nach n-iarann áth nó muileann
Ach á mbaint ins a' gharraí
Agus á bhfágáil ar a teinidh.

The potatoes are the love of my
heart
They don't require a kiln or mill
Only to be dug in the field
And left on the fire.

In agricultural terms the potato remained disease-free in the
Irish context. It also did everything the much vaunted turnip
did; it was a root crop which replaced fallow, a winter crop
for livestock, and a valuable reclaiming agent in previously
untilled ground. It facilitated the development of the spail-
pín system, which regularly supplied harvest migrants from
poorer to richer areas: the differential harvest time (2–3
weeks) between east and west, and between upland and
lowland, allowed seasonal migrants to save the crops in richer areas, and then return to harvest their own crop.

The potato was nutritious: with milk added, it formed a
balanced diet, containing adequate amounts of protein, car-
bohydrates and minerals. Its high energy value and low fat
content made it a healthy food source. It also remained palatable even as part of an extremely monotonous diet. Those
who relied totally on potatoes were consuming a stone a day
– about fifty to eighty potatoes; over a fifty year career of
eating potatoes, this meant consuming a million potatoes.

The seventeenth century witnessed the transformation of
the lazy bed from being a receptacle for oats to being one for
the potato. The lazy bed could be minutely adjusted to soil
type, altitude, slope conditions and rockiness: (this explains
the great variety of Irish spade types). Its flexibility allowed
steep, irregular or inaccessible slopes to be cultivated areas
which could never have been brought under the plough. As
Samuel Hayes explained in 1797, writing about mountainous
areas in County Wicklow: 'Potatoes certainly may be cultivated in ground too moory, stony or too much covered with
brush and furze to afford wheat in the first instance. In such
ground, the potato must be produced in the common ridge

21

or furrow, or lazy-bed way. The crop is often very consider-able in such circumstances, with a sufficient quantity of good dung and in some soils with lime or ashes, but the labour is very great.'

The lazy bed was environmentally efficient, a brilliantly ingenious method of absorbing both an unrestricted labour supply, and nutrient sources like manure, sand, seaweed and peat. Spade cultivation of this type absorbed about five times as much labour as ploughing, twenty times as much as stock-rearing; in that sense, it was a massive soak for surplus or under-employed labour. But it was efficient. Spade culti-vation of potatoes tripled the yield over ploughing, and in the 1840s, Irish yields were twice those of France. Therefore the lazy bed system was a safety-valve in a high-pressure demographic regime.

Population expanded rapidly in those favoured parts of the west of Ireland where potato cultivation could be added to access to hills (for rough grazing), to bogs (for turf) and to the seaside for seaweed, sand and the *cnuasach trá* (shore-food). Given these amenities, families had access to cheap food, fuel and housing (which could be easily constructed using only local materials – stones for walls, clay for floors, 'wreck' timber for rafters, oats or bent grass for thatch). Such areas were a poor man's paradise in the late eighteenth cen-tury. With little material expectations before the consumer revolution, there were remarkably few formal barriers to early marriage and family formation. In the absence of the old elite, there was little influence exerted by the new land-lord class in social norms; similarly, the institutional church and formal education were weak in the newly settled areas. Alongside the lack of negative influences, there were also positive inducements to marriage (in the form of cheap food, fuel and housing) and the ready availability of land (albeit poor or marginal). This can be contrasted to the population picture in the environmentally favoured big farm areas of Leinster and Munster, where social and economic constraints depressed the demography.

An Irish proverb succinctly expressed the dominant west of Ireland attitude: 'Dá mbeadh prátaí is móin againn, bheadh ár saol ar ár dtóin againn'. An outsider caught the same sentiments in *Letters from the Irish Highlands of Connemara* in 1824:

> If they have turf and potatoes enough, they reckon themselves provided for; if a few herring, a little oatmeal and above all the milk of a cow be added, they are rich, they can enjoy themselves and dance with a light heart after the day's work is over.

Alongside the potato and the lazy bed cultivation system, a third principal determinant of the west of Ireland settlement pattern was the rundale and clachan system. A clachan (or *baile* or 'village') was a nucleated group of farmhouses, where land-holding was organised communally, frequently on a townland basis and often with considerable ties of kinship between the families involved. Although the misleading English word 'village' was often used to describe the *baile*, these clusters of farmhouses were not classic villages, in that they lacked any service functions – church, pub, school or shop. While the houses might have adjacent individual vegetable gardens (*garraí*), they were surrounded, on the best available patch of land, by a permanently cultivated infield – a large open field, without enclosures, with a multiplicity of 'strips' separated by sods or stones, in which oats or potatoes were grown. Each family used a variety of strips, periodically redistributed, to ensure a fair division of all types of soil – deep, shallow, sandy, boggy, dry. Outside the infield, and generally separated from it by a sturdy wall, was the outfield – poorer, more marginal, hilly or boggy ground which was used for common pasture and turbary. An occasional reclamation might be made in the outfield for the purpose of growing potatoes (especially when the population grew). The grazing was organised communally using the old Gaelic qualitative measure (the 'collop' or 'sum') to define the amount of stock each family was allowed to have on the pasturage (so as not to overstock it). Occasionally, if the outfield spread into high mountain pastures, cattle might be moved there in the summer, attended by young boys or girls who lived in summer huts. This was called the *buaile* and was especially important for butter-making.

This type of settlement became practically universal on the poorer lands of the west of Ireland in the pre-Famine period. They were an ingenious adaptation to the environmental conditions of the west of Ireland, where tiny patches of glacial drift were frequently embedded in extensive areas of bog or mountain. Collective use of the infield maximised utilisation of the limited amount of arable land provided by those drift pockets. Because it was permanently cultivated, the infield's fertility had to be maintained by drawing on the non-arable outfield for resources – manure, sods, peat and especially seaweed.

Economic development, underpinned by the potato, rundale and clachan, and the lazy bed, engineered a massive shift in population density from east to west, from good land to poor land, and from port hinterlands and river valleys to bog and hill fringes. The density of the population in the mid-nineteenth century had been completely transformed since the mid-seventeenth century. Massive potato-aided reclamation, intensive sub-division of rundale shares and expansion into previously unsettled areas were all part of the surging demographic profile of Ireland in the post-potato period. Between 1600 and 1845, Ireland's population surged from one million to eight and a half million, with four million additional people being added between 1780 and 1845.

The new areas of settlement were concentrated along the ragged Atlantic fringe, and on bog and hill edges. Rundale villages, powered by the potato, acted as a mobile pioneering fringe; the spade and the spud conquered the contours. On the mid-seventeenth century Down Survey maps, settlement limits were at c. 500 feet; by 1840, they had climbed to 800 feet – an important consideration in a country of fragmented uplands like Ireland.

Two final observations are appropriate here. The west of Ireland was a zone of settlement discontinuity, not of continuity. It was not an archaic but a very modern society, whose very existence was underpinned by a relatively novel development – the extensive infiltration of the ecological interloper – the potato. One might also wonder if the potato ultimately destroyed the pre seventeenth-century balance between tillage and pasture in these environmentally frail areas. Traditionally, land use had been regulated not by permanent possession of a precise piece of land but by abstract rights – the *cuibhreadh* or share, which was determined by a balance between kinship affiliations, lease obligations and environmental constraints. These were dictated by the qualitative estimation of the carrying capacity for livestock, which then allowed for the precise quantification of grazing rights (sums and collops). These in turn defined tillage rights in the infield, on the basis that manure was the key to the sustainability of the system. The balance of pasture and tillage was determined traditionally – i.e., by that blend of necessity and experience which embodied the legacy of accumulated environmental experience. The equilibrium of land use prior to the potato emphasised pastoralism at the expense of tillage. In the west of Ireland, the spread of the potato deranged the traditional balance between tillage and pasture.

These issues came into increasingly sharp focus in the aftermath of the Napoleonic wars, when a sharp depression hit the area. Agricultural prices halved, the fickle herring deserted the west coast (where they had been abundant between 1780 and 1810), the linen industry was dislocated by the advent of factory-spinning and weaving – a succession of hammer blows, accentuated by a series of wet summers and bad harvests. By 1822 the region was facing a Famine situation, with a 'bitter harvest of misery and disappointment'.

The problem faced by these communities was that their prospects were essentially limited. While a minimum existence was underwritten by the potato, their room to manoeuvre was limited as expectations increased. Called forth by a unique *conjuncture* of forces, they were trapped in restricted circumstances once those conditions altered. The shrinking pre-Famine economy was squeezed by a relentless demographic regime. Its trauma lay ahead, but with too limited time for readjustments. With the improved position of pastoralism on the lowland areas, the declining demand for agricultural labour, and more attentive landlord surveillance of sub-division, there were few places left to go but to the high mountain or wet bog.

The combination of a distressed proto-industrial sector and a volatile agricultural situation gave rise to a great shifting under-class in Irish society in the immediate pre-Famine years. In Ballina in 1835, a commentator noted: 'If you were going among them for twenty years you would not know their faces, they come and go so fast.' Their existential marginality was mirrored in their settlement marginality. This period witnessed the explosive expansion of cabin shanties on the edge of towns, bogside squatter colonies like the Erris 'troglodytes' or the wretched settlers oozing into the wet deserts of the Bog of Allen, voracious assaults on commonages, or on the limits of cultivation which were pushing up over 1,000 feet.

The cumulative impact of these changes strengthened dangerous tendencies within the society. Firstly, in the pre-Famine period, the more solvent tenants tended to emigrate, thereby simplifying and weakening the social structure. Secondly the prolonged depression drained existing capital resources and damaged resilience in the face of crisis years. Thirdly, the weakening of other cash inputs forced tenants to sell all their oats production, and dragged them increasingly towards dependence on the potato and indeed into dependence on the inferior lumper variety, which was initially called the 'Connaught lumper'. The ecological knife-edge was thereby constantly sharpening, pushing those communities ever closer to the potato precipice. Between 1810 and 1845, there was a decline of potato varieties in favour of the lumper – a high bulk variety which could tolerate poorer soils, and above all else required little manure. The resulting dense monoculture was also more susceptible to disease. Once oats became a cash crop and left the diet, the dependence on the potato was dangerously deepening, especially as the emaciated economy was squeezed by an inexorable demographic regime.

The post-Napoleonic collapse impacted perniciously on the cottier class, who now found themselves under relentless pressure. Farmers no longer had the same demand for labour, as the terms of agricultural trade swung more towards pastoral rather than tillage production. The sharp decline in agricultural prices also depressed already minimal wages, in effect pushing it towards a pure potato wage. The labourer's position, economically redundant, socially marginal, was even further eroded by his lack of any legal foothold on his conacre ground. Farmers could peremptorily refuse to renew the verbal contract for conacre ground, or evict and distrain, without any legal restraint. For those close to the poor, it was these mini-landlords ('tiarnaí beaga') rather than the landlord class per se who were the worst enemies of the agricultural labourer. In 1844, Fr Michael Fitzgerald, the parish priest of Ballingarry in County Limerick, described how a gentleman farmer had cleared his land of cottiers, in the interest of efficiency. 'There are now beautiful fields and pastures there, but these beautiful fields are the sepulchres of the poor.' He also accused the big farmer of lacking a social conscience:

> If he possessed honest feelings, he ought to be ashamed of his Durhams and his South Downs and his interminable fields of corn, tilled by miserable serfs (more miserable than the fellahs of Egypt or the blacks of Cuba), and occupy the place from which human happiness and human enjoyment were rooted out and exterminated.

But the potato, as well as being a lifesaver was also a hard taskmaster. Asenath Nicholson described a scene near Roundstone, County Galway, in 1845:

> The poor peasants, men, women and children were gathering seaweed, loading their horses, asses and backs with it, to manure their wretched little patches of potatoes sown among the rocks. 'Three hundred and sixty-two days a year we have the potato,' said a young man to me bitterly, 'the blackguard of a Raleigh who brought them here entailed a curse upon the labourer that has broke his heart. Because the landlord sees that we can live and work hard on them, he grinds us down in our ways and he despises us because we are ignorant and ragged.'

In these circumstances, a failure of the crop would cause disaster; repeated failures would simply decimate the population. The unprecedented attack of *Phytopthora infestans* destroyed one-third of the crop in 1845; the combined impact of blight and the failure to sow the crop led to the yield being lower by three-quarters in 1846 and 1847 and one-third in 1848. Massive mortality and emigration ensued: one million died and two million emigrated in the next two decades, cruelly paralleling the three million 'potato people' who were totally dependent on the now fickle tuber in the immediate pre-Famine period. These deaths were disproportionately concentrated in the areas of new settlement dominated by rundale and clachan, and by the lumper potato. In the dense huddles of poor quality housing, disease had a field day. From a sample of 7,000 people who died in West Cork in 1847, we know that 44% died of fever, 34% of starvation and 22% of dysentery. The clachan settlements were decimated. At Liscananaun, in the parish of Turloughmore in County Galway, the swollen clachan had 114 houses and 688 people in 1841: by 1851, this had been shrunk to 46 houses and 257 people – only one-third of its pre-Famine size. A similar devastation emerges from close study of clachans right across the west of Ireland in the Famine period.

The response of the United Kingdom government to this devastating crisis was dominated by its perception of the potato as literally the root of all Irish evil. There was a prevalent ideological antipathy to the potato as a 'lazy root', grown in 'lazy' beds by a 'lazy' people. The potato itself was an inferior food in a civilisational sense, which pinned the Irish poor to the bottom of the cultural ladder, accentuating the negatives associated with their race ('Celtic') and religion (Popery). The potato, in this point of view, was 'the crop which fosters, from the earliest childhood, habits of indolence, improvidence and waste'. 'No other crop produces such an abundance of food on the same extent of ground, requires so little skill and labour either to rear it or prepare it for food, and leaves so large a portion of the labourer's time unoccupied.'

One response to the Famine then was to see it as an opportunity to replace the backward, degenerate potato as a food-source by a 'higher form', like grain, which would forcibly elevate the feckless Irish up the ladder of civilisation. By linking food, race and religion (the Potato, Paddy

28

and Popery) in a stadial view of civilisation, the Famine could then be interpreted benevolently as an accelerator effect conducive to a policy of agrarian anglicisation. Simultaneously, by linking Celtic inferiority and the obstinate Popery of the Irish poor, it could interpret the Famine as ultimately being caused by moral not biological failings.

These viewpoints, shared by senior politicians, key administrators and influential journalists, encouraged an extreme reluctance to intervene in Ireland; the British establishment could and did argue that in doing so, it was simply acting in accordance with God's plan. In a society increasingly soaked in evangelicalism, this argument was decisive in carrying the dominant strand of British public opinion with it in its view that Ireland should be let starve for its own good. That viewpoint hardened even more in the aftermath of the 1848 Young Ireland rebellion, interpreted as a sneaky stab in the back of the empire. Wood, the minister in charge of the purse strings at the height of the Famine, was sanguine: 'Except through a purgatory of misery and starvation, I cannot see how Ireland is to emerge into a state of anything approaching to quiet or prosperity.' Trevelyan agreed: 'Even in the most afflicting dispensations of providence, there was ground for consolation and often even occasion for congratulation.' Framed within these perspectives, the paradox of the Irish Famine, commented on by Gladstone in 1847, became more explicable: 'It is the greatest horror of modern times that in the richest ages of the world and in the richest country of that age, the people should be dying of Famine by hundreds.'

The Famine victims themselves interpreted the disaster in social, not in religious or moral terms:

Is ní h-é Dia cheap riamh an obair seo
daoine bochta do chur le fuacht is le fán.

or

Mo thrua mór uaisle a bhfuil móran coda acu
gan tabhairt sásaimh san obair seo le Rí na ngrás
Ach ag feall ar bhochta Dé nár bhfuair riamh aon saibhreas
Ach ag síor obair dóibh ó aois go bás.

Similarly the Irish poor lamented the passing of the potato;

> Ba iad ár gcaraid iad ó am ár gcliabháin
> Ach is é mo dhiobháil iad imeacht uainn
> Ba mhaith an chuidheacht iad is an t-údar rince
> Bhíodh spóirt is siamsa againn in aice leo.

or

> Ba mhaith liom an práta, dob fháil is dob fhairsing é
> Chun é a roinnt ar bhochtaibh Dé.

But the emigrant Irish, coming in contact with an American society undergoing the consumer revolution, had little hesitation in rapidly embracing its values. A Kerry woman who settled in Philadelphia in the post Famine period noted of her adopted land:

> Bíonn mairtfheol aorach ar phlátaí china
> bíonn gin Cubánach 's caoirfheoil aird
> 's nach ró-bhreá an phrae sin 's é fháil gan aon locht
> ná a bheith in Éirinn ar lumper bhán'.

> There's the best of beef there on china plates
> mighty mutton and Cuban gin
> And isn't that much better grub than to
> be stuck in Ireland on the lumper spud.

The assault on the potato as a food source was accompanied by an onslaught on the rundale and clachan system, in the belief that only individual farms would encourage initiative and self-reliance. The clachans needed to be dispersed to break the cultural moulds which sustained mutual aid (comhar na gcomharsan) and thereby fostered a debilitating dependency. The privatisation and linearisation of landscape spread a logical lattice of ladder farms over the west of Ireland, obliterating the earlier informal networks of the rundale system. As early as 1845, some landlords had begun to implement this new landscape policy, including George Hill at Gweedore and Lord Leitrim at Milford, both in Donegal. A contemporary description catches the new system being implemented on the Leitrim estate:

> The country is being divided into long straight farms, by long straight fences, running up to the mountains, the object being

to give each farmer a pretty equal division of good and bad land, and to oblige him to reside on his farm. Formerly the land was divided by rundale, as it is called; a dozen people possessed alternate furrows in the same field, something similar to the ridge and furrow system in England on an extended scale. The system was necessarily attended with every evil, and improvement precluded. The agent is endeavouring to eradicate it by the means before-mentioned, and has given each tenant three years to build his house and his outside fences. These long straight fences are partly made, partly lock-spitted and in many places not laid out, and as the measure has met with great opposition it is difficult to say when they are likely to be completed.

Those new attitudes can be contrasted to the cohesive cultural moulds of the *baile* system of settlement, whose values were succinctly expressed in the proverb *Is ar scáth a chéile a mhaireann na daoine.* Hely Dutton described such villages in Galway in 1808, concluding that they led 'to such strong attachments, generally strengthened by intermarriages, that though they may have some bickering with each other, they will, right or wrong, keep their companions'. In this intimate face-to-face world, communication skills were highly valued, and a rich oral culture was encouraged – the non-material performing arts, like singing, dancing and storytelling emerged as the prized art forms, creating a satisfying interpretation of the culture. All this life was intricately interwoven with the cohesive quality of rundale life, with its communal, customary and contextual modes of organisation. The vivacity and gaiety of the society, as well as its hospitality, was constantly commented on by pre-Famine visitors.

These changes also entailed a massive dislocation of the culture itself, symbolised by the rapid erosion of the Irish language in the reorganised areas. This change is neatly caught in a vignette by William Wilde in a visit to Lough Inagh in Connemara, where he saw the tally-stick in operation [a stick around the children's neck which was notched if they were caught speaking Irish]. Wilde asked the father:

if he did not love the Irish language – indeed the man scarcely spoke any other; 'I do,' said he, his eyes kindling with enthusiasm; 'sure it is the talk of the ould country, and the ould

31

times, the language of my father and all that's gone before me – the speech of these mountains, and lakes, and these glens, where I was bred and born; but you know,' he continued, 'the children must have larnin', and as they tache no Irish in the National School, we must have recourse to this to instigate them to talk English'.

A certain amount of iron entered the Irish soul in the Famine holocaust. Malachi Horan, a small farmer at the Dublin end of the Wicklow mountains near Tallaght, commented that the Famine's main effect had not been to create poverty – 'they were used to that' – but that it made the people 'so sad in themselves ... and that it made many a one hard too'. Edith Martin (the Galway half of the Somerville and Ross partnership) expressed similar sentiments: 'The Famine yielded like the ice of the northern seas; it ran like melted snow into the veins of Ireland for many years afterwards'. At the end of the century John Millington Synge commented on the omnipresent Famine shadow that still fell across the Wicklow Glens, and the three shadowy countries 'that were never altogether absent in the old people's minds – America, the workhouse and the madhouse'. The widespread dislocation lent credence to James Fintan Lalor's claim that the Famine represented 'a deeper social disorganisation than the French Revolution – greater waste of life, wider loss of property – more of the horror with none of the hopes'.

This assault on rundale and clachan was also accompanied by an assault on Irish landlordism itself; the British establishment welcomed the bankruptcy of Irish landlords, whom they saw as equally feckless as the Irish peasantry. If they were replaced by a new breed of hard-headed English and Scottish owners, occupying newly cleared estates for large-scale cattle or sheep ranching, so much the better. *The Times* noted (somewhat prematurely): 'In a few years a Celtic Irishman will be as rare in Connemara as a Red Indian on the shores of Manhattan'. But the Encumbered Estates Act was designed to facilitate the easy transfer of land from Irish to English and Scottish landowners who would transform the society, culture, politics and economics of Ireland.

As landlords set their faces against rundale and clachan,

and against the partnership leases which underpinned it, and as the Encumbered Estates machinery created a new landlord group with ambitious agrarian plans in mind for the west of Ireland, the large scale grazier tenant became a preferred option. By the end of the century, it was estimated that of 190,000 acres in Connemara, 60,000 (one-third) were held by 90 graziers. Across Connaught as a whole, the graziers leased the level limestone lowlands, while the rundale farmers were tolerated only on the bog and mountain fringes. In Roscommon, for example, the celebrated plains of Boyle were dominated by the bullock and virtually devoid of people, while the bog-pocked south of the county was strewn with clachans. The glaring environmental and social asymmetries were to be a powerful stimulus to the Land League, and later to the anti-grazier United Irish League. A Connemara priest, Rev. James Kelly, attacked the grazier system as a parasitic attack on the very core of Irish society itself.

> It is lying like a nightmare over the land and over the people and they are anxious to get that off their dreams and off their waking and working moments; and although by some noble and interested lords, the graziers are called the backbone of the country, [they] must be regarded as an invertebrate class ... They are actually like tuberculosis on the constitution: they are spreading out on the vitals of the people.

The incompatible existence cheek-by-jowl of the contrasting systems of rundale and grazier farming was the obvious landscape expression of an economic, social and political dichotomy which the Famine had lain bare. That dichotomy dramatically symbolises the contrasting responses to the Famine, while forcing consideration of a colonial context which we have too often ignored in our recent analyses of nineteenth-century Irish life.

THE GREAT FAMINE AND IRISH POLITICS

S.J.CONNOLLY

THE PERIOD 1845–52 WAS NOT one short of political incident, confrontation and even drama. It began with the final phases of the movement for repeal of the Act of Union, the secession from that movement of the Young Ireland party, and the armed insurrection by the Young Irelanders in 1848; later came the emergence, from 1849, of a new movement for the defence of Irish farmers, the Tenant League, and the election in 1852 of what appeared at the time to be a strong new party for the defence of Irish interests in the United Kingdom parliament. Yet there remains a striking disassociation between all of these developments and the background against which they unfolded: a six-year holocaust of crop failure and disease, in which something like one million people died of fever and starvation, another million fled the country, and perhaps the same overall total again survived for long periods on the very edge of starvation. The splits, regroupings and new departures, the intense debate over points of administrative or legal detail, the passionate conflicts on issues of abstract principle: all seem equally set apart, as if by a wall of glass, from the unprecedented disaster unfolding in the Irish countryside.

One main reason for this disassociation lay in the structure of the political system. Since the beginning of 1801 Ireland had been governed, under the Act of Union, as part of the United Kingdom. Executive power lay in the hands of a lord lieutenant and chief secretary, both of whom were appointed by, and responsible to, the British cabinet. Within the United Kingdom parliament Ireland was represented by 105 M.P.s out of a total of 656, as well as by representative Irish peers sitting in the House of Lords. These Irish M.P.s were, like the rest of the House of Commons, drawn almost entirely from a small social elite. Parliamentary candidates, even when standing under a clear party label, were generally expected to fund their own campaign. They also had to be able, if elected, to spend a substantial part of each year in London, maintaining the lifestyle appropriate to a member of parliament. There was in any case a formal qualification, requiring members to have an income from property of at least £600 per year in the case of county constituencies, £300 per year in the case of boroughs. In 1835 the future Chartist leader, Feargus O'Connor, then Repeal M.P. for County Cork, was required to give up his seat because he did not meet this qualification. Voting also involved a property qualification. Following the Reform Act of 1832 about one person in every eighty-three was qualified to vote. The Franchise Act of 1850 brought this up to one in every forty. Small numbers, combined with the absence of a secret ballot, left voters vulnerable to intimidation from landlords and other social superiors, as well as open to the temptations of direct or indirect bribery. For all of these reasons parliamentary politics remained very largely the preserve of the wealthy and leisured few. Seventy per cent of the members who sat for Irish constituencies between 1832 and 1859 were landowners or sons of landowners. The next largest occupational group, perhaps fifteen per cent of the total, were professional men, among whom lawyers were by far the largest element.

The dominance of parliamentary representation by men of fortune did not, however, mean that popular opinion had no political role. The Irish electorate may have been small, vulnerable to the pressures of deference, coercion and corruption, and confined in the choices laid before it. Yet the system could work only with its participation, and at least its passive consent. Over the preceding twenty years, moreover, a mainly Catholic middle class had begun to mobilise the latent political potential of that electorate for its own purposes. The process had begun with the campaign for Catholic emancipation in 1823–9, and had continued with further agitations for political reform, the overhaul of the tithes system, and repeal of the Act of Union. All of these movements had benefited from the gradual growth of political sophistication associated with rising living standards, better communications and the spread of literacy. The result was a political system in transition. Politics was still very largely a rich man's game; but it was no longer a game that rich men could play with reference to themselves alone. Instead parliamentarians, or would-be parliamentarians, though themselves still drawn overwhelmingly from the privileged classes, nevertheless found it necessary to take some account of a newly awakened popular opinion, however imperfectly and episodically that opinion was expressed through the electoral system. The muddled and inconsistent nature of their attempts to do so was nowhere more evident than in the failure of any political grouping to frame an effective response to the unprecedented challenge of the Famine crisis.

FROM THE 1830S TO the 1860s the majority of M.P.s returned for Irish constituencies identified themselves with one of the two major British political parties, Liberal or Conservative. In 1841, for example, Ireland returned forty-three Conservatives and forty-two Liberals, in 1847 forty-two Conservatives and twenty-five Liberals.

The Conservatives (still sometimes referred to by the older party label Tories) were the traditional defenders of the established order in church and state. As such they could count on the support of the majority of Protestant voters. In much of Ulster this alone was enough to give them electoral dominance. But Conservatives also proved remarkably effective in organising the Protestant vote even in other regions, particularly in the towns of Leinster and Munster, where a limited urban franchise gave the Protestant artisan class an electoral potential well beyond its share of the overall population. In addition Conservatives, as the natural party of the landed class, could count on the greater part of whatever electoral influence landlords were able to exercise over tenants and other dependants. The Liberals, still sometimes referred to, particularly when the more conservative sections of the party were in question, as the Whigs, were the party of moderate reform. Their supporters included a small group of aristocratic Irish families, such as the Charlemonts and Fitzwilliams, for whom Whiggery was partly a matter of political principle and partly of family tradition, a dwindling minority of mainly more affluent Ulster Presbyterians, and sections of the Protestant middle classes of the other three provinces. Since none of these groups was numerically very large, the electoral strength of Irish Liberalism lay over-whelmingly in the Catholic population. But the Protestant Liberals nevertheless enjoyed a prominence in the party wholly out of proportion to their numbers. In 1832, for example, no less than thrity-five of the forty-three Liberals returned for Irish seats were Protestants. And even in the parliamentary session of 1851–2, when there was no rival Repeal party to provide an alternative identity for Catholic parliamentarians, Protestants made up thirty-two of the seventy-one Irish M.P.s classified as Liberals.

The third major political grouping among Irish M.P.s at Westminster was the Repeal party, led by Daniel O'Connell, whose aim was the repeal of the Act of Union and the restoration of an Irish parliament. In the general election of 1832 Ireland had returned forty-two Repeal M.P.s. Between 1834 and 1840 O'Connell had suspended his demand for repeal in order to support a minority Liberal government, in exchange for reformist legislation and the extension to Irish Catholics of a larger share of public patronage. But from 1840, faced with the imminent replacement of the Liberals by a Conservative ministry under his old enemy, Sir Robert Peel, O'Connell once again took up the Repeal campaign, inside and outside parliament. The new movement got off to a slow start, reflected in the reduced number of Repeal M.P.s returned in 1841. By 1843, however, the campaign had gathered momentum, and a series of great public demonstrations, the 'monster meetings', commencing in March of that year, raised popular excitement to new levels. On 7 October government banned the meeting planned for the following day at Clontarf outside Dublin. O'Connell's unresisting acceptance of the ban did not, as is sometimes claimed, mark the end of his movement: the Repeal party remained a significant force for a further four years. But his anti-climactic surrender did mean an inevitable loss of momentum, particularly when government followed up its advantage by having O'Connell and other leaders tried for conspiracy and imprisoned for four months, until released on appeal in September 1844.

The Repeal movement was a complex coalition, taking very different forms at different levels of society. For the Catholic middle classes the repeal of the Act of Union was a practical strategy for the return of control of day to day affairs to Irish hands, the regeneration of the Irish economy, and further progress towards full practical equality with Protestants. To the Catholic lower classes, on the other hand, repeal, like Catholic emancipation ten years earlier, was the symbol of a vaguely conceived but passionately imagined transformation of the whole social and political order. A ballad confiscated by police in County Galway in July 1843 summed up the potent mix of millenarian expectation and resentment of religious and social oppression from which popular Repealism drew its strength:

> Since Luther lit the candle we suffered penury
> But now it is extinguished in spite of heresy,
> We'll have an Irish parliament, fresh laws we will dictate,
> Or we'll have satisfaction for the year of ['98].

Such language was in sharp contrast to the democratic radicalism of Daniel O'Connell. It contrasts even more sharply with the character of the men who represented the cause of repeal in the United Kingdom parliament. Political opponents may have tried to present O'Connell's followers as down at heel interlopers. But the truth was that their social origins were only slightly different to those of other members. Forty-six M.P.s, excluding O'Connell and members of his immediate family, sat as Repealers between 1832 and 1847. Of these twenty-three were described as primarily landowners, while eleven others combined landownership with trade, legal practice or commissions in the army. The remainder were mainly prosperous lawyers or merchants.

As with the Liberals, equally, a party heavily dependent on Catholic votes nevertheless included among its parliamentary representatives a disproportionate number of Protestants, thirteen out of thirty-nine in 1832. Both these apparent anomalies reflected the practical constraints on participation in electoral politics already mentioned. In a number of cases, in fact, it was clear that the difficulty of finding suitable candidates had compelled the Repeal leadership and local organisations to accept as their standard bearers men who were at best patriotic Liberals, at worst mere political adventurers, for whom the cause of repeal was never more than a vote catcher. The parliamentary Repeal party thus reflected, in a particularly acute form, the contradictions that characterised the political system as a whole, at this transitional stage in the movement from elite to democratic politics.

The Irish Liberals and Conservatives did not entirely fail to respond to the emergency of the Famine. At the beginning of 1847, as dissatisfaction grew with the inadequacies of government relief measures, a conference of Irish M.P.s, landowners and others met in Dublin. They passed resolutions calling for the public works schemes that now constituted the main form of relief to be directed to more productive purposes, and also for some measure to ensure that tenants vacating a holding would be compensated for any improvements made during their occupancy. Eighty-three peers and M.P.s, including both Liberals and Conservatives as well as Repealers, agreed to act together as a party to promote these proposals. The mood of national unity, however, lasted only a few months. The proposed Irish party split when Conservative M.P.s backed a scheme for large scale public investment in Irish railways, while Liberals supported the government in voting it down, with Repealers voting on both sides. It collapsed entirely when most of its members opposed a bill to extend the scope, and therefore potential cost to Irish tax-payers, of the Poor Law. Thereafter the main way in which non-Repeal M.P.s sought to use their influence was in opposing the Liberal government's half-hearted proposals for economic restructuring and for a modest reform of the law on landlord and tenant. Initial outrage at the failure of

39

government to deal more effectively with the crisis gave way to a determination, in the last resort, to resist any proposals likely to cost Irish landowners money.

Daniel O'Connell, the leader of the Repeal party, was in principle willing to advocate a far more radical response to the Famine crisis. As early as November 1845 he called for the prohibition of food exports, and his other suggested remedies included a tax on absentee landlords to finance relief works. None of this, however, translated into a coherent political strategy to prevent mass starvation. Throughout 1845–6 the Repealers remained highly critical of what were to seem, in retrospect, Peel's relatively successful efforts to cope with a limited crop failure. They did, it is true, support Peel's bill to repeal the Corn Laws, the system of duties on imported food that kept up the price of domestic agricultural produce. But even then O'Connell threatened at one point to sacrifice the bill, and the prospect of cheaper food for Ireland, in order to defeat a second measure, a tough coercion bill that sought to curb rising rural disorder by collective fines on disturbed districts and a rigid curfew backed by the penalty of transportation. At the end of June 1846 O'Connell joined with the Liberals, and with Tories in revolt against Peel's abandonment of agricultural protection, to bring down the government. He went on to express initial confidence in the public works schemes with which the new Liberal government, under Lord John Russell, replaced Peel's food depots. As the appalling inadequacy of the public works as a means of preventing starvation and the spread of disease became clear, Repeal spokesmen became increasingly bitter in their criticism both of the government's failings, and of the callousness of the landlord class. Yet the party continued to give general parliamentary support to the Liberal government. In February 1847 its members voted for the Poor Relief (Ireland) Bill, replacing the public works with outdoor relief (soup kitchens) administered under a temporarily extended poor law, despite the manifest inadequacies of the scheme. At the end of 1847 some Repealers even supported a new repressive measure, the Crime and Outrage Bill.

Several explanations can be offered for the failure of the Repeal movement to respond more effectively to the disaster of the Famine. It is important to remember that, by the time the potato crop first failed in 1845, O'Connell himself was already in rapidly declining health. He died on 15 May 1847, his place as leader being taken by his far less effective son John. Secondly there was the inhibiting effect of the overarching assumption that Ireland's economic and social problems were a direct result of the Act of Union. If the only real solution lay in repeal and the re-establishment of a separate Irish legislature, then the detail of individual relief measures within the framework of the United Kingdom became to some extent irrelevant. Thirdly, responses to the relief programmes of successive governments were shaped by a restrictive pattern of party alliances. The fact was that the Repeal party, despite its ostensibly separate existence, never wholly escaped from being part of the radical wing of the British Liberal party. Some of its parliamentary representatives had sat as Liberals before repeal became an issue; most were to do so again after the Repeal movement had fallen apart. O'Connell himself, partly through past experience and partly through a deep personal antipathy towards Peel, was never able to conceive of the Conservatives as anything other than enemies. This stance, shared by most other Repealers, left the movement pathetically tied to the Liberal government even as it presided over policies that sacrificed growing numbers of Irish lives to the doctrines of free market economics. Finally, and perhaps most importantly, there was a limit to the radicalism to be expected from a parliamentary group whose members, almost as much as those of their Liberal and Conservative counterparts, were solidly based in the propertied classes. O'Connell himself argued for measures to give the tenant farmer greater security of tenure, and to provide employment for the labourer by compulsory tillage. But he set his face firmly against any radical restructuring of the ownership of land, while many of his supporters were unwilling to go even as far as he did in circumscribing the rights of property.

In August 1847 the various Irish political groupings

were in theory called to account for their performance by the announcement of a general election. The Conservatives, split into rival factions by Peel's abandonment of the Corn Laws, returned thirty-one protectionists and eleven Peelites, the Liberals twenty-five M.P.s and the Repealers thirty-eight, two of them members of the breakaway Irish Confederation. Such an outcome, in the aftermath of what had been the worst season of the Famine, only confirms the inability of the electoral system of mid-nineteenth-century Ireland to force an adequate response, from any section of the political elite, to the disaster unfolding throughout rural Ireland.

WHAT, THEN, OF POLITICS outside the electoral system? Ribbonism, descended from the Defender movement of the 1790s, still existed as an underground conspiracy organised round some vague concept of a future national revolution. But its membership was mainly among urban artisans and other wage earners, and it never in practice moved beyond the role of a Catholic secret society for mutual defence. Pre-Famine rural Ireland had also had an active, and at times highly effective, tradition of agrarian protest. Such protest, however, had been an attempt to protect the position of the labourer, cottier and small occupier within the existing agrarian system: secret societies like the Terry Alts and the Rockites were aptly described in 1836 as a vast trade union for the protection of the Irish peasantry. As such they were unable to respond to what was in effect the collapse of the whole framework of economic relationships within which they had operated. There was more violence during the Famine than is sometimes recognised, especially during 1845–6, before prolonged distress had weakened the will to protest. But this took the form mainly of the seizure or theft of food, rather than any attempt at systematic resistance to the policy of government or landlords.

The only real alternative to Liberals, Conservatives and Repealers was the Young Ireland movement. 'Young Ireland', originally a derisive nickname, was a term first applied to a group of literary minded intellectuals associated with the *Nation* newspaper, launched in October 1842. Initially a part of the Repeal movement, the Young Irelanders were already drifting, by the time the Famine began, into open conflict with O'Connell. As young, assertive and self-confident newcomers, they resented O'Connell's autocratic leadership and his tendency to favour an inner circle dominated by sycophantic favourites and untalented members of his own family. As supporters of a nationalism that would embrace both Catholic and Protestant, they criticised O'Connell's willingness to associate repeal with exclusively Catholic interests, notably when he followed the Catholic bishops in condemning the government's scheme for non-denominational university education (the so-called 'Godless Colleges', at Cork, Galway and Belfast). Most of all the Young Irelanders attacked O'Connell's willingness, after the set-back at Clontarf, to consider suspending the demand for repeal in favour of a renewed tactical alliance with the Liberals. The confrontation came in July 1846. O'Connell, whether out of genuine alarm at the recent bellicose language of some of the Young Ireland group, or as a calculated manoeuvre to rid himself of unwelcome critics, demanded that members of the Repeal movement adopt resolutions repudiating the use of violence in any circumstances. Although the Young Irelanders had at that stage no plans for insurrection, they were unwilling to accept so sweeping a declaration. Instead they withdrew from the movement and set up their own organisation, the Irish Confederation. They took with them a small body of supporters, mainly drawn from among the artisans of Dublin and other towns, but mass support remained solidly with O'Connell.

Young Ireland's secession took place just two weeks after reports that blight had again been detected in the year's potato crop. Yet the threat of a second season of famine played little part in the programme of the new movement. Having criticised O'Connell for turning Repeal into a narrowly Catholic movement, its leaders, particularly William Smith O'Brien, saw the split as an opportunity to rally the Protestant propertied classes to a cause now liberated from thraldom to demagogues and priests. Their response to the continuing crisis of the Famine was thus to call, not for any compulsory transfer of resources to those in desperate need, or for measures to force property to meet its responsibilities, but rather for a patriotic union of classes. By the second half of 1847 a newcomer to the movement, James Fintan Lalor, had begun to outline a radically different strategy: beginning with the principle that absolute ownership of Irish land was vested in the people of Ireland, so that the rights of landlords must be subordinated to the common good, he argued that the cause of Irish self-government should be linked to the popular demand for land reform, 'like a railway carriage to a train'. His arguments were in turn taken up by John Mitchel, one of the most militant of the Young Ireland spokesmen. The result, however, was merely to highlight the social conservatism of the Young Ireland leadership. Smith O'Brien and others refused to sanction any linking of social and political agitation, leading Mitchel to secede and set up his own newspaper, the *United Irishman*, in February 1848, with Lalor as a leading contributor.

In the end, of course, Smith O'Brien and others abandoned the quest for a union of classes in favour of a popular rising. The background of continuing famine, and of frustration at the failure of either government or Irish landowners to respond effectively to the crisis, undoubtedly played a part in their decision. Yet it is revealing that the main impetus for the move towards more militant language and tactics that became evident in the first half of 1848 was not the continued spectacle of mass starvation, but the news of revolution on the streets of Paris, and its subsequent spread across continental Europe. Even then, moreover, Smith O'Brien and his colleagues were finally pushed into action only when it became clear that the government intended to move against them, and that their alternatives were to attempt a rising or to submit quietly to arrest, prosecution and certain conviction. The resulting insurrection was a feeble affair. Smith O'Brien, in County Tipperary, attracted a crowd several thousand strong, but these dispersed after an inconclusive shoot-out with two small detachments of police. His instruction to those who flocked to his banner to go home and return with four days' supply of food demonstrated that the Young Irelanders' lack of a coherent military strategy was matched only by their ignorance of the realities of the countryside in which they sought to raise armed rebellion.

By the time that Young Ireland disappeared, following the failure of its insurrection and the subsequent arrest and transportation of several leaders, the Repeal party had also disintegrated. Most Repeal M.P.s moved without undue difficulty into the Liberal party, of which they had in reality always been a semi-detached wing. From the autumn of 1849, however, a new political initiative began. This had its roots in two parallel developments. The first, commencing in Callan, County Kilkenny, in October 1849, was the formation of Tenant Protection Societies in Leinster, Munster, and some parts of Connacht. The second was the revival from early 1850 of a movement among farmers in Ulster to secure legal protection for 'tenant right', the customary entitlement of an outgoing tenant to receive a payment from his successor. A conference in August 1850, attended by representatives from both north and south, established an Irish Tenant League.

At this stage the movement was an extra-parliamentary one. Its leading spokesmen in the south were three journalists, Charles Gavan Duffy, a former Young Irelander and still editor of *The Nation*, Dr John Gray of the *Freeman's Journal*, and Frederick Lucas, the English convert who edited the Catholic periodical, the *Tablet*. The northern tenants had one parliamentary spokesman, the County Down landlord William Sharman Crawford, but he sat as radical M.P. for the English constituency of Rochdale. In 1851, however, a quite separate issue, the introduction of an Ecclesiastical Titles Act prohibiting Catholic ecclesiastics from assuming titles taken from places in the United Kingdom, provoked a group of Irish M.P.s to come together as an informal party, generally known as the Irish Brigade. By August the Brigade had agreed with Sharman Crawford and the League to take up the issue of land reform. The alliance was formalised after the general election of July 1852, when forty-eight of the newly elected members subscribed to a pledge binding them to oppose any government that did not include in its programme a bill to secure tenant right.

At first sight the creation of an independent Irish Party with tenant right as its central demand seemed to herald the birth of a wholly new kind of politics. The reality was more modest. The triumph of 1852, in the first place, did not extend to Ulster. There the linking of the tenant cause with the Catholic campaign against the Ecclesiastical Titles Bill was enough to undermine the initial enthusiasm of Protestant farmers. Only one Ulster constituency, Newry, returned a Tenant Right candidate; even Sharman Crawford was defeated in County Down. Elsewhere too the triumph of popular politics was more apparent than real. Reform of the electoral franchise in 1850, roughly doubling the proportion of the population entitled to vote, had certainly contributed to the success of the Independent Irish Party. But nothing had happened to make it easier for those who were not men of substantial means to compete for parliamentary seats. Of the forty-eight Independents returned in 1852, no less than twenty-four were landowners or sons of landowners. Another fifteen were professional men, once again mainly lawyers. To a large extent, in fact, the Irish Party was drawn from the existing parliamentary class, many of whose members took up the banner of independent opposition in the same pragmatic spirit in which some of them had earlier become nominal Repealers. It is thus hardly surprising that, once they were safely installed in parliament, and once tenant protest and indignation at the Ecclesiastical Titles Act had begun to subside, many should have dropped away. Already by 1853 the original forty-eight supporters of Independent opposition had dwindled to around twenty-five; by 1855 there were no more than a dozen.

Nor was it only at parliamentary level that appearances were deceptive. At first sight the formation of the Independent Irish Party might appear to be the long-awaited political response to the Famine, giving voice at last to those who had borne the brunt of the prolonged disaster. The main victims of the Famine, however, had been the rural poor. Destitution and population loss had been heaviest in the western counties, and everywhere it had been the smallholders and cottiers who had died or been forced off the land. The Tenant League, on the other hand, was dominated by substantial farmers from the prosperous eastern counties. Well over half the delegates at the August 1850 conference came from the four counties of Meath, Dublin, Wexford and Kilkenny. These substantial tenants were spurred into action when bad harvests in 1849 and 1850 exacerbated the problems caused by a fall in wheat prices. Prices had fallen partly as a result of the repeal of the corn laws, but also because of the end of the Famine food shortages. In this sense the Tenant League represented, not the victims of the Famine, but its beneficiaries. And once prices recovered, with the commencement from 1853 of a world wide economic boom that was to last for more than two decades, tenant militancy melted away.

At the same time it would be wrong to single out the Tenant League and the Independent Irish Party for having thus focused on what was, from the point of view of those most affected by the Famine, the largely irrelevant issue of tenant right. The fact was that all political groupings, on those occasions when they did try to take account of the problems of rural Ireland, confined themselves almost exclusively to the same issue. In 1845, for example, Peel's Conservative ministry introduced a measure to compensate vacating occupiers for improvements made during their tenancy, only to abandon it in the face of landlord opposition. The proposals put forward by the short lived 'Irish party' of early 1847 likewise centred on compensation for improvements, as did the whole series of half-hearted attempts at remedial legislation put forward during the Famine by the Liberal government. Repealers went somewhat further, calling not just for compensation but for some greater measure of security of tenure. O'Connell, for example, talked at different times of repealing post-Union legislation that had made evictions easier to arrange, and of restricting the right to recover unpaid rents by legal process to those landlords who had granted their tenants twenty-one year leases. Even Fintan Lalor and Mitchel, the agrarian radicals, based their proposals on the concept of what would later be called the dual ownership of the soil by landlord and tenant. All of these proposals would have contributed in differing degrees to reducing what were by any standards the glaring inequalities between a privileged landlord class and the farmers on whose enterprise and labour their wealth depended. But their relevance to the main victims of the Famine, the smallholders, cottiers and labourers who were more commonly the subtenants and employees of the farmers than the direct victims of landlord exploitation, is more open to question.

Why did the issue of landlord-tenant relations so dominate contemporary thinking? In part it can be seen as the triumph of abstraction over reality. To the uninvolved theorist the contract between tenant farmers and their landlords was more visible, and of apparently greater significance, than the multitude of small scale, informal transactions that dominated the lives of the majority. In part it was a flight from the impossible to the possible. Revision of the law of landlord and tenant was formidable but feasible. In the absence of large scale industrialisation, on the other hand, it was difficult to envisage any future for the huge body of labouring poor that did not involve mass dispossession and emigration. Finally, there were considerations of practical politics. The position of the tenant farmer class may have been less desperate than that of the rural poor. But it was on the former, not the latter, that any attempt to develop an effective popular political movement would have to be based. This was all the more important because many of the measures that might conceivably have been proposed to alleviate the condition of the labourer, cottier and smallholders could have done so only at the expense of the farming class. At one point, for example, Daniel O'Connell suggested that holders of large grazing farms should be required to set aside a minimum proportion of their land for tillage. The proposal confirms O'Connell's stature as a politician of greater perception, and more genuine radicalism, than any of his leading contemporaries. But the fact remains that such a solution, if followed through, would have been deeply uncongenial to the graziers and large farmers that were one of the main pillars of O'Connell's political movement.

What, finally, was the effect of the Famine on Irish political life? In the short term, it has been suggested, the catastrophe may well have weakened nationalist politics, casting doubt on the feasibility of the goal of a self-governing, prosperous Ireland. In the longer term, however, there can be little doubt that the crisis contributed substantially to the growth of nationalist sentiment. To subsequent generations the Famine was proof of the inability or unwillingness of Great Britain to give Ireland the government it required. In 1861 John Mitchel, now in American exile, published *The Last Conquest of Ireland (perhaps)*, in which the charge against British government rose from incompetence or callousness to genocide: the deliberate promotion of mass starvation as a means of completing Ireland's political subjugation. Two decades later the evocation of mass starvation and forced emigration became part of the attack on the twin targets of landlordism and British government developed by Parnellite nationalism. To appreciate fully the significance of the Famine, however, it is also important to remember the audience to which that nationalism addressed itself. Of the main victims of the potato blight, the cottier and smallholder had by the 1880s largely disappeared, while the landless labourer remained as part of a shrinking and subordinate minority. The tenant farmers had thus become the dominant social class in a predominantly rural Ireland. This meant an audience for popular politics that was more prosperous, more sophisticated, and more independent than had been the case in the 1840s and earlier. It also meant that a political rhetoric that equated the cause of the tenant farmer with that of the Irish people had gained much greater credibility. In both these ways the transformation of social structure brought about by the Famine helped to make possible precisely that coherent fusion of political and economic grievances that had so wholly eluded every Irish political grouping during the disaster itself.

THE OTHER GREAT IRISH FAMINE

DAVID DICKSON

IN THE AFTERMATH OF THE Irish Great Famine no public monument was erected to the memory of its victims – although the sesqicentenary commemorations may rectify this. It is ironic that within a ten-mile radius of Dublin there are at least two prominent monuments associated with a much older famine – the obelisk on the top of Killiney Hill, and the extraordinary 140-foot high structure known as Conolly's Folly between Celbridge and Maynooth. These landmarks were erected during the great crisis of 1740–41, the one on Killiney by a minor south Dublin Catholic gentleman, John Mapas, the other near her great house by Catherine Conolly, widow of the most powerful commoner in early Hanoverian Ireland. It is true that obelisks were part of the repertoire of fashionable Palladian demesnes, but the association of two of the most conspicuous examples with philanthropic action and with such dissimilar sponsors point to the singularity of the crisis that precipitated these initiatives.[1]

In trying to establish a context for the Great Famine, we can derive considerable insight by travelling back to that other 'great' famine a century before. Nearly all the early commentators and writers on the Famine of the 1840s, including Trevelyan, Wilde and O'Rourke, were aware of the earlier crisis, but its existence and that of some ten other major Irish famines that occurred over the previous 500 years have truly been overshadowed.[2] We should of course not be too surprised at the almost complete loss of oral tradition and public memory relating to earlier crises, for popular awareness of the Great Famine has been conserved not just because by the enormity of the disaster, but because it

50

remains the most recent catastrophe in Irish history, blotting out recall of older horrors, and also because (unlike all earlier recorded disasters) it occurred in a blaze of publicity and affected a precociously politicised society.

We have but the most fragmentary knowledge of nearly all the other famines of the last millennium in Ireland – defining the word famine as a lengthy period of collective hunger which affected large parts of the country, and which was associated with, or succeeded by, a pronounced surge in the death rate – and we can only speculate as to the mortality levels in any famine before 1700. But taking a long view of Irish famine from the thirteenth to the nineteenth centuries, we can detect two features uniting medieval and early modern crises – a highly uneven distribution pattern of such outbreaks over time, and a tendency for them to be associated with war. Crises clustered in the first half of the fourteenth, the first half of the seventeenth and the first half of the eighteenth centuries. As far as we can tell each such malign phase ended not with a whimper, but with a 'super-crisis': in the fourteenth century with the Black Death, in the seventeenth century with plague and famine during the Cromwellian reconquest, and in the eighteenth century with the disasters of the 1740s. War and unusual climatic instability seem to have been ingredients of the most crisis-prone periods, but the entry of bubonic plague into the catalogue of disaster was fortuitous: most life-threatening epidemics and pandemics that have afflicted Irish people were subsistence-related, but the incidence and virulence of plague, as of smallpox and influenza, were unrelated to the state of the harvest or the adequacy of human diet. Nevertheless, in Ireland as elsewhere, malign coincidence seems to be a necessary ingredient of truly calamitous famines, with extraneous factors – war, plague, or economic crash – being required to turn times of trial into trend-changing catastrophes.

The severity of the mid-seventeenth-century crisis remains tantalisingly opaque; Sir William Petty's near contemporary estimate that between the outbreak of the 1641 rising and *pax Cromwelliana* in 1652 over forty per cent of the population were lost by the 'sword, plague and famine' is unacceptably high, but his suggestion that two-thirds of the losses during these years were caused by the plague of 1649– 53 is more plausible.[3] A few apocalyptic contemporary references hint at the horrors of those years: it was said of Co. Clare in June 1652 that 'the people die under every hedge there, and [it] is the saddest place ... that ever was seen'; a later estimate of the impact on Connacht was that 'upwards of one-third of the population was swept away'; and it has recently been conjectured that about half the houses in Dublin were deserted in the early 1650s. The prolonged anarchic state of the country and the movement of rat-infested armies prevented the enforcement of the most rudimentary public health controls, but it was the combination of plague and famine-induced dysentery which proved so fatal.[4]

The return of warfare on an even larger scale in 1689–91 brought with it a wave of camp- and famine-induced fevers, particularly in the inland counties that were the major theatres of the war. But serious as this was, the cost of 'the war of the two kings' was far more in terms of property destruction and livestock losses than of human mortality. The comparatively swift resolution of the war no doubt helped. In the following two decades, dominated by great wars in the world outside, Ireland was only moderately affected by the harvest crises that traumatised the country's neighbours – Scotland in the mid-1690s, France both in the early 1690s and in 1708–10, years of extremity which lodged in the French peasant consciousness until at least the Revolution.[5]

Ireland was less fortunate in the 1720s. The decade associated with the Drapier's damning indictments of the governance of Ireland started with two bad harvests and ended with three that were worse.[6] But compared with the 1650s, the country was now more commercialised, the economy more diverse, the volume of foreign trade transformed, many towns greatly enlarged, and the infrastructure improved. It was also far more populous: as far as we can tell, the population of most Irish counties had more than doubled since the 1650s.[7] Ironically the grain failures and food shortages of the 1720s appear to have hit the modernised sectors of the economy quite disproportionately: lowland Ulster and the Dublin region (although it is not inconceivable that distress elsewhere, notably in Connacht, was overlooked and under-documented in the official sources).[8] Appalling weather, international commercial depression, and the stresses of unbalanced growth gave rise to a pauper and fever-stricken inflow into the cities; the fledgling Dublin press carried a litany of reports of famine epidemics. These helped to stir up voluntary action, and numerous subscriptions were raised to finance food purchases for the poor. In addition, the government for the first time became involved in organising grain imports. And there was an unprecedented civilian emigration: as many as 15,000 may have departed for the American colonies during the decade, most of whom were Protestants coming from rural Ulster.[9]

The famine death toll of the 1720s, bad as it was, would have been a great deal worse had it not been for the potato. Its cultivation as a garden crop had spread very considerably since the mid-seventeenth century; it had become the dominant winter food of poorer households in Munster, and in parts of Connacht and Leinster by the early eighteenth century. This of course did not insulate the poor from the impact of bad grain harvests, since oatmeal, whether boiled or baked, remained the near universal summer food; furthermore, potato prices were highly sensitive to the movement of grain prices, and could be forced up when oats supplies were expected to run short. But the now widespread consumption of the potato did provide a cushion against catastrophic famine in the wake of the many wet summers and bad grain harvests of the late seventeenth and early eighteenth centuries – until, that is, the fateful Christmas of 1739.

On 27 December temperatures across Ireland fell far below freezing point and a frost, made all the more unbearable by a week of strong easterly gales, set in. What ensued, here and across most of north-western Europe, was – and remains – the most severe period of extreme cold on record. In the translated words of Seaghan Ó Connaire, the parish priest of Cloyne, Co. Cork, 'The Gaels were not all weakened in Ireland/Until from the sky came the harsh east winds which left/us in woe, pain, in debt and hardship'.[10] The Arctic weather lasted almost without remission for seven weeks, keeping the interiors of most houses below freezing, and was followed by an extraordinary set of freak seasons – starting with a cold and rainless spring. By late May it was said that the 'grass and corn were all burnt up and the fields looked as red as foxes'; a cool dry summer was followed by the coldest autumn in two centuries and then by a snowy winter; there was drought but little heat in the summer of 1741, and normal rainfall patterns only returned nearly two years after the first 'great frost'.

Such a bizarre sequence of climatic aberration was hard enough for a poor agricultural society to cope with, but it was the overnight disaster of 27–28 December 1739 that toppled the first domino and precipitated the crisis: all but the potatoes about to be consumed were still in the ground where they had grown, or were stored in shallow pits; such was the frost that nearly all the tubers were frozen and thereby rendered inedible. There followed the first great potato-centred crisis in Irish history, and one made all the worse by the knock-on effects of the strange weather – hypothermia and a collapse in standards of personal hygiene, a huge mortality of cattle, sheep and horses, and a sharp recession in economic activity in the towns. And as if all this was not enough, the outbreak of war in 1740 between Britain and Spain put a great damper on overseas trade and the demand for Irish beef and butter. Much of the seed corn was consumed in the early months of the potato scarcity, and so the cereal and potato acreage sown and harvested in 1740 was greatly down on that of normal years. And because it was a continent-wide crisis, the usual sources of emergency grain to top up Irish supplies, southern and eastern England, and the southern Baltic – were not able to make up the deficit on this occasion.[11]

The population of the country on the eve of this crisis was in the region of 2.4 millions. After the first round of deaths from the cold and starvation, tens of thousands were reduced to begging, to wandering along the highways, and to collecting the classic foods of famine: docks, cresses, nettles, seaweed, and the blood drawn from live cattle. The combination of indigestible and unsustaining food and of dangerously unhygienic living conditions gave rise in the later months of 1740 to a series of overlapping epidemics – typhus, relapsing fever, and dysentery (known then as the bloody flux or *flusc fola*) – with mortality peaking in 1741, *bliadhain an áir*, the year of the slaughter. The Dublin papers in the early months of 1741 commented repeatedly on the march of the killer epidemics across at least three of the four provinces.[12]

It has been a familiar characteristic of all major Irish famines for the death rate to remain far above normal levels after the food supply position has begun to improve; thus thousands were to die even after the gathering in of the relatively abundant harvest of 1741. We have no precise aggregate evidence as to how many died in the crisis, but it is certain that the worst of the suffering was in the south and the west, and that Ulster escaped the great mortality. At least a fifth of the population of Munster, and probably between 12.5 and 16 per cent of the population of Ireland overall, died from famine-related causes, with children and the old being disproportionately represented.[13] In absolute terms this would put the total of crisis victims at between three and four hundred thousand; in relative terms it would suggest that the famine was at least as severe and probably rather more so than the Great Famine itself.

It is worth reflecting further on the differences between these two great disasters. First of all, their duration: the 1740s crisis plumbed the depths *despite* the fact that it lasted only two years, whereas the 1840s crisis was so serious *because* it spanned six.[14] Secondly, the wider context: the great frost was a common European disaster, caused by a freak sequence of abnormal seasons; the 1840s famine was precipitated not by bad weather but by plant disease (with all the virulence of a plague), and its effects were felt only in the relatively small number of regions across Europe where the potato had come to play centre-stage in popular diet. War was a crucial part of the lethal cocktail of 1740–41, as indeed it had been in the worst seventeenth-century moralities; by contrast, the United Kingdom was at peace in 1845, although the Irish crisis was later exacerbated by external factors: the political crisis in Westminster in 1846, commercial recession, wretched cereal harvests and the whiff of international revolution in 1847–48.

Another contrast is geographical: many of the acutely distressed districts in 1740–41 were among the most naturally fertile areas of the country – Tipperary, east Cork and Limerick – and while such areas were also badly affected in the Great Famine, the real blackspots of the 1840s were in regions of lower soil fertility and congested population. Just as the crisis of the 1720s had borne heavily on the vulnerable groups within the modernised zones of the east and north, that of the 1740s can be seen as hitting hardest the new class of near-landless cottiers created by the land-engrossing cattlemen and sheep-masters of lowland Munster. Such families were truly the victims of unbalanced economic development.[15]

In the course of the 1740–41 crisis, there was a huge influx into the southern cities, initially in search of food. Some went further; there was a small rise in the number of emigrants to the American colonies from Dublin and Cork in 1741; the pre-existing channels of seasonal migration – to harvest work in England and the cod fisheries off Newfoundland – were also much busier.[16] But overall there was no transformation in migration as a result of the crisis; cheap transatlantic fares and mass migration were far in the future, and only emerged as a possible response to domestic crisis in the second quarter of the nineteenth century. Emigration became an option, indeed the option, for all but the poorest victims in the next calamity.

The almost complete absence of official documentation on the earlier crisis, compared with the vast public archives and officially sanctioned printed record of the Great Famine a century later points to another more fundamental contrast. No Irish administration, whether in the 1740s or the 1840s, had any appetite for large-scale intervention in the welfare of the crown's subjects, both operating within minimalist definitions of the function and moral parameters of the state; if anything, leading figures in the Irish executive in the 1740s such as Archbishop Boulter were less concerned as to the dangers of government involvement in emergency preventive action in times of famine than were politicians and administrators in Whitehall and Dublin Castle a hundred years later, certainly those of a Whiggish disposition. But whatever about their respective mindsets, the Irish government of the 1740s was far less able to intervene than their successors in the age of Peel and Russell; the eighteenth-century public service had been far smaller, and apart from the revenue service and the army, the authority of the state was entirely mediated through the gentry, the Established Church clergy, and municipal corporations. Irish government by the 1840s was bigger, more centralised and had far more efficient eyes and ears throughout the country. With a national police, an army commissariat and a Board of Works, Dublin Castle had an entirely different range of options if confronted by emergency.

Most important of all, the country from 1839 was endowed with a national poor-law system, financed by local taxation but run with an almost military degree of standardisation in the early years. In the 1740s there had been neither a national nor a comprehensive local system of provision; a non-statutory poor law, whereby the old and infirm received regular alms, operated under the auspices of Church of Ireland vestries in the larger towns and in rural parishes where a fifth or more of the inhabitants were members of the Established Church. But this was of little relevance in an emergency, and the Catholic Church, lacking coherent organisational structures, was in no position to step into the breach. From early in 1740 there was a remarkable flurry of voluntary but uncoordinated initiatives on the part of urban corporations, ad hoc committees, landowners (or their agents), and Protestant clergy; these followed the Ulster precedents of 1727–29 but were on a much larger scale. Most of these consisted of the subsidised or free distribution of meal; a few involved direct employment, along the lines of the Killiney and Castletown schemes.

The internal history of local relief and its effectiveness

57

remains unknown, but the motivation underlying it was more complex than simply timely displays of public spirit and philanthropy. Among the wealthier classes there was an awareness of the link between hunger and the collapse in public health, and a very well-founded fear of social disorder in the towns; such considerations helped to motivate local elites into action.[17] Food riots, usually directed against the houses and storehouses of middlemen hoarding grain, had erupted in Dublin and Cork on several occasions in the early eighteenth century, and in 1740 and 1741 there were repeated disturbances from Sligo to Cork, with fatalities on at least one occasion.[18]

It was fears of this nature that lay behind the gradual extension of the state into preventive and emergency procedures when confronted by harvest failure and the threat of a re-run of 1740. These had a strongly urban bias, and were designed to moderate fluctuations in grain prices, implying quite wrongly of course that all subsistence problems were tied to the outcome of the grain harvests. Arrangements in Dublin were the largest and most elaborate: just as in 1740 some 8,000 had been fed by the city workhouse, its successor institution was used to support over 5,000 in 1784 and 20,000 for some weeks in 1800.[19] From the 1750s governments intervened in the grain trade with greater freedom, and parliament passed a series of acts to enable the establishment of publicly-funded county workhouses ('houses of industry') in the 1770s. However none of the bad years in the second half of the century became full-scale crises, and it was not until the end of the Napoleonic wars and the miseries of 1816–17 that the limitations and deficiencies of relief arrangements were recognised and partially addressed by the innovative Chief Secretary, Robert Peel.[20]

A final point of contrast between the two great famines brings us back to the question of memory and public history: the victims of 1740–41 belonged to a turbulent world where catastrophic turns of fate were only too well known; everyone in their fifties and older would have recalled the horrors of the Jacobite wars, and many younger folk would have been aware of the French famine thirty years before; those who could read the contemporary Dublin newspapers were being given depressing reports of distress from across northern Europe. (Indeed the death rate in parts of Scandinavia turned out to be as high as those in Ireland in the early 1740s.)[21] Nobody saw in the huge Irish carnage a scandal when the weather was so obviously to blame; the generosity of some landlords might be questioned, but nobody faulted government for what had happened. Yet it was remembered: William Harty, writing eighty years later, said that the events of 1740–41 had 'made an impression so indelible that even after the lapse of more than half a century, I have heard the old describe them with feelings of horror'.[22]

The second great famine hit a much altered society: for all the demonstrable problems of the poor, it was possessed of far greater administrative and economic resources than had been the case a century previously; the literate public were a great deal more numerous and better informed as to social conditions at home and abroad. But compared with the gentry-dominated world of the 1740s, the political nation of the 1840s was riven by divisions political, religious, and generational over the country's future. All however could agree that it was an outrage that Ireland, a metropolitan province of the richest kingdom in the world, should be brought to its knees by famine in an era of comparative peace and relative plenty. When that sense of outrage was distilled by the likes of John Mitchel, the last Great Famine was invested with a political as well as a social significance that erased older memories and longer perspectives.

FOOD AND FAMINE

E. MARGARET CRAWFORD

The Potato Crop 1846

Alas! the foul and fatal blight
Infecting Raleigh's grateful root,
Blasting the fields of verdure bright,
That waves o'er Erin's favourite *fruit*.
The peasant's cherised hope is gone
His little garden's pride is o'er,
Famine and Plague now scowl upon
Hibernia's fair and fertile shore.

(ANONYMOUS)

THUS PENNED AN ANONYMOUS POET in *The Illustrated London News* in 1846.[1] It was a feeble verse to describe a terrible disaster: the last Great Famine to occur in the British Isles and one of the last in Western Europe. Between 1845 and 1849, the Irish potato crop failed in three seasons out of four. The devastation was caused by a fungal disease, *phytophthora infestans*, commonly called potato blight. Since the potato was the staple food, frequently the only food, of the Irish poor, the effect was catastrophic. A million people died, another million emigrated, and a terrible legacy was born.

A unique feature of Irish society in the early nineteenth century was the manner in which the potato dominated diets of at least one-third of the population. Contemporary estimates of consumption, ranged from seven pounds to fifteen pounds a day. A particularly detailed pre-Famine dietary survey described large meals of potatoes consumed morning, noon and night, washed down with skimmed milk or buttermilk.[2] Such high dependency on one food explains the enormity of the crisis when disease ruined the crops.

As the extent of the blighted crop emerged, any good parts of the potatoes remaining were retrieved for consumption. Even diseased potatoes were soaked, skimmed of the bad matter and used to make boxty bread (potato bread) or boiled and eaten though with painful consequences. The administration in Dublin initially nurtured the hope that diseased potatoes could be salvaged. To this end a Scientific Commission was set up in 1845 to advise on ways of preserving the potato crop. It included the botanist, Dr John Lindley, editor of the *Gardeners' Chronicle*, who in September 1845 had delayed publication of that journal to make the dramatic announcement of the arrival of potato blight in Ireland, Dr (later Sir) Lyon Playfair, Professor of Chemistry, and Professor Robert Kane the most distinguished Irish scientist of the day. Among the suggestions the Commissioners considered was:

> the ... conversion of potatoes into potato-flour, or into starch and pulp, [which] may afford a suitable employment to certain classes of inmates of the workhouse; and the [Poor Law] Guardians will have the goodness to consider the means by which [these] wishes ... can be carried out.[3]

The necessary implements and machinery were supplied, along with exact details on the method of processing. A Minute Book of the South Dublin Union records the setting up of the apparatus in the workhouse yard.[4] The scheme foundered on practical difficulties with the drying apparatus. In any case, the task facing the government was beyond such technical tinkering.

The fundamental problem can be set out with stark simplicity. The potato crop of 1845 was about one-third deficient. In 1846 three-quarters of the crop was lost. Yields were better in 1847, but little had been sown in the previous season since seed potatoes were so scarce. In 1848 yields again were only two-thirds of normal.[5] Thus there was a yawning gap in food supplies, far beyond the ability of chemistry to plug. But, could policy have succeeded where science failed? There is an enduring belief that the government could have engineered a switch to other foods. In order to test the hypothesis we need to consider the options.

Before 1700 the two main sources of food for the masses

of the population were pastoral products and grain. The moist and cool climate of Ireland provided an ideal environment for the rearing of livestock, and hence the production and consumption of meat, offal, milk and butter. Oats were grown extensively in Ireland; barley, wheat and rye grew in more favoured regions, mainly for export. Oats were incorporated into diets in a wide variety of ways. For example, oaten bread, porridge, and butter rolled in oats. Of these, the most commonly eaten was porridge. In the nineteenth century oatmeal porridge augmented the potatoes and milk diet in the north of Ireland and along the eastern seaboard as far south as county Dublin. Besides porridge, there were oatmeal cakes, oatmeal dumplings and sowans – a mixture of crushed oats steeped in water – sometimes called cherrins. At times oatmeal was simply dampened and eaten raw. Other grain dishes included flummery, a mixture of grain chaff and boiled water, rye porridge, or indeed any grain made into porridge. Cereals, meat and butter continued to be widely consumed among the better off during the eighteenth and early nineteenth centuries, but the poor potatoes largely took their place as more and more meat, butter and grain were exported. On the eve of the Famine, however, cereal-based foods were not available to most of the poor, who neither grew grain nor had the money to buy it. Yet it was a grain with an exotic name, and from a foreign land which provided the main relief food during the Famine crisis. This alien food was Indian meal.

Indian meal is made from maize by grinding and milling the whole maize grain. The cultivation of maize originated in the New World, but had been transported across the Atlantic by returning explorers during the sixteenth century and became established in Mediterranean countries where climatic conditions suited its growth. Maize is generally more drought resistant than wheat, and gives a higher yield per acre. Furthermore, it matures quickly. For these reasons maize has acquired the reputation of being a poor man's cereal.

Indian meal was first introduced into Ireland in 1800 as a relief food for the poor when potatoes were in short supply, although some historians have indicated that it was a new import to Ireland in 1846. According to Cecil Woodham-Smith, 'no trade in Indian corn existed: it was virtually unknown as a food in Ireland'.[6] There is, however, ample evidence of Indian meal being eaten by the poor prior to 1846. In July 1800 the Rev. Vaughan Sampson, recorded the arrival of a schooner carrying a cargo of Indian meal.[7] In the same year John Hancock of Lisburn imported a consignment of 200 tons of Indian meal from Philadelphia to be sold to distressed families.[8] There were sizeable imports of Indian corn and meal during 1800 and 1801, much less in 1802, and none between 1803 and 1826. However, in the distressed year of 1827 Indian meal was imported again. Humphrey O'Sullivan, a school teacher in Callen, County Kilkenny, noted in his diary on 12 May 1827 that 'Indian meal has come in from America: many people like it well: it will keep down the cost of living for the poor'. Again on 27 June 1827 he wrote, 'we were distributing Indian meal today ... the spirit of the Gael is very much broken'.[9] Such references suggest that Indian meal was consumed only when domestic crops failed. During the 1830s and the early years of the 1840s imports amounted to little more than an annual trickle.

Aware of the impending distress, Robert Peel on behalf of the government, purchased Indian corn for £100,000 in the autumn of 1845. The American cargo was to be stored in numerous depots ready for release as the crisis deepened. Sales commenced in March 1846 to those people who could afford a penny for a pound of meal.[10] Private traders were excluded, and local relief committees were permitted to purchase Indian meal only when local prices were rising. By 1847, however, the price of Indian meal had doubled, by which time private merchants had taken over. Even at the enhanced price Indian meal was cheaper than oatmeal, hence its attraction as a substitute for the potato.

The use of Indian meal initially had a major drawback. It could not be processed like home-grown grains because it was particularly hard and so it had to be chopped in steel mills instead of being ground. In addition, it was susceptible to sweating and overheating; consequently unloading and processing had to be done quickly on arrival in Ireland. Early consignments were of old, dry and inferior corn, which exacerbated the technical difficulties of milling it into a digestible form. Other difficulties further frustrated its acceptance. Most people did not know how to cook Indian meal; some tried to eat the meal raw, because they lacked fuel for cooking. As William Wilde pointed out: 'the poor were totally unacquainted with the mode of preparing ... Indian meal ... for food: indeed in many instances, they ate the former raw. Some had no fuel, others were too hungry to carry it home, and all were ignorant of the mode of preparing it either as stirabout or bread.'[11]

The consequences of consuming inadequately ground and incorrectly cooked Indian meal were painful. The flint-hard grain was sharp and irritating, and capable of piercing the intestinal wall. Little wonder it was so unpopular with the Irish, who called it 'brimstone' on account of its bright yellow colour. So strong was the feeling against this foreign food that even workhouse paupers sometimes refused to eat Indian meal, believing they were being poisoned.[12] According to Woodham-Smith, 'attempts to introduce ... [Indian meal] into workhouses to replace potatoes caused riots'.[13] However, as the 1846 season advanced, and dearth intensified, the hungry population was compelled to overcome its dislike of Indian meal. Indeed so widespread did its consumption become, that supplies were very quickly exhausted.

The spectacle of cart loads of wheat, barley and oats continuing to be exported under armed guard, from Ireland while the peasantry starved is an indelible picture in the minds of Irishmen. Associated with this powerful image is the belief that prohibition of grain exports would have averted famine. This is largely myth, although as with all myths it contains a kernel of truth.

It is indeed true that cereal exports continued during the Famine, although it is often forgotten that total exports fell during the Famine years. In fact Ireland became a net importer of grain. Secondly, the government was ideologically committed to free trade; to believe that it could have interfered with private markets is simply anachronistic. Thirdly, even had it done so, the starving peasantry had no money to purchase grain had it been diverted into the home market; it would have had to be given away. Finally, the loss of potatoes was so great. If we translate the potato shortage of the four seasons 1845–49 into calories, the shortfall was twenty-three per cent. Even had all exported grain been directed into domestic consumption, all potatoes and grain previously used for feeding animals or employed to make alcohol and starch used to feed people, and even allowing for imports of Indian meal, there remained a net calorie deficit of the order of twelve per cent.[14]

What else was available? In coastal districts of Ireland, fish, usually herring, complimented the potato diet when in season. Why then, did fish not make a greater contribution to alleviating the starving during the calamitous seasons? Some travellers commented on the inclement weather preventing fishermen from casting their nets. Other commentators such as, William Edward Forster, a Quaker, travelling in the west tells us that initially herrings were unsaleable, 'the people having been so accustomed to use them with potatoes'.[15] More fundamentally, though, few fishing people were able to catch fish, having pawned their fishing nets. In addition, the restricted supply and subsequent high price of fish banished it from the poor man's table.

More easily accessible sea foods were limpets and seaweeds which could be gathered at low tide.[16] So intense was the harvesting of limpets that rocks were picked clean. Several varieties of seaweed were eaten. Carrageen moss and dulse were the most common. Traditionally seaweed was generally cooked, though dulse was often dried and eaten raw. In times of famine beaches were stripped bare of the tidal crop.

Early in the 1846 season, when the diseased state of the potato crop became apparent, inhabitants in mountainous regions, where the growing of grain was impossible, killed grazing sheep.[17] While the mutton lasted the people were well nourished, but all too soon stocks were exhausted and Famine conditions appeared. Such was the desperation of the starving that carrion was consumed with little thought about the diseased state of carcasses.[18] O'Rourke cites the case of a family near Claremorris, County Mayo, whose horse died, after which it was flayed and the carcass left for dogs and birds to feed upon. However, so intense was the family's hunger that they too ate the decomposing carrion.[19]

Cabbage, turnips and swedes were poor alternatives for the potato. They were incapable of providing the nutritional requirements to sustain health. Nevertheless, cabbage and turnips were both used as substitute foods.[20] When all else failed many people resorted to eating weeds. Hungry people had eaten charlock and nettles long before the Great Famine. In 1757, when there was severe starvation in many parts of Ireland, the Rev. Philip Skelton recorded how the hungry subsisted on boiled prushia, which was described as 'a weed with a yellow flower that grows in corn fields'.[21] This was probably charlock, a member of the cabbage family and was commonly found growing in corn fields. A plant of one to two feet tall, it had bright yellow flowers, which perhaps explains the comment that those who ate the weed acquired a yellow hue to their skin. In 1849 English travellers in the west, expressed shock on finding the starving population subsisting on corn-weed and nettles.[22]

As the intensity of the Famine increased various philanthropic groups set up soup kitchens. The Society of Friends was in the forefront of this activity. Their first soup-shop was in Charles Street, Upper Ormond Quay, Dublin, and opened on the 23 January 1847. Others soon followed in towns, cities and rural districts. More soup kitchens were opened by other organisations. The British Relief Association, Father Mathew in Cork, and religious houses, as well as some local gentry, were all involved in soup distribution.

The Society of Friends had an average daily demand of 1,000 quarts of soup at Charles Street, though on some days more than 1,500 quarts were distributed.[23] The Friends' recipe was 120 lbs of good beef, 27 lbs rice, 27 lbs oatmeal, 27 lbs split peas, 14 ounces of spices with a quantity of vegetables and water.[24] A quart of soup cost 1 penny, or, with a piece of bread, 1½ d. The soup shop was open six days a week and provided two distributions of soup daily.[25] The soup served

on the Grattan estate was made to a different recipe. It contained 1 ox head (without the tongue), 28 lbs turnips, $3^1/_2$ lbs
onions, 7 lbs carrots, 21 lbs pea-meal, 14 lbs Indian corn-
meal, and enough water, to make 120 gallons; the result was
described as vile and inedible.[26] Moreover, despite their
hunger, many of the starving complained that the soup
offered increased their suffering because it caused bowel
complaints.

Noting the obvious success of the Society of Friends'
soup kitchens, the government reluctantly changed its policy. From the beginning of the Famine it had clung to the
principle that the poor could be relieved at public expense
only if they entered the workhouses. As the crisis deepened
public works were commenced to provide employment for
the poor. Projects such as road building, pier construction
and land drainage provided a means to earn money with
which to buy food. The schemes, however, were unable to
cope with the enormous numbers of distressed people. As
the public works schemes failed, and workhouses became
grossly over-crowded, another temporary operation was set
up to supply food directly to the starving without cost or the
imposition of a 'work test'. The Temporary Relief Act, or
'Soup Kitchen Act' as it was popularly called came into force
in February 1847. Reluctantly the government recognised
that a network of soup kitchens would feed the starving
more cheaply than public works projects.[27]

At local level, the soup kitchens were under the control
of the poor law unions, and a district relief committee was
responsible at the smaller unit of the electoral division. A
long list of rules and regulations were drawn up. For example, those applying for relief were to be classed into four
categories: (i) the destitute, helpless, or impotent; (ii) destitute, able-bodied though not holding land; (iii) destitute,
able-bodied and holders of small tracts of land; (iv) earners
of very small wages. Only the destitute were to be fed free;
those earning wages which were insufficient to purchase
food at market prices could receive relief at a low cost. Children aged nine years and under were given half rations.

What constituted 'soup' was also a matter of debate. In

the opinion of the Relief Commissioners, soup was any food cooked in a boiler, and distributed in a liquid state, thick or thin, and whether composed of meat, fish, vegetables, grain or meal.[28] The regulations specifying permitted food rations varied too. A ration was set at 1 lb of bread or 1 lb biscuit, or 1 lb meal or flour of any grain, or 1 quart of soup thickened with meal, plus a quarter ration of bread, biscuit or meal. A pamphlet was prepared by Sir Randolph Routh, of the Commissariat Office, Dublin Castle, one of the Relief Commissioners, containing 'the best recipes [he] could procure'.[29] These recipes included ox cheek soup, pea soup, and 'soup without meat'. In addition, the pamphlet provided instructions for the making of breakfast from Indian Meal, directions for using Indian meal without grinding, and on the use of rice, a bread recipe, along with commentaries on scotch barley, beetroot, parsnips and much more besides.[30]

Controversy surrounded whether the kitchens should supply cooked or uncooked food. The Relief Commissioners opposed the dispensing of uncooked food for several reasons. Firstly, the opportunities for fraud were great. For example, in the Union of Ballinrobe the County Inspectors of Weights and Measures seized a set of scales and weights, and placed them in the custody of the police because they were 'irregular'.[31] Secondly, recipients all too often sold their uncooked rations in order to purchase tea, tobacco or alcohol. Thirdly, the Central Board of Health provided practical grounds for issuing cooked food. It pointed out that, through ignorance or lack of fuel, paupers tried to eat raw Indian meal and then suffered intestinal disorders. Fourthly, experience had shown that only the really destitute applied for cooked food rations, and so cooking was an effective way of keeping costs down. There was, however, resentment towards cooked food, the destitute being sensitive to the indignity of receiving relief in that form. On the other hand, the setting up of a soup kitchen, staffing it and supervising the cooking of the soup entailed more effort than some unions were prepared to undertake. Consequently uncooked food was dispensed in some areas notwithstanding the disadvantages.

The task of supplying up to three million meals daily was a daunting one. Organisation was important if the scheme was to succeed. For advice, the government consulted the famous French Chef of the Reform Club in London, Monsieur Soyer. His brief was to concoct a palatable, low cost and nutritious soup. Soyer arrived in Dublin with a fistful of recipes, his model kitchen and apparatus. A building was erected to house this kitchen in front of the Royal Barracks, near Phoenix Park. French cuisine had come to aid Ireland's hungry.

Soyer composed a series of recipes, all impressively economical.[32] His recipe No. 1. contained $\frac{1}{4}$ lb. leg of beef to 2 gallons of water, 2 oz dripping, 2 onions, and other available vegetables, $\frac{1}{2}$ lb seconds flour, $\frac{1}{2}$ lb pearl barley, 3 oz salt and $\frac{1}{2}$ oz. brown sugar. The total cost was 1s. 4d. Recipe No. 2 was even cheaper at under £1 per 100 gallons, and apparently that included the cost of fuel.[33] For flavour mint, bay leaves, thyme and marjoram were recommended.[34] These recipes provoked criticism from a variety of sources. The nutritional value of his meatless soup was questioned. Such was the debate that scientists analysed the soups. Paradoxically, one scientist, John Aldridge, concluded that Soyer's most expensive broth was the least nourishing, while the cheapest was the most nutritious.[35] A correspondent to *The Times* described Soyer's soup as 'preposterous', pointing out that the debilitating effects of a solely liquid diet were well known to the medical officers of our hospital, prisons, and other public establishments.[36] The medical journals entered the fray also. *The Lancet* agreed that, while there was nothing wrong with Soyer's soup, nevertheless it could not be considered as a food able to sustain the 'manufactory of blood, bone and muscle which constitutes the "strong healthy man".'[37] In fact, filling famine-bloated bodies with watery soup did more harm than good.[38]

The workhouses by their very nature became inextricably involved in the Famine crisis. As early as October 1845 a General Order was issued permitting Guardians to 'depart from the established dietaries by substituting the use of oatmeal, rice, bread or other food in lieu of potatoes'.[39] As

Famine conditions intensified one Board of Guardians after another reluctantly ceased to use potatoes, replacing them with cereal foods. Many workhouses served Indian meal mixed with oatmeal and made into stirabout. Several served only Indian meal, often in very large quantities. For example, in the Cashel workhouse the daily ration was 16 oz raw weight; at Lisnaskea it was 20 oz.[40]

As the grip of the Famine intensified more and more ratepayers defaulted, and as a result many unions became bankrupt. Cheques were dishonoured, consequently contractors refused to supply food, and diets deteriorated still further. The effects of severely curtailed rations soon became evident in the physical appearance of the paupers. In January 1847, the Rev. Richard Gibbons, shocked after visiting the Castlebar workhouse, wrote to the Under Secretary for Ireland, Mr T. N. Redington, 'I am pained to have to state that almost every individual [is] showing striking signs of haggard and famished looks; the provisions, oaten or Indian meal, are supplied very irregularly'.[41]

By the end of 1847 chaos reigned in many workhouses. One extreme case, the Ballinrobe workhouse, was the subject of much correspondence. No food was in its kitchen nor eaten in the dining hall. Instead, paupers got their food rations raw in the morning and cooked them in numerous locations throughout the building: in the infirmary, the dormitories, the day room, the nursery, and on fires often lit in rooms without chimneys. The correspondent painfully described conditions as 'a picture of demi-savage life'.[42] So bad had workhouse diets become in the late 1840s that inmates committed crimes in order to get transferred to the relatively better conditions of the gaols. The Inspector-General of Prisons complained that, 'insubordination in workhouses [was] committed solely for the purpose of obtaining gaol dietary'.[43]

By 1848 variations in the menus were almost as numerous as the number of workhouses, indicating that the Commissioners in Dublin had lost control over prescribing the diet. Local conditions rather than edicts from headquarters dictated the menu, with the most destitute areas providing very frugal fare. Throughout the country Indian meal had been adopted in place of potatoes, with no other vegetable supplied as an alternative, although about one-third of workhouses served soup, in some cases described as vegetable soup, in others as broth or meat soup.[44]

As diets deteriorated, so the incidence of nutritional deficiency diseases increased. Earliest to appear was scurvy caused by a deficiency of vitamin C. Initially the ailment was diagnosed as of a 'gastro-enterite' nature caused by the eating of diseased potatoes.[45] Some doctors, however, quickly recognised the symptoms as land scurvy.[46] Scurvy soon became widespread throughout Ireland. Medical records abound with descriptions of red, spongy, swollen and bleeding gums, swollen, painful and discoloured joints, as well as purple discoloration of the skin, all symptomatic of scurvy.[47]

Unquestionably, the cause of scurvy was the absence of potatoes from the diet. The huge quantities of potatoes eaten by the Irish before 1845 ensured a rich daily intake of vitamin C. The failure to replace potatoes with another anti-scorbutic vegetable left the population vulnerable to scurvy. But, if the vitamin C content of the diet was so good when food supplies were adequate why did scurvy appear so quickly when the potato failed? There are two answers. The first is that vitamin C is not a storable vitamin and so man cannot build up reserves. Secondly, the population was conditioned to high levels of vitamin C and so deficiency symptoms appeared early in the crisis. The widespread appearance of the disease in the workhouses eventually prompted the Poor Law Commission to issue a circular on the subject in July 1849.[48] The circular attributed scurvy to insufficient vegetables and milk in the diet. Lack of vegetables in the daily fare was indeed the source of the problem, but unfortunately their directive to the Boards of Guardians was not totally sound. The Commission recommended the inclusion of *well cooked* vegetables, so ruining the vitamin C content of the meals before the paupers ate them.[49]

Along with scurvy there were other vitamin deficiency diseases present in Ireland. A prolonged lack of vitamin A results in xerophthalmia, which damages sight, particularly of children. Although not identified at the time, the dietary

71

evidence and medical reports confirm the presence of xero-phthalmia.[50] Reference to William Wilde's historical survey of diseases in Ireland reveals that an eye affliction which contemporaries called ophthalmia (an infectious eye disease) had long been endemic in Ireland.[51] We lack adequate dietary evidence for earlier episodes, but it is certain that in 1849–50 many people diagnosed as having ophthalmia were in fact suffering from xerophthalmia. The Poor Law medical records provide the clearest evidence.[52] In 1849 the Poor Law Commissioners were greatly alarmed by an epidemic which they described as ophthalmia in the workhouses. It was particularly rife in the overcrowded and insanitary estab-lishments of the south and west and was especially common among children under fifteen year of age.

Two Dublin specialists Professor Arthur Jacob and Dr (later Sir) William Wilde were asked by the Poor Law Commissioners to investigate the disease. Comparison of the symptoms described in Wilde's report with the clinical manifestations of xerophthalmia is revealing. First, he noted the highest incidence was among children.[53] In the Tipperary workhouse ninety-six per cent of cases were children whose ages ranged from four to fourteen years. Only fourteen patients were adults.[54] Secondly, Wilde reported clinical symptoms which correspond to those of the vitamin A deficiency disease, xerophthalmia.[55] Thirdly, the nutritional analysis of diets served to children in the workhouses during the Famine years demonstrates a severe lack of vitamin A. Menus consisted of Indian meal, oatmeal, bread, and gruel, with skimmed milk or buttermilk.[56] The substitution of buttermilk or skimmed milk for whole milk, exposed the children to the effects of vitamin A deficiency,[57] as both are poor sources.[58]

Left untreated, xerophthalmia ultimately results in blindness. Often blindness occurs in one eye only. This pattern once again reflects that found by Wilde. Finally, the strongest evidence we have for vitamin A deficiency among the workhouse children comes from the treatment pre-scribed by Wilde. Three times in his report he recommended cod liver oil: 'the plentiful use of ... which medicine a large supply should at once be procured, and a tablespoonful given to each child, two or three times a day.'[59] Wilde's prescription predated by sixty years the general recognition that cod-liver oil was effective treatment for vitamin A deficiency.

There were probably other vitamin deficiency diseases, including pellagra, which is common among populations existing solely on Indian meal. But the hungry and emaciated were vulnerable to a host of infections such as typhus, relapsing fever and cholera. Among the widespread sickness the more subtle signs of nutritional deficiency went largely unnoticed.

Could the Great Famine have been avoided? In the sense that its immediate cause was a fungus that all but obliterated the basic food of the bottom third of the population, the Famine was a 'visitation of God'. The British government's reaction was tardy and trite, though in fairness, it was dealing with a catastrophe outside its normal experience. It is also easy to mock the spectacle of a French born chef being plucked from the comforts of a London club to solve the problems of the starving peasantry. But the fact remains that neither a Frenchman's soup nor an exotic Indian meal did more than soften the loss of the once friendly potato. The real question to ponder is why the potato had become so prominent in the diet of the Irish in the first place.

FAMINE, FEVER AND THE BLOODY FLUX

LAURENCE M. GEARY

WILLIAM R. WILDE, IRELAND'S LEADING nineteenth-century medical historian, described fever as a malignant presence, one which lurked in holes and corners of the island, ever ready like an evil spirit to break out upon the slightest provocation. According to Wilde, this particular malady had been 'the great element of destruction' in Ireland for hundreds of years, an assessment which would have found few dissenting voices among his medical colleagues.[1]

Fever was endemic in pre-Famine Ireland and flared up periodically into nation-wide epidemics. There was a widespread awareness of the contagiousness of the disease and its ability to leap class and social barriers. Characteristically, fever began among the poor and spread to their social superiors, among whom it proved much more lethal. The disease impinged on rural and urban dwellers, and affected cities, towns and villages, as well as the isolated cabins of the cottiers and agricultural labourers. Fever had a devastating impact on the already precarious existence of the poor. Each attack, with the weakness it left behind, lasted about six weeks and, with successive family members being struck down, fever might persist in a poor man's cabin for months on end. Thus, it had a major pauperising influence, often reducing the poor to absolute penury, a point given graphic emphasis by a labourer from County Cork, who informed the poor inquiry commission in the 1830s that 'a heavy fit of sickness takes the bed from under a man and strips his family almost naked'.[2] An eminent nineteenth-century Dublin physician summed up the popular reaction to epidemic fever when he claimed that it was to be feared above all other diseases. 'It is worse than plague,' he said, 'for it lasts through all seasons. Cholera may seem more frightful, but it is in reality less destructive ... Civil war, were it not for its crimes, would be ... a visitation less to be dreaded than epidemic fever."[3]

The prevalence and perniciousness of fever in the eighteenth and nineteenth centuries and the threat it posed to rich and poor alike provoked considerable debate on its causation and diffusion. Some physicians, notably the contentious and controversial Dominic John Corrigan, argued that the coincidence between malnutrition and infection in Ireland was so great that famine and fever were cause and effect. He claimed that famine was common to all the major fever epidemics that had occurred in Ireland since the beginning of the eighteenth century, from which he deduced that famine was their common cause. This was dismissed as sheer conjecture by many of his contemporaries, who stated that the profession was unaware of the dietary implications of insufficient and poor quality food, beyond the fact that such deficiencies weakened an individual physically and if taken to extremes caused death by starvation. They thought that famine was an aggravating or predisposing, rather than the sole or paramount, cause of epidemic fever, observing that fever often raged in times of plenty and subsided or was entirely absent when privation existed or was on the increase. Finally, they argued, a common causative factor, such as famine, could not account for the symptomatic variations which occurred, often in the course of the same epidemic, including the presence or absence of jaundice and spontaneous nose bleeds.[4]

It is now known that these discrepancies resulted from the frequent concurrence during famine of two distinct infections, typhus fever and relapsing fever. The epidemiology of the two diseases is very similar. Both are caused by microorganisms, transmitted by the human body louse. The typhus infection can enter the body through scratches on the skin, through the conjunctiva, or by inhalation, while relapsing fever is generally contracted through the skin. Typhus symptoms include high temperatures, prostration, mental confusion, and a characteristic rash. In cases which are not going to recover, death usually occurs from heart failure about the fourteenth day. High temperature, generalised aches and pains, nausea, vomiting, nose bleeding and jaundice are features of relapsing fever. The fever ends after five or six days with a sharp crisis attended by profuse sweating and exhaustion. The symptoms return after about a week and there may be several such relapses before the disease runs its course.[5]

Typhus and relapsing fever propagate most actively in conditions which favour lice infestation, notably in the squalid and overcrowded residences of the poor. The relationship between famine and fever is complex, but there is no direct nutritional connection. Subsistence crises and famines created the ideal social conditions for the generation and diffusion of louse-borne and other epidemic infections. Increased vagrancy and mendicity, seemingly inevitable consequences of food shortages in Ireland, were responsible for the dissemination of infected lice throughout the country. It was social dislocation and the disruption of normal living patterns caused by famine which transformed the nation's endemic fever into destructive, terrorising epidemics.[6]

Historically, epidemic fever in Ireland was preceded, accompanied or followed by certain other diseases, notably bacillary dysentery and smallpox. Dysentery and fever, which were popularly known as 'the disorder' and 'the sickness', were described by one authority as inseparable companions.[7] Another claimed that their epidemic concurrence at various times in Ireland and, to a lesser extent, their constant co-existence as endemic diseases, was a striking feature of the natural history of the country.[8]

The term 'dysentery' was formerly applied to any condition in which inflammation of the colon was associated with the frequent passage of bloody stools. Hence, its earlier designation, 'the bloody flux'. The term is now restricted to amoebic dysentery, which is almost entirely confined to tropical and sub-tropical countries, and to bacillary dysentery, an infectious disease which may occur sporadically or in epidemics. The disease is caused by the dysentery bacillus and the infection is spread by flies, by direct contact, or by pollution of the water by faeces infected with the bacillus. Symptoms vary from those of a mild attack of diarrhoea to those of an acute fulminating infection. The duration of the diarrhoea varies from a few days to a fortnight, depending upon the severity of the attack. There may also be nausea, aching pain in the limbs, and shivery feelings, while there is always fever. An attack cannot develop except through the agency of the specific bacillus. However, anything which causes an intestinal upset, such as unsuitable food, predisposes to infection. Dysentery is rendered more virulent by famine and by the concurrence of other exhausting diseases. At one time, mortality rates were as high as fifty per cent during epidemics.[9]

Dysentery is strongly conditioned by nutritional status, but smallpox, the third of the epidemic triumvirate which had ravaged Ireland for generations, is so virulent that it acts independently of nutrition.[10] As with fever, it was the social consequences of famine, especially the increase in vagrancy, which provided the ideal conditions for the propagation and diffusion of this highly infectious disease, one which killed, disfigured, blinded and terrorised countless thousands in Ireland and elsewhere in pre-modern and modern times.

The coincidence between dearth and disease, which many eighteenth and nineteenth century doctors noted, was indeed striking. Famine and fever occurred in Ireland in all but two decades of the eighteenth century, most seriously in 1740–41, when, according to one anonymous pamphleteer, fever, dysentery and smallpox 'swept off multitudes of all sorts; whole villages were laid waste by want and sickness and death in various shapes; and scarce a house in the whole island escaped from tears and mourning'.[11] Estimates of the mortality vary from 80,000 to five times that number. Modern historians tend to the upper reaches, suggesting that between 250,000 and 400,000 people died of hunger and disease during these two years. Proportionately, this is an even higher death rate than that of the Great Famine a century later.[12] The next major fever epidemic followed in the wake of the 1798 rebellion. It was fuelled by climatic extremes, deficient and poor quality harvests, and rapidly rising food prices. The state of the poor in the principal Irish towns at the turn of the century was wretched in the extreme. It became even more so after the fall of Napoleon, when wartime buoyancy was followed by severe economic depression, a downturn which triggered the most extensive and virulent fever epidemic in Ireland between the great famines of the 1740s and the 1840s.

While doctors differed over causation, there were some aspects of fever which were largely beyond dispute, such as the contagiousness of the disease, its tendency to appear at times of social upheaval or economic crisis, and its consequences. These recurring features may be illustrated by referring to any eighteenth or nineteenth century fever epidemic. I have chosen that which occurred between 1817–19 simply because it is better and more accessibly documented than any of the others. Two substantial contemporary histories were compiled, the first by the Dublin physicians, John Cheyne, a pietistic Scot, and Francis Barker, professor of chemistry at the University of Dublin.[13] Their work was complemented by that of another Dublin medical practitioner, William Harty, whose approach was sharper and more critical of the government's response.[14]

The winter of 1815–16 had been unusually prolonged. It was followed by a cold, wet summer which resulted in a very late and depleted grain harvest. The quality of the corn that was saved was very poor, as was the straw used for bedding. Potatoes were small and wet. Turf could not be harvested because of the incessant rain and the shortage of fuel resulted in imperfectly cooked food, damp clothing and bedding, inadequately ventilated rooms, and a deterioration in personal and domestic hygiene. Similar climatic conditions, with the same distressing consequences, prevailed in the following year. The hardship caused by inclement weather and poor harvests was compounded by the bankruptcies, growing unemployment and falling wage rates which characterised the post-Napoleonic period. The price of potatoes, oatmeal and bread, the staples of the poor, increased alarmingly, particularly in Dublin.

The scarcity and cost of potatoes and grain reduced the

rural population to grubbing in the fields and hedgerows for whatever they could find growing wild, including herbs of various kinds, such as rape, borage, mustard, nettles, water cress, kale, which was normally fed to cattle, and prasha bui, the colloquial name given to the leaves of the wild turnip. There were food riots in several urban centres, just as there had been during previous shortages. A mob attempted to prevent oatmeal being exported from Galway. Corn mills and stores were attacked in Limerick and various efforts were made to seize food in Dublin. Bakeries and other provision shops were plundered, while individuals delivering bread were robbed in the streets.[15]

Almost inevitably, the age-old pattern of fever succeeding food shortage was repeated. The disease appeared epidemically in some places in late 1816 and was prevalent throughout Ireland by the spring of the following year, diffused to the country's outermost reaches by multitudes of wandering beggars. It was a common observation that the numbers tramping the roads of Kerry during the years 1817–19 were so great that the whole country appeared to be in motion. The indigent from Kenmare and other impoverished areas of the county streamed into north Cork and took up residence wherever they could. According to Dr Galway of Mallow, 'every farmer's outhouse was occupied by groups of squalid creatures, who were shortly seen to crawl out, begging alms in all stages of typhus fever'. The situation was no different in other parts of the country. Kilkenny was said to be 'inundated with mendicants from every part of Ireland'. More than 200 people a day crossed the river Bann eastwards at the bridges of Toome and Portglenone, from the beginning of May to the middle of July 1817, most of them driven by 'the utmost extremity of want'. In that same month of July, some 1500 strangers were soliciting alms in the parish of Donegore, County Antrim. Migrants were seldom refused a night's lodging in most parts of the country and thus, according to Barker and Cheyne, 'the humane and hospitable dispositions of the people of Ireland mainly contributed to introduce contagion into their dwellings'.[16]

Assemblies of any kind were regarded as foci of contagion. Wakes, funerals, weddings and patterns were condemned for the role they played in spreading fever. Soup kitchens attracted considerable censure also. The promise of a free meal drew large numbers of the destitute and the hungry, many of them fever-stricken, into cities and towns, and thus facilitated the transference of infected lice to new victims. Some medical practitioners believed that food depots, by relieving hunger, were instrumental in suppressing fever, others that they contributed to its dissemination by assembling large crowds of paupers. There was no such ambiguity regarding wakes. During the traditional forty-eight hour mourning period, friends, namesakes and relatives assembled to pay homage to the memory of the deceased and to indulge in the copious supplies of whiskey, snuff and tobacco that were generally available on these occasions. It was part of the Irish tradition that even the most lowly in life should be so honoured in death. The survivors would have considered themselves eternally disgraced if the customary homage had not been paid to the memory of the deceased.[17] There was considerable irony in the fact, as a County Clare clergyman observed, that those who would not go near a house while the fever stricken occupant was alive were prepared to spend the whole night there after his death.[18]

The enormity of the 1817–19 epidemic overwhelmed the existing resources and made computation difficult. There were huge discrepancies in morbidity and mortality estimates, just as there had been in 1740–41. William Harty concluded that some 800,000 of the total population of almost 6,000,000 had contracted fever and that 44,300 died of the disease. In making his calculations he allowed for the acknowledged deficiencies in the admission and mortality registers of temporary and permanent fever institutions. Record-keeping was as rudimentary as much of the accommodation that was hastily provided for the stricken. There were no statistical returns for some counties, such as Mayo and Donegal. An inestimable number of individuals died in many parts of the country where there were no medical institutions of any kind. Many of the infected were tended at home or, more likely, consigned to one of the primitive isolation-shelters which dotted the countryside. As a result, Harty was forced to resort to what he called 'conjectural calculation', but, he insisted, there was sufficient data to enable him 'to approach the truth', to deduce 'a probable estimate of the extent and mortality of this disease'.[19] Such fudging did not deter the pioneering Irish social historian, Kenneth Connell, who considered Harty's figures 'a fair guide'. However, as the latter had underestimated the country's population by almost 1,000,000, the numbers for the sick and dead needed to be inflated to about 850,000 and 50,000 respectively, according to Connell.[20] In reality, Harty's figures were little more than guesswork, and Connell's reasons for accepting them are unconvincing. It is surprising that he did not even refer to Barker and Cheyne's estimates. They concluded that one-quarter of the country's population, some 1,500,000 in all, were stricken by fever between 1817 and mid-1819 and that some 65,000 died. They based their calculations on reports they received from various parts of the country and on the proportion of deaths to hospital admissions.[21] As such, they are as questionable as Harty's.

The quarter of a century which followed the 1817–19 fever epidemic was marked by repeated failures of the potato crop and recurring outbreaks of infectious disease. This debilitating cycle culminated in the cataclysm of the Great Famine, when all the features of the 1817–19 epidemic recurred, but with added, almost apocalyptic, violence. The traditional estimate that the famine of the late 1840s was responsible for some 1,000,000 excess deaths has been corroborated by recent research.[22] Relatively few died from actual starvation, the majority succumbing to diseases which were collectively described by one medical observer as 'a sort of famine poison'.[23] The great despoiling infections were typhus, typhoid and relapsing fever, dysentery and diarrhoea, severe measles, and smallpox of a 'peculiarly malignant character', which, according to the Board of Health, prevailed very extensively in 1849.[24] Cholera, which affected Ireland pandemically in 1848–49, was not one of the fevers of the Great Famine. Its appearance was coincidental but it contributed to the overall distress and mortality.

The loss of nearly one half of the potato harvest of 1845 did not cause undue distress and it was not until the general failure of the crop in the following year that infection began to spread. Most parts of the country experienced the onset of epidemic fever during the winter and spring of 1846–47, although there were some variations. The disease appeared in Ahascragh, County Galway, as early as April 1846, while parts of Donegal were not affected until November of the following year. By the middle of 1847, one-third of the population of Cork consisted of those who had been pouring into the city from all parts of the county since the previous October, individuals who were described as 'shadows and spectres, the impersonations of disease and famine'. All parts of the country were not similarly affected. A few areas in County Down, for instance, appear to have escaped epidemic fever altogether.[25] In general, death from starvation and disease was highest in the far west, high in Munster and south Ulster, and very low in Dublin and east Ulster.[26]

Doctors blamed the outbreak of fever on hunger and its social consequences, on the almost tangible misery, distress and despondency which appeared to be everywhere. There was a complete disintegration of the social norms, the only reality being the desperate search for sustenance. Hygiene was neglected, clothing and bedding were pawned or left unchanged for months on end, and displaced families, who had abandoned their holdings, or been evicted, congregated together in vacant cabins throughout the country. The sick and dying clamoured for admission to the workhouses, while the jails and bridewells were filled to overflowing. Dirt, neglect and gross overcrowding generated fever, which was diffused in a variety of ways, by vagrancy, by the intermingling of the infected, the convalescent and the healthy at soup shops, food depots and public works. Even those who were barely able to crawl out of their makeshift beds were compelled by the direst necessity to report for work on the roads, where, according to one County Kilkenny doctor, they occupied themselves 'in industrious idleness' and in infecting their susceptible work-mates.[27]

The epidemic fever of the late 1840s was popularly

known as 'famine fever', 'starvation fever', 'the fever', the 'relapse fever of 1847', 'five days' fever' and 'road fever', because it was said to have originated with the vast numbers of vagrants, mendicants and migrants on the public roads. Relapsing fever was the prevalent disease among the poor and the destitute, while the higher social classes tended to contract the more deadly typhus fever, particularly those who were more exposed to infection, notably clergymen, doctors, members of relief committees and those connected with the administration of the poor law.[28] The mortality rate from typhus was also more pronounced among the middle and upper classes than it was among the poor. In the words of Dr Carroll of Waterford, fever fatality increased in the ratio of the rank and respectability of the individuals attacked.[29] A distinctive feature of famine fever, one on which several doctors commented, was the peculiar smell which clung to the clothes and bodies of the poor. A County Clare physician observed that 'the sooty and peat-smoke odour of former times' had given way to a more offensive, sickening and readily recognisable one. This emanation was described by a doctor in west Cork as 'a cadaverous suffocating odour', a 'peculiar mousy smell', which was 'always the forerunner of death'.[30]

Among the poor, dysentery and diarrhoea were the most frequent and most fatal complications of famine fever. According to Dr Daniel Donovan of Skibbereen, County Cork, chronic dysentery, or 'starvation dysentery' as it was sometimes called, was almost universal among the destitute. He categorised this affliction as the most complicated and loathsome of diseases, one which was infinitely more lethal than cholera. Donovan recorded the symptoms of chronic dysentery as he had witnessed them in one of the worst affected areas of Ireland during the terrible winter of 1846–47. He noted that the pulse was almost entirely absent, that the extremities were livid and cold, the face haggard and ghostlike, the voice barely audible and reminiscent of the cholera whine. Anasarca of the feet, legs, scrotum and penis developed and very often sloughing of the mouth, tongue, throat and nostrils. The smell from evacuations was very offensive,

83

almost intolerable, and was similar to that of 'putrid flesh in hot weather'. The discharges continued unabated until the body wasted to a skeleton. The patient, although extremely debilitated, retained his faculties to the last and expired without a struggle. Donovan carried out more than 100 post-mortem examinations of individuals who had succumbed to this terrible malady. He was surprised not that so many should die from chronic dysentery but that any should survive, given the extremely disorganised state of the bowels.[31]

This deadly infection was attributed to the potato substitutes which the starving were compelled to eat, to the pickings of field, hedgerow and shoreline, and especially to the immoderate consumption of raw or partially cooked Indian meal by individuals who had neither the knowledge, firing or restraint to prepare it properly. A County Dublin dispensary doctor testified to 'the violent attacks of colic, dysentery and diarrhoea' he had witnessed following the use of this food.[32] One of his colleagues in west Cork thought that the dietary transition from modest quantities of turnips and sprats to excessive amounts of 'highly nutritive' Indian meal almost goaded the digestive system into disease.[33] The board of health concurred. They advised the relief commissioners in March and again in May 1847 against doling out uncooked food to the hungry, on the moral ground that it was often exchanged for money, tea or tobacco, and, more importantly, because the consumption of raw or inadequately cooked Indian meal, oatmeal, or rice was responsible for the dysentery and diarrhoea which were wreaking such havoc throughout the country. Reports from the board's medical advisers suggested that the dispensation of cooked food had a marked effect in checking bowel complaints and, they added, the districts most free from disease were those where this policy had been adopted.[34] An anonymous reviewer of the health commissioners' post-Famine report to the lord lieutenant castigated 'the bungling officials connected with the relief works' for failing to realise that starving paupers seldom had the fuel or the utensils to cook the food they were given. He concluded that the distribution of raw Indian meal to starving, debilitated, often homeless beggars was about as useful as a daily ration of river sand.[35]

Like other relief workers, medical practitioners were pre-occupied and disturbed by the rending scenes of misery and distress which confronted them on a daily basis and which they were largely powerless to alleviate. They were perplexed by the inability of medicine and the inadequacy of their art to check the pestilence which raged around them.[36] Doctors knew that dearth and disease were closely linked. They were also aware that they did not have the antidote, that there was little they could do to counteract illness which originated in squalor and starvation.[37] The political intervention they sought was overtaken by the natural. Famine-related death and emigration depleted the reservoir of disease in Ireland and the incidence of fever and other infectious diseases was significantly reduced in the wake of the disaster. It was one of the ironies of the Great Famine that the virtual extirpation of the underclass which harboured illness and infection rendered the future safer for the survivors and their children.

Acknowledgement
I would like to acknowledge my indebtedness to the Wellcome Trust, whose generous support facilitated the research on which this essay is based.

IDEOLOGY AND THE FAMINE

PETER GRAY

AT THE HEART OF RECENT HISTORICAL controversies over the Great Famine has been the question of responsibility. In the last few years a number of historians have questioned what had come to be the orthodox view that the governments of the day did all that could reasonably be expected of them within the constraints of the time. 'Revisionist' historians writing since the 1950s have been accused of adopting a tone of 'generosity and restraint' when considering the state's response to the crisis.[1] Criticism has been fuelled by Brendan Bradshaw's plea that the emotive and catastrophic aspects of the Irish past be re-incorporated into academic history-writing.[2] These new developments in the study of the Famine have re-opened many old debates, while by no means endorsing the populist-nationalist interpretations encapsulated by Gavan Duffy's charge that the Famine was 'a fearful murder committed on the mass of the people'. Rather, they have sought to transcend the sterile polarity between nationalist 'mythology' and revisionist debunking, by taking seriously the bitter popular and folk traditions of the Famine, and by questioning the soothing platitudes which have appeared in some accounts.[3]

The role of British government has come under renewed scrutiny as to the extent it can be held responsible for the Famine mortality of over one million in five years. This is a complex issue, as it is subject to other important considerations such as the bureaucratic capabilities of the early Victorian state. These matters are dealt with in detail elsewhere – what concerns us here are the ideological motivations and constraints on ministers, and the effects of these on the formation of policy. The focus will be on the Whig-liberal government that presided over the worst years of the Famine from mid-1846 to mid-1849.

Ideology is understood here as the framework of ideas – the world-view – that moulded how individuals and groups perceived the problems that faced them. Ideological constructions circumscribed the interpretation of such catastrophes as the potato blight and the resultant famine. They were significant in determining what were acceptable modes and levels of response to the crisis, giving legitimacy to some and not others. Ideology must also be considered in a dynamic sense as the competition of rival ideas for supremacy in the political sphere. The political fault-lines were numerous and shifting: between Great Britain and Ireland, between class groupings in each country, between administrators and politicians, between, and more importantly within, political parties. The importance of ideologically-driven individuals in formulating policy has been recognised by previous writers; Cecil Woodham-Smith's spirited if somewhat narrow castigation of Charles Trevelyan being the classic case.[4] But if the role of ideology is to be properly understood, it must be linked to a detailed study of the political history of the Famine years, and of the broader public and intellectual context of British politics.[5]

The allocation of responsibility for actions a century and half ago poses serious historical problems. Historians risk falling into gross anachronism in attempting to pass judgement on long-dead individuals. Yet, while allowing for an inevitable present-oriented bias on the historian's part, the attempt should be made. The question then arises whether intentions or consequences should be the criteria for judgement. Any neglect of the adverse consequences of policy may be treated as culpable, if it can be shown that these were public knowledge. Yet it is the active intentions of policymakers that may be considered more reprehensible. An evaluation of responsibility thus requires an understanding of the debates of the time, and the existence of articulated and feasible alternatives to the policies actually implemented. That such choices were perceived to exist in the later 1840s, and that they were linked to ideological differences, is suggested by Lord Clarendon's agitated appeal to the prime minister in August 1847: 'We shall be equally blamed for keeping [the Irish] alive or letting them die and we have only to select between the censure of the Economists or the Philanthropists – which do you prefer?'[6]

BEFORE CONSIDERING SOME OF the crucial decisions taken by the government, the main ideological and political groupings should be sketched out. The tradition which has often attracted most attention is that of classical political economy. Classical economic thought had, over time, become increasingly technical in expression and posed difficulties even for well-educated laymen, but its authority as an 'orthodox' system was augmented by this very abstruseness. Its leading practitioners in the 1840s were anxious not only to refine economic theory, but to translate it into policy. They included Nassau Senior, G. C. Lewis, Robert Torrens and Richard Whately. Politically, they were associated with the 'Bowood set' presided over by the Whig Lord Lansdowne and which included Lord Monteagle and other 'moderate liberals'. Orthodox economists were, however, partisans more of policy than of party, and, in common with their 'moderate' colleagues, often looked as much to liberal Conservatives such as Sir Robert Peel.[7]

While Malthus and Ricardo had been pessimistic about Irish over-population and under-development, the next generation of economists were generally more hopeful about the development of agricultural resources and productivity at a rate higher than the growth of population.[8] Encouraging capital investment in land became their priority, along with securing guarantees of security for freedom of outlay and certainty of return. To be successful, a re-organisation of landholding was essential, as they held that only large-scale capitalist farming on the English model could be efficient. Greater productivity would provide increased and more regular employment for labour; higher expectations and consumption would be made possible by the replacement of subsistence crops by wages.[9] The classical economists did not look to *laissez-faire* (or complete non-intervention) as a prescription for Irish woes; there was a consensus that Ireland could not follow the English path to development without aid. Government action was thought legitimate to build a public infrastructure and provide education, and both the Irish Board of Works and National Education system had strong orthodox support. Indeed, the poor inquiry chaired by Senior's friend, Archbishop Whately, reported in 1836 that more remunerative works, and some assisted emigration were vital for Ireland.[10] Not surprisingly, a number of 'improving' Irish landowners came to put their trust in classical prescriptions.[11]

The relief of destitution, whether endemic or due to exceptional causes, was a greater problem for orthodox thinkers. Senior and his associates resolutely opposed the extension of a compulsory poor law to Ireland, on the grounds that in such a poor country, it would drain scarce resources away from employment into 'useless' relief to the able-bodied. Moreover, Irish living conditions were thought so bad that no workhouse or labour test could prevent abuses.[12] Their failure to prevent Whig governments introducing first a limited Irish poor law in 1838, and then extending this as the central plank of Famine-relief policy in 1847, demonstrates the limited influence of Senior and his allies over policy-making at pivotal times.[13] Orthodox economics was more important in the broad appeal of its arguments for rejecting 'visionary' experiments affecting existing property rights, and for producing a climate of opinion that prioritised economic development over the relief of suffering, even in conditions of social catastrophe.

Several variant forms of economic thought were at least as significant. What became known as the 'Manchester school' was more radical, extreme and optimistic. It drew on general principles of orthodox thought, such as the desirability of free trade and *laissez-faire*, popularised them and rendered them more dogmatic.[14] Lacking any outstanding theorists, this group was committed to campaigning for changes in state policy, and was most influential among the politicised middle classes and in the liberal press. The Anti-Corn Law League was its initial focus; after 1846 it turned towards a more direct assault on landowners and their social privileges as obstacles to economic development.[15]

This class antagonism differentiated the Manchester school from orthodox thinkers, but more important was their adherence to a labour theory of value – the doctrine that capital is merely accumulated labour. From this flowed the idea that economic backwardness stemmed not from under-capitalisation, but from restrictions on the freedom of labour and the use of resources. When applied to Ireland these ideas rejected Malthusian pessimism entirely: Ireland was seen as potentially an extremely wealthy country that could support several times its current population. What was required were measures to force Irish landowners to employ the poor, and a 'free trade in land' to facilitate their replacement by agricultural entrepreneurs if the current owners failed.[16] Manchester-school economics appealed primarily to radical politicians and their constituencies, but a number of leading Whig-liberals were also drawn towards its optimistic dynamism and faith in progress.

A second offshoot from classical economics was that associated with a smaller group of heterodox writers in the 1840s. Theoretically more sophisticated than the Manchester school, they shared much of its optimism and criticism of aristocracy. They differed most in their support for alternative models of Irish development to that of crude Anglici-sation. William Thornton, John Stuart Mill and George Poulett Scrope agreed that it was the relationship of landlord and tenant that lay at the root of Irish economic back-wardness: all looked positively on the alternative model of peasant proprietorship existing in other European countries and in the Channel Islands. Once predatory landlordism had been restrained and peasants secured in their holdings, they believed the 'magic of property' would create the necessary motivation for investment and exertion from below. Detailed suggestions as to how such a revolution in agrarian power-relationships could be brought about were more trouble-some, but all these writers agreed that the Famine presented the government with an opportunity to intervene to recon-struct Irish society, preferably by confiscating waste and

90

uncultivated lands for reclamation by the rural poor.[17]

This heterodox argument coincided with an increasingly vociferous popular agitation in Ireland for land reforms.[18] For a number of Whig politicians anxious to defuse the cry for Repeal by granting a measure of 'Justice to Ireland', such ideas were particularly attractive. Lord John Russell and his Lord Lieutenant, Lord Bessborough, had a reputation for reformist co-operation with O'Connell. They identified themselves with the populist or 'Foxite' tradition of Whiggery rather than with orthodox liberalism,[19] and were anxious to introduce 'some great scheme' for Ireland in 1846.[20] The intensification of the Famine was to expose both the limitations of this commitment and their political weakness, but the interventionist leanings of this group of senior Whigs should not be underestimated.

All these schools of thought interpreted the Famine disaster in the light of their own diagnoses of the 'Irish problem' and plans for Irish reconstruction. The very scale of the crisis tended to push each towards an inflexible insistence on their own preferred panaceas. These economic ideologies were in turn variously affected by a pervasive religious mode of thought, which tended to reinforce such rigidity. This was Providentialism, the doctrine that human affairs are regulated by a divine agency for human good.[21] More an interpretative language than a unified body of thought, Providentialism took several forms. What concerns us here is the extent to which ideological stances on the Famine were validated and intensified by the widespread belief that the potato blight had been sent by God for an ascertainable purpose.

Ultra-Protestants predictably saw the blight as divine vengeance against Irish Catholicism and on the British state that had recently committed such 'national sins' as endowing the Catholic seminary at Maynooth.[22] Yet as this faction was effectively marginalised in the national politics of the later 1840s, anti-Catholicism played little explicit part in goverment policy during the Famine. Many more interpreted the 'visitation' as a warning against personal and national pride and extravagance, and as an inducement to engage in

charitable works for Ireland. The state gave some endorsement to this view by instituting a 'national day of fast and
humiliation' and supporting the establishment of the British
Association for relief in early 1847.[23] For some, like the indefatigable American Asenath Nicholson and numerous Quaker groups scattered across Ireland, the Christian duty of
charity continued to dominate their actions throughout the
Famine. But for many in Britain, charitable feelings existed
alongside a strong desire to see the fundamental changes in
Ireland they believed would prevent any need for repeating
such private generosity.[24]

What gave Providentialism some degree of ideological
coherence was the existence of a Christian political economy
that had evolved alongside the classical tradition in economics. Clerical economists such as Chalmers, Sumner and
Copleston had a profound influence over a British social elite
that was imbued with the ethos of evangelical Protestantism.
They urged governments to remove restrictions to economic
freedom less to promote economic growth, than to subject
individuals to the moral discipline of the 'natural economic
laws' instituted by God.[25] 'Direct' acts of Providence, such as
the potato blight, could be interpreted in this tradition as
special 'mercies', sent to oblige men to remove artificial obstacles to the divine order. Sir Robert Peel's tying of the
potato blight of 1845 to the policy of removing the Corn
Laws can be read in this light.[26] The British obsession with
free trade in food from 1846 reflected the power of this ideological connection.[27]

Many of the better-known Christian political economists
were conservative and evangelical, and were most influential over Peel and his followers. Yet as with classical economics, popularised and radicalised forms of the doctrine
had a greater impact on the early Victorian middle classes
and their political leaders. Providentialism blended with
Manchester school economics to produce a moralistic reading of the Irish crisis, that put the blame for the state of Irish
society squarely on the moral failings of Irishmen of all
classes. Consequently the Famine was welcomed as an God-
given opportunity to enforce a policy that would transform

Irish behaviour.[28] Moralism was embraced by Whig-liberals such as Earl Grey, Charles Wood, Sir George Grey and the civil servant Charles Trevelyan, who sought to place themselves at the head of radical public opinion, and who were deeply infused with evangelical piety. The political consequences of this were summed up by Trevelyan in October 1846:

> I think I see a bright light shining in the distance through the dark cloud which at present hangs over Ireland ... The deep and inveterate root of *Social* evil remain[s], and I hope I am not guilty of irreverence in thinking that, this being altogether beyond the power of man, the cure has been applied by the direct stroke of an all wise Providence in a manner as unexpected and unthought of as it is likely to be effectual. God grant that we may rightly perform our part and not turn into a curse what was intended for a blessing.[29]

There were other influences and ideologies operating in British politics in this period. Protectionist Toryism was released from Peel's constraining influence when the Conservative party split in 1846, but remained on the defensive in the following years. Policy initiatives on Ireland tended to be individual efforts and directed mainly at shoring up the beleaguered Irish landowning elite. Lord George Bentinck's proposed railway scheme in February 1847 lacked the solid support of his Protectionist party and was denounced by radicals as a subsidy to landowners and by Peel as an infringement of fiscal orthodoxy, and was heavily defeated.[30] Where British Tory intellectuals did consistently attack the liberal consensus, it was to criticise the principle of free trade, not to advocate greater relief spending to meet the distress 'which the heedlessness and indolence of the Irish had brought upon themselves'.[31] At the other extreme, British working-class radicalism was in abeyance as an organised force until the Chartist revival of 1848. Some working-class political leaders sympathised with the radicalism of the Young Ireland movement, and particularly with the ideas of James Fintan Lalor,[32] but it is unclear just how far this extended. Many radical periodicals aimed at the lower classes adopted a staunchly moralist and anti-landlordist position.[33]

In assessing the motivations for government action, it is always necessary to consider not only the ideological and political forces, but the nature of administrative practice and organisation. Much of what any government does in response to imperative problems is to follow procedures laid down by precedent, and this was to some extent true of reaction to the Irish Famine. The policy adopted by Peel's government in 1845–6 owed much to earlier famine-relief actions and reliance on existing structures. Yet the continuities can be overstated. Underlying Peel's response was a belief that the potato failure of 1845 heralded the beginning of a profound social transformation in Ireland, and that the repeal of the Corn Laws created a new context for Irish development.[34] All leading politicians grasped that the Great Famine required new directions in policy.

Government officials in Ireland were no more immune to the prevailing moods of opinion than were ministers. Commissariat officers often expressed the conviction that relief measures should, as one put it, 'as far as it is possible, have a view to the future, however discouraging they may be in *initio*, and be mainly directed towards developing the productive and remunerative powers of the country'.[35] Nevertheless, administrators on the ground in Ireland were also developing a particular ethos of their own, that to some extent counter-balanced the orthodox or moralist obsessions with the economy as a whole. A Benthamite concern for the efficient operations of institutions established for specified purposes – to distribute food, to organise public works and to provide relief through the poor law – stressed the immediate and the welfare aspects of state action rather than the long-term consequences. The impact of this administrative ideology was curbed by Trevelyan's dictatorial omniscience at the Treasury and frustrated by lack of resources and resistance from local notables, but it became the dominant attitude of a Dublin Castle executive increasingly at odds with London.[36]

THE SECOND AND TOTAL potato failure fell on a new Whig-liberal minority government led by Lord John Russell that was far from ready for the task. The ministry itself was more a coalition of 'reformers' than a unified party with a shared ideological position, and it was subject to shifting political balances in parliament and in the country at a time of widespread agitation and flux. Irish policy was a point of contention for the various factions associated with the ideologies outlined above. Virtually the government's only shared commitment was to upholding free trade against any revived Protectionist threat. The ideological power of this doctrine, when combined with the political imperative of keeping intact the government's main *raison d'être*, conspired to rule out anything more than marginal tinkering with the Irish food supply.[37] The consequences of this refusal to intervene in the terrible winter of 1846–7 were fateful.[38]

In the aftermath of the 1846 failure it was widely believed in British political circles that Ireland could never return to its previous condition, and that a great and inevitable 'social revolution' was under way. Political debate centred on the question of how to relieve the poor threatened by starvation, in such a way as to prevent the recurrence of famine. Opinions varied according to attitudes towards Irish landlordism and widely divergent beliefs about the size of the Irish wages-fund: that is, the amount of capital it was thought possible to mobilise within Ireland for the employment of labour. Irish landlords themselves argued that this was normally at an absolute minimal level, and demanded state help to promote private as well as public development.[39] English Conservatives and moderate liberals usually agreed that the wages-fund was low and that long-term aid through work projects and drainage loans were desirable, while remaining critical of the lax attitudes of many Irish landlords.[40] Russell's circle were not averse to state investment in the Irish infrastructure, but they shared a tendency with moralists and radicals to see the wages-fund as high, believing that landlords and large farmers were squandering or hoarding their resources, which they had amassed by ruthlessly exploiting the peasantry.[41] Moralists parted company with others in claiming that the destitute population

95

could be supported and the economy reconstructed simultaneously by measures of economic coercion. It was not enough for relief measures to provide the poor with the means of survival, they should do so in such a way as to discourage a culture of dependency and coerce the proprietors into undertaking their moral responsibilities.[42]

If the moralists sought to control Irish policy from 1846, they did not have it all their own way. Adjustments made to the public works legislation inherited from Peel were limited and were intended to eliminate abuse and manipulation by landlords and farmers. Against strong resistance from Wood (now Chancellor of the Exchequer), Bessborough succeeded in extending the scope of the works to include some projects of private interest, but this was insufficient to stem the growing dissatisfaction with the system on all sides.[43] By December 1846, reports of the horrors of mass starvation at Skibbereen and other places demonstrated that traditional forms of relief were failing.[44]

The initiative behind the radical departures agreed in January 1847 came not primarily from politicians but from the professional administrators. Thomas Larcom, then a senior relief official in the Board of Works, argued that labour and relief should be kept conceptually and practically apart. Relief through public works had produced little of value at vast expense, had drained labour from agricultural cultivation, and had failed to prevent the masses of 'helpless' and 'impotent' poor from suffering high mortality.[45] Bessborough and Russell conceded that the scale of the 1846–7 crisis demanded humanitarian aid in food, followed by the permanent extension of the poor law to give a right to relief to both the able-bodied and helpless destitute.[46] The principle of relief by means of the poor law attracted a degree of consensus in January 1847 because it meant different things to different people and because the existing system was clearly indefensible. It was only on the implementation of the extended poor law from September 1847 that the huge gulf of interpretative differences became manifest.

The temporary relief act of February 1847, establishing government supervised and assisted soup kitchens issuing free rations to the destitute, was an unprecedented innovation, but a temporary and transitional one. The political circumstances that allowed the act to pass also constrained its acceptability to a fixed period of time. British public opinion, saturated by graphic accounts of Famine horrors in the press, and stirred by a genuine, if ill-informed and temperamental humanitarian sensibility, was prepared to accept a degree of state intervention until the next harvest (so long as Irish ratepayers would ultimately be liable). The feeling remained strong that responsibility still lay with the proprietors who had tolerated and exploited the rise of a potato-dependent 'surplus' population, and that they should be made to pay for the costs of social transition.[47] This was the logic, shared by most parliamentary liberals, that lay behind the decision to throw relief on the poor law as soon as that 'exceptional' season ended. What was at issue in the session of 1847 was whether any concessions should be made to landlords in the working of the act, and what degree of government help for economic reconstruction should be provided.

Despite moralist pressure that assistance should be kept to a minimum to shock proprietors and people into a programme of ameliorative self-help, a Land Improvement Act was passed to give loans to proprietors. These were taken up by only a few large solvent landlords, but the legislation neutralised Peelite and moderate opposition to the extended poor law.[48] Russell's waste land reclamation bill, drawn up in co-operation with his Foxite colleagues Bessborough and Morpeth, was central to his personal legislative plan in 1847. The scheme was a radical one – to create peasant proprietors on Irish waste lands compulsorily purchased and reclaimed with help from the state. This bill was in line with the Foxite view of the limitations of landlords' rights, and was similar to schemes advocated by John Stuart Mill and by Poulett Scrope. However, the measure was first trimmed in cabinet by moderates anxious for the full security of property rights, and then savaged in parliament by Peel and Lord Stanley as an unwarranted interference in the sphere of private enterprise, and Russell was forced to drop it.[49] When considered in the light of the sympathy expressed by Russell and Bessborough for a form of tenant-right which was far in advance of the negative views of most British politicians,[50] this initiative calls into question the assumption frequently made that Whigs were inherently more dogmatic and rigid in their adherence to economic orthodoxy than Conservatives.

The 1847 poor law bill was rejected in principle by orthodox thinkers; Senior had become convinced by this time that the potato-failure had left Ireland over-populated by a redundant mass of two million people, and that there were no 'safe' means of giving outdoor relief.[51] His position was, however, compromised by its close association with the intransigent opposition of Irish landlords led by Monteagle and Whately, which did nothing but confirm the government's and parliament's insistence upon the bill.[52] The character of the measure was, however, substantially altered by amendments forced on the government by Stanley as the English Conservatives' price for allowing it through the house of lords. Chief amongst these was William Gregory's infamous quarter acre clause, which denied relief to tenants holding more than a quarter of an acre of land, and which turned the act into a charter for land clearance and consolidation.[53] A cabinet majority of moderates and moralists supported the Gregory clause as a weapon necessary for forcing the pace of transition to an Anglicised social and economic structure, and Russell was persuaded to accept it as a spur to greater cultivation.[54] It was bitterly resented by Edward Twisleton, the chief poor law commissioner in Ireland, as a major cause of extensive misery and death, and after an intensive struggle it was partially mitigated in the interests of tenants' dependants in May 1848.[55]

It is generally agreed that the British government deserves most criticism for abandoning Ireland with only the inadequate poor law for support from the autumn of 1847, in effect leaving the country to the workings of 'natural causes'. Vast American imports made food readily available, and the state had proved its administrative capacity by providing up to three million daily rations in summer 1847 and at an unexpectedly low cost, yet little was done to meet the widespread destitution that continued to summer 1849 and beyond.

For at least part of the explanation we must look to the strengthening of the moralists' hand in policy-making. Two significant changes took place in August 1847 simultaneously with the running down of the soup kitchens. Firstly, a general election produced heavy Protectionist losses and a small majority of Whig-liberal M.P.s. This did not necessarily strengthen Russell's position, as many of the new M.P.s were middle-class radicals who looked to Cobden, Bright and Hume for leadership, and several ministers were defeated in popular constituencies.[56] Russell drew the conclusion that 'we have in the opinion of Great Britain done too much for Ireland and have lost elections for doing so'.[57] As the radicals came to hold a balance of power, Wood and Grey were further empowered. The Chancellor's comment that '*the struggle* in Ireland is to force them into self-government ... our song ... must be – "It is your concern, not ours"', chimed with the dominant British mood.[58] Secondly, the potato did not fail in 1847; few were planted and few harvested, but the apparent absence of any direct sign of Divine intent allowed Trevelyan to declare that the Famine was over, and that no further extraordinary measures could be justified.[59]

Popular feelings on this were reinforced by the British banking crisis and financial crash of October 1847, which further boosted middle-class radicalism in its obsessive drive to retrench state expenditure. Government relief in Ireland was particularly targeted.[60] Wood was thus not overly dismayed by the defeat of the 1848 budget, which had included a substantial increase in British income tax to meet the weight of Irish and defence expenditure, and which had been introduced by Russell. The setback allowed him to use the excuse that 'the British people have made up their minds to pay no more for Irish landlords' to reject Clarendon's increasingly frantic appeals for more aid.[61] Russell's attempts to circumvent this obstacle by means of a state loan were blocked in cabinet by an alliance of moralists threatening a revolt of 'distressed English manufacturers' and moderates rejecting any additional taxation on Irish land or incomes.[62]

There is no doubt that traditional anti-Irishness played a

role in this British hostility; racial and cultural stereotypes were common in the press.[63] An upsurge of agrarian violence in late 1847, and the nationalist activity culminating in the abortive rebellion of 1848, further convinced many of Irish ingratitude for English 'generosity' in 1847.[64] Yet the most striking aspect of British opinion was the inclusion of Irish landowners in this moral censure. When the potato failed again in 1848, the dominant view was that Providence had again intervened to discipline all classes into the exertion and self-reliance necessary to maximise the use of undeveloped Irish resources.[65]

This is the political context in which we should see Clarendon's outburst to Russell quoted above. On his arrival in Ireland in July 1847, the new Lord Lieutenant shared many of the assumptions of Wood and Grey.[66] His conversion was rapid and profound; within a few months he had come under the influence of the senior Irish administrators based in Dublin Castle, and shared their view that the saving of human life was imperative (although to Clarendon perhaps more for political than humanitarian reasons).[67] While continuing to defend the broad outlines of government policy when pressed by Irish landlords, he demanded increased grants to assist the impoverished areas where the poor law was collapsing, and to help improving landlords through assisted emigration and other remedial measures.

The correspondence between Clarendon and Russell reflected not antagonism but increasingly a shared concern. The two men collaborated in drawing up remedial proposals, with Russell travelling to Dublin in September 1848 to finalise their plans.[68] Nevertheless, although the prime minister was prepared to threaten resignation in early 1849 if the cabinet rejected his assisted emigration proposals, this and all his other plans proved abortive.[69] Russell had lost authority over his cabinet, and found his own position increasingly marked by confusion and indecision in the face of ideological certainty.[70] On the failure of anything but the most modest of measures, he fell back on self-justifying rhetorical defences based on his continuing antagonism towards proprietors, and on the 'inevitability' of mass suffering.[71] Unable to choose between the imperatives of philanthropy and economy, Russell sought to steer an untenable middle course, and in the process presided over the decimation of the Irish people.

If what Clarendon denounced as 'the extreme doctrines of the Economists' had triumphed in the cabinet,[72] they were not unchallenged in parliament. After nearly three years of passive support for Russell's measures, Peel called in March 1849 for the abandonment of 'demoralising' outdoor relief on the poor law, the introduction of a fixed maximum rate, and a return to the principle of remunerative public works to support the poor and assist improving landlords. Prompted by Russell's failure to propose any remedial measures at the start of the 1849 session, and angered along with Clarendon at the apparent abandonment of the west to starvation, Peel was also concerned at what he took to be the total exhaustion of the wages-fund there.[73] However, it is doubtful that this part of Peel's plan, even had it not been so repugnant to majority parliamentary opinion, would have been effective in saving many lives. The administrators of the Board of Works and poor law commission had no intention of easily accepting a return to the system discredited in winter 1846–7, and of abandoning the principle of the separation of labour and relief. Their argument was reinforced by the fact that the majority on outdoor relief in the west were in the swollen classes of widows, orphans and the infirm whose vulnerability would be increased by a further upheaval in the organisation of relief.[74]

Two other elements were strongly stressed in Peel's 1849 plan, but in contrast to the first, these attracted a wider degree of parliamentary consensus. One of these was that Ireland must demonstrate a degree of exertion before Britain could be expected to give further aid. Preferring the extension of the income tax to Ireland (as did Russell), but thinking it inexpedient at present, Peel urged instead the imposition of a rate-in-aid levied on all the poor law unions in Ireland for the support of the western distressed unions, in return for further loans. His other recommendation was for a strong measure to force the sale of encumbered estates in the west to new, active proprietors. The language Peel used in advocating this – suggesting a 'new plantation' of Connacht by British landowners and capitalist farmers – clashed with some Whiggish sensibilities, but it was this initiative that led to the major legislative enactment of 1849. Moralists like Wood had long been committed to an encumbered estates bill as the best mode of facilitating social transition in the west by sweeping away the existing irresponsible or in-debted owners and replacing them with men of different values and available capital. To Wood, as to Peel, 'free trade in land' was the logical climax of response to the Irish crisis that had made 'free trade in corn' so vital in 1845–6.[75]

In retrospect, the most realistic alternative to the moralist relief policy was presented by the Irish executive and admin-istration under Bessborough and Clarendon. Although bound by the constraints of early Victorian administrative thinking, the Irish administration was probably the most ad-vanced and interventionist in Europe, and was staffed by committed and conscientious men of high quality such as Larcom, Griffith, and Twisleton. These officers recognised that the crisis of relief after 1847 resolved ultimately into a question of money skilfully distributed via reformed and ef-ficient structures to specific areas and needs. Their bitterness at the state's unwillingness or inability to respond effectively to the ongoing crisis is demonstrated by Twisleton's decision to resign over the termination of all direct parliamentary subsidies and the planned imposition of the rate-in-aid in spring 1849. Writing to Russell on 12 March, Clarendon ex-plained Twisleton's motives: 'He thinks the destitution here is so horrible, the indifference of the House of Commons to it so manifest, that he is an unfit agent of a policy that must be one of extermination.'[76]

The policy pursued from autumn 1847, against the op-position of Irish opinion and the advice of expert admin-istrators in Ireland, can only be condemned as adding pro-fusely to the country's misery. It is difficult to refute the in-dictment made by one humanitarian English observer in the later stages of the Famine, that amidst *an abundance of cheap food ... very many have been done to death by pure tyranny'.*[77]

102

The charge of culpable neglect of the consequences of policies leading to mass starvation is indisputable. That a conscious choice to pursue moral or economic objectives at the expense of human life was made by several ministers is also demonstrable. Russell's government can thus be held responsible for the failure to honour its own pledge to use 'the whole credit of the Treasury and the means of the country ... as is our bounden duty to use them ... to avert famine, and to maintain the people of Ireland'.[78]

Yet to single out the government alone for blame is to oversimplify. Alternative policies proposed by members of the governing elite in England might have some effect in reducing mortality levels, but what ruled these out was the strength of the British public opinion manifested in parliament and particularly in the commercial and industrial constituencies. During the Famine years the British economy went through a crisis that mobilised an assertive middle-class political opinion. Amid the confusion, those most in line with this sentiment, and those (as in the cases of Wood and Trevelyan) ready to exploit it, were at a political advantage. Thus the ideas of moralism, supported by Providentialism and a Manchester-school reading of classical economics, proved the most potent of British interpretations of the Irish Famine. What these led to was not a policy of deliberate genocide, but a dogmatic refusal to recognise that measures intended 'to encourage industry, to do battle with sloth and despair; to awake a manly feeling of inward confidence and reliance on the justice of Heaven',[79] were based on false premises, and in the Irish conditions of the later 1840s amounted to a sentence of death on many thousands.

THE ROLE OF THE POOR
LAW DURING THE FAMINE

CHRISTINE KINEALY

THROUGHOUT THE COURSE OF THE FAMINE years, 1845–52, the permanent system of poor relief in Ireland played a pivotal role in the provision of relief. Initially, the function of the Poor Law was perceived as subsidiary to the government's specially introduced relief schemes but, after 1847, the Poor Law was officially transformed into the main organ for Famine relief. The debate regarding the introduction of a Poor Law to Ireland and its role during a period of extraordinary distress, provides an interesting insight into attitudes towards poverty, poor relief and famine in the middle of the nineteenth century, especially in understanding the response of politicians and officials in Westminster and Whitehall to the successive years of Famine in Ireland.

A national state system of poor relief was introduced into Ireland in 1838. Its introduction followed years of debate regarding the nature of Irish poverty and the most effective way of alleviating it. The debate linked poverty inextricably with contemporary concerns regarding over-population. The belief that Ireland suffered from over-population was given weight and intellectual respectability by influential economists such as Thomas Malthus and Nassau Senior. Ireland's poverty was seen as a threat to Britain's prosperity unless a solution was found. This debate on Irish poverty was concurrent with concern in England regarding the mounting costs and demoralising effects of the so-called 'old' Poor Law.[1]

In 1833, the government appointed a Commission of Inquiry under Richard Whately, Archbishop of Dublin and leading political economist. After three years, the Commission concluded that an estimated two and a half million persons required assistance for a few weeks of each year. They suggested that an extensive schedule of improvement schemes and emigration programmes should be introduced. Significantly, the Commission rejected an extension to Ireland of the amended English Poor Law of 1834, which was based on the workhouse 'test'.[2] The recommendations of the Commission were unwelcome to influential figures within the government, the cost being seen as a major deterrent. Instead, the Whig government sent George Nicholls, an English Poor Law Commissioner, to Ireland. Nicholls was told to limit his investigation to the relief of 'destitution' and not the relief of 'poverty', and to report on the suitability of the workhouse system being extended to Ireland. Nicholls supported an extension of the English Poor Law to Ireland and a bill based on his report was passed for Ireland in 1838. As a consequence, a system of poor relief was transposed from the wealthiest and most industrially advanced economy of Europe to one of the least industrially developed parts, with little attention being given to the local characteristics prevailing in the country.[3]

In addition to the relief of destitution, the Poor Law was regarded as playing a vital role in the transition of the Irish economy from one based on subsistence potato-growing and small holdings, to one based on wage labour and a more capitalised system of agriculture. The Whig government believed that the workhouse system could play an important role in the transition period. At the same time, it was hoped that the introduction of a stringently administered system of poor relief would also improve 'the character, habits and social condition of the people' – all prerequisites for the desired influx of capital to the country.[4]

Although the Irish Poor Law was closely modelled on the 'new' English Poor Law it differed in a number of key respects. Firstly, relief could only be administered within the confines of a workhouse: outdoor relief being expressly forbidden. Secondly, no 'right' to relief existed. Finally, a Law of Settlement, which had been an integral part of the English Poor Law since the seventeenth century, was not introduced in Ireland. These provisions indicated that from the outset,

105

Irish paupers were to be treated differently – and, in fact, more harshly – than their counterparts in England.[5] The rationale was that if a more liberal provision of relief was permitted in Ireland, the resources of the country would be swallowed up. Both Poor Laws, however, made a distinction between the 'deserving' and the 'undeserving' poor, and regarded their mutual function as being the relief of 'destitution' rather than the alleviation of 'poverty'. Moreover, relief provided under the two Poor Laws was based on the common principle of less eligibility, that is, that any relief provided had to be less attractive than that available to an independent labourer. This was to be achieved through a monotonous diet, enforced labour, and strict regimentation, classification and segregation within the workhouses. This 'test' of destitution was regarded as essential in Ireland, with its many potential paupers.[6]

The Poor Law legislation was implemented with impressive speed. This was partly due to the determination of the Whig government to avoid the problems and opposition that had appeared in England after 1834.[7] Within a few years of the Law being introduced, the country was divided into 130 new administrative units known as unions, each of which contained a centrally located workhouse, built to a standard design. Approximately 100,000 paupers could be accommodated within these buildings. Guardians were nominated and elected and rates had been assessed and levied. By the beginning of 1845, 118 workhouses had opened their doors to paupers seeking relief who, following an interview with the guardians, were bathed, classified and clothed in workhouse uniform, and then segregated according to age and gender. The workhouses, however, were far from full; the Dunfanaghy workhouse in County Donegal, for example, contained only five inmates. Furthermore, the anticipated influx of able-bodied paupers never materialised; the vast majority of workhouse inmates being there by virtue of their old age, infirmity or youth.[8]

George Nicholls, the architect of the Irish Poor Law, was appointed the first Poor Law Commissioner for Ireland.[9] Nicholls, regardless of his advocacy of the reformed Poor

106

Law, was aware of its chief limitation, that is, its inability to provide sufficient relief during a period of acute distress or famine.[10] Bad harvests and subsistence crises were, however, an integral part of the agricultural cycle in Ireland. Regardless of this fact, the new Poor Law did not include any provision for periods of extraordinary distress, limiting relief, at all times, to that which could be provided within the confines of the workhouses.

In 1839 and 1842, there was localised, yet severe, distress in some parts of Ireland. In both of these years, the Poor Law Commissioners were resolute that the Poor Law should not be extended, even for a temporary period. They informed the government that they 'could not deviate in the slightest degree from the course the act prescribed'.[11] Consequently, the relief provided to alleviate these periods of distress was kept totally separate from the permanent system of relief.[12] The experiences of 1839 and 1842, however, exposed the unsuitability of the new legislation to deal with periods of prolonged or exceptional distress. Firstly, the Irish Poor Law, by excluding the possibility of outdoor relief, was constrained in the amount of relief it could provide by the capacity of the workhouses; secondly, as only destitute persons were deemed eligible for relief, small-holders who required short-term assistance were excluded from its provisions; and thirdly, the principle of local chargeability, by which each electoral division was liable for its own rates, meant that the fiscal burden invariably fell most heavily in the districts which were most seriously effected by the distress. These factors meant that the Poor Law introduced in only 1838, was ill-prepared to meet the challenges which confronted it after 1845.

THE APPEARANCE OF POTATO blight in the autumn of 1845 was unexpected yet unexceptional. Potato diseases and blight were not unusual and the appearance of a previously unknown fungus throughout Europe was not regarded with undue alarm. The government, led by Sir Robert Peel, acted promptly, invoking traditional relief measures, although on a larger scale. In recognition of the unusualness of the blight, and because he was anxious to obtain an accurate picture of the extent of the disease, Peel appointed a Scientific Commission under Lyon Playfair.[13] Although there were demands for the ports to be closed, the British government was not willing to undertake such a radical measure. For Peel, however, the crop shortages in both England and Ireland provided an ideal opportunity to attempt a repeal of the controversial Corn Laws – something that he had wanted to do since his election in 1841. This was achieved, in a diluted form, by the summer of 1846, which was too late to have any impact on the importation of cheap corn to the country.[14] By that time, poor harvests throughout Europe meant that less corn was available generally, whilst the purchase of corn by other European governments reduced the small surplus even further.[15]

As the impact of the blight would be most apparent in the following spring and summer, the government had time to put in place a system of temporary relief. To a large extent, the measures adopted were similar to those employed during earlier periods of distress, although the scale was larger. The government imported a small quantity of additional food into the country, and relief committees and public works were established.[16] In regard to the Poor Law, the precedents established in 1839 and 1842 were invoked, the government again making a clear distinction between temporary relief measures necessary to meet the exceptional distress, and the permanent system of poor relief.[17]

The financial implications of employing the Poor Law on a more extensive basis were also considered in 1845. Poor Rates were raised at the level of electoral division; the more paupers that an electoral division sent to a workhouse, the higher the rates. Poor Rates were a relatively new tax and the government did not want to antagonise the taxpayers. Widespread resistance to the rates had occurred in 1843, resulting in a change of policy which exempted all occupiers valued at less than £4 from payment of Poor Rates.[18] Within Peel's government, it was generally accepted that the burden that could be placed on the local rates was finite and would be insufficient to finance a period of exceptional distress.

Instead, it was believed that privately raised funds should be used to compensate for the deficit. This policy was confirmed by the Home Secretary, Sir James Graham, who stated:

> It could not be expected, that by a compulsory rate, on the basis of poor rates, introduced suddenly, any large fund could be obtained for the relief of the poor in Ireland during the present scarcity'.[19]

An exception to the principle of maintaining a separation between permanent and temporary relief was made in regard to the treatment of fever victims. Fever generally followed periods of shortages yet medical provision remained sporadic and geographically uneven. Increasingly, the Poor Law played a significant role in providing a medical safety net in some of the poorest parts of the country. Each workhouse possessed its own infirmary, and since 1843, Poor Law Guardians had been given the authority to treat victims of fever who were poor but not necessarily destitute. Following the 1845 blight, boards of guardians were empowered either to acquire or to erect a separate building for the treatment of fever victims. This provision, which was widely adopted, was borne from the income of the local Poor Rates.[20] This meant that the local rates, from the outset of the Famine, were financing essential medical relief within their locality rather than merely poor relief.

The impact of the blight on the numbers of workhouse inmates was gradual. In December 1845, the workhouses had contained just over 38,000 paupers. By the end of March 1846, as the impact of the food shortages began to be felt, the number had increased to almost 41,000, and by June had reached in excess of 51,000. Despite this increase, the workhouses were still less than half full.[21] The guardians of the Lowtherstown workhouse, which had contained only 4 paupers at the end of 1845, attributed the under use of their facilities to the harshness of the regulations within the workhouses, particularly the prohibition of tobacco. They warned the central authorities that the local people would 'perish from famine' unless the regulations were changed.[22] Day-today life within the workhouses also changed little in the first year of blight, an exception being in regard to the diet: the widely used potato diet being replaced in sixty-nine workhouses by rice, soup, bread, oatmeal or corn.[23] Overall, therefore, the Poor Law emerged from the first year of potato blight relatively unscathed although as the summer of 1846 progressed and as the system of temporary relief was being wound down, reports of even more widespread blight made a second year of extraordinary distress inevitable.

IN RESPONSE TO THE second more widespread appearance of blight of 1846, the government decided to rely again on temporary measures to provide the additional relief; public works were to be the main means of providing assistance with relief committees playing a secondary role. This policy reflected the newly-installed Whig government's assurance that it would keep its role as a purchaser and importer of additional foodstuffs to a minimum. Again, the Poor Law was expected to play a subsidiary role in the provision of relief. However, in recognition of the anticipated increase in distress, local guardians were asked to base their estimates for the coming year on the expectation that the workhouses would be full. It was envisaged that the greatest demand for workhouse relief would come from old and infirm persons who were unable to obtain employment on the public works scheme.[24]

The complacency of the Poor Law authorities in responding to the demand for relief was quickly shown to be wrong. The first appearance of blight had had little impact on the take-up of workhouse relief, but in the second year of distress, demand for this relief was both early and substantial. By the end of 1846, over half of the workhouses were full and having to refuse admittance to paupers. A shortage of capacity was due partly to the unprecedented scale of distress, but also to the slowness with which the temporary relief measures were being implemented in many of the most distressed areas. Unusually cold weather, high food prices and low wages, all further limited the effectiveness of the public works as the main vehicle for the provision of relief.

A sharp increase in disease, emigration and mortality in the winter and spring of 1846–47 resulted.

Inevitably, the inadequacy of the government's relief schemes placed an additional and unexpected burden on the permanent system of poor relief. This pressure continued until the spring of 1847, when three-quarters of the workhouses were full. The opening of soup kitchens, and the importation of additional food supplies into the country, greatly relieved pressure on workhouse accommodation in the summer of 1847, although soup kitchen relief could be refused if the local workhouse was not full.[25]

The demands being placed on the workhouses demonstrated the limits of the Poor Law system. The prohibition of outdoor relief and the deliberate exclusion of a 'right to relief' in the 1838 legislation meant that if a workhouse became full, the responsibility of the Poor Law to provide relief had ended. A dogmatic interpretation of the Law was favoured by Edward Twistleton who stated that:

> I confess that it does not appear to me that the responsibility of deaths from starvation outside the workhouse rests either with the Board of Guardians or the Commissioners.[26]

For boards of guardians, confronted with an unrelenting demand for workhouse relief, the situation was less straightforward. Many of them – due to a combination of compassion and fear – provided relief in ways categorically prohibited by the legislature. Additional paupers were admitted to the workhouse, or a variety of forms of outdoor relief were provided. These actions horrified the central Commissioners who believed that the most fundamental aspiration of the Poor Law Act was being contravened.[27] Conciliatory and threatening tactics were variously employed by the Poor Law Commissioners to dissuade the guardians from continuing with these illegal forms of relief. The inadequacy of the government's temporary relief measures were apparent, however, to many of the local administrators. The Galway board of guardians urged the government to respond more generously to the food shortages on the grounds that:

In so general a calamity, the state should contribute its fair
proportion of the General Burden, a principle recognised by Sir
Robert Peel last year.[28]

The worsening situation did result in a modification in the
role of the Poor Law. In December 1846, the guardians were
directed to obtain additional workhouse accommodation.
This was viewed as a preferable alternative to providing outdoor relief. At the same time, the government emphasised
that they would not provide any financial assistance for this
purpose, but that all additional accommodation would have
to be financed from the local Poor Rates. This change of
policy was initiated by the government, and it did not have
the support of the Poor Law Commissioners. In a con-
fidential letter to the government, Twistleton stated that the
local unions did not possess the resources to meet any additional demands on their now overstretched finances. Twistleton's advice was rejected by the Home Secretary who informed him:

> Many persons liable to be rated are ... placing their money in
> the Savings Banks, and by their refusal to employ any labour-
> ers in the cultivation of their land, are increasing the existing
> distress. To acquiesce in their exemption from the burden,
> legally and morally attaching to them, would, I think, be most
> objectionable in principle and most injurious in effect.[29]

At this stage also, the government was considering more far-
reaching changes to the Poor Law system. These changes
were partly in response to the failure of the public works, regardless of high expenditure by the government. More importantly, however, many leading members of the government were increasingly of the opinion that during a period
of extended shortages and distress, relief would be effective
and economical only if it was financed from local resources.[30]
The administration of the Poor Law, with its emphasis on
local responsibility and local chargeability, was viewed as an
ideal mechanism for shifting the responsibility from central
to local resources. Concurrently, there appeared to be a hardening of public opinion within England and sectors of Ireland towards Irish distress. This contributed to a determina-

tion to force the Irish landowners to take a greater responsibility for the provision of relief in their localities.

Within Britain, this feeling was exacerbated by an influx of Irish paupers into the ports and towns, which meant that Irish distress was viewed as a double burden on British tax payers. *The Times*, for example, began to argue increasingly for less government intervention in the affairs of Ireland, especially in the provision of Famine relief, declaring that 'There are times when something like harshness is the greatest humanity'.[31] Moreover, this hardening of attitude was evident in a number of Irish newspapers, which argued for less government intervention in Ireland. The conservative *Dublin Evening Mail* regarded Irish distress both as a financial encumbrance and as a threat to British political stability. It regarded the Poor Law as a necessary protective measure for the British government and claimed, 'It is for the preservation of Great Britain that we dwell so much upon the subject of Irish distress, and the means of preventing a constant recurrence of it'.[32]

In January 1847, the government began to implement major changes in both the temporary and permanent systems of relief, signifying a departure both from the traditional mechanisms and from the philosophy of Famine relief. In February 1847, the Temporary Relief Act was rushed through parliament, providing for the establishment of soup kitchens throughout the country to replace the public works. Neither money nor wages were demanded in return for the food, making the relief provided under this act the most liberal available at any period during the course of the Famine. This was reflected in the take-up of relief: at its maximum, over three million people were receiving rations from the soup kitchens. The three categories who were eligible for free relief were, destitute helpless persons, destitute able-bodied persons not holding land, and destitute able-bodied persons holding small portions of land. Wage earners could purchase the soup rations but not at less than cost price.[33]

Like the public works, the Temporary Relief Act was generously financed, £2,255,000 being voted by parliament.[34] Two features of the act were significant: firstly, the act was an interim measure until permanent changes could be made to the Poor Law; secondly, although the money allocated for the soup kitchens appeared to be liberal, approximately half had to be repaid out of the local Poor Rates. In effect, this meant that from early 1847, the British government was endeavouring to transfer the financial responsibility to local taxation via the mechanism of a revised Poor Law.

In summer 1847, whilst soup kitchen relief was at its peak, the government was steering through parliament major changes to the Poor Law. The ensuing debate in parliament dominated British political life during the early part of 1847 moving the Irish Famine to centre stage of parliamentary issues. The determination of the Whig Party to end Irish dependence on British resources was undoubtedly influenced by the approach of a general election in the summer of 1847. Furthermore, British public opinion had hardened against such a protracted demand for aid, and a monetary crisis in 1847 had given weight to the Treasury's call for financial retrenchment and rectitude. The economist, Nassau Senior, believed that after two years of coming to the assistance of Ireland, British generosity had been exhausted. He explained:

> The English resolved that the Irish should not starve. We resolved that, for one year at least, we would feed them. But we came to a third resolution, inconsistent with the first, that we would not feed them for *more* than a year. How then were they to be fed in 1848? ... The answer, according to English notions, seemed obvious: Of course they must be supported by poor rates.[35]

The decision to make the Poor Law responsible for the provision of all relief after August 1847, and the corresponding transfer of the fiscal burden from central to local resources, was viewed with alarm by many Irish landlords. As Table 1, on the next page, demonstrates, since 1845 the increase in the level of poor rates had been substantial.

Although an Irish party was formed in parliament to resist these changes, ultimately it had little impact.[36] At this stage, a small yet powerful group within Westminster were

Table 1: Amount of Poor Rate Collected in 1846, 1847 and part of 1848

	1846 £s	1847 £s	1848 £s	% increase 1846–7	1847–8
January	36,229	52,439	194,054	44.7	270.0
February	41,885	47,264	187,064	12.8	295.8
March	38,909	52,561	138,449	35.1	63.4
April	38,436	63,110	111,981	64.2	77.4
May	31,230	64,865	114,518	107.7	76.5
June	30,630	59,436	121,571	94.0	104.5
July	24,185	62,097	85,450	156.7	53.7
August	17,173	53,389		210.9	
September	21,510	73,358		241.0	
October	26,805	121,255		352.4	
November	36,639	151,684		314.0	
December	46,440	168,860		263.6	

[Figures based on information provided in 'Summary of Financial Returns, State of the Unions and Workhouses in Ireland', Fifth Series, British Parliamentary Papers, 1848 (919), p. 674.]

determined that the Famine should be used as an opportunity to bring about long-desired changes within the Irish economy. The Poor Law, with its dependence on local taxation, was viewed as an effective way of penalising landlords who were absentee or had allowed their estates to become sub-divided.[37]

To facilitate the extended role of the Poor Law, outdoor relief was permitted. It was, however, subject to various controls and could only be provided with the prior consent of the Poor Law Commissioners. Overall, these restrictions meant that entitlement to relief was more restricted than it had been in the previous two years. Able-bodied paupers who were in receipt of outdoor relief were required to work for at least eight hours each day, on a task 'as repulsive as possible consistent with humanity'.[38] The new legislation also established a separate Poor Law Commission in Dublin under Edward Twistleton. Simultaneously, the powers of the central commissioners were extended, providing them with the ability to dismiss recalcitrant boards of guardians. In the eighteen months after the act was introduced, thirty-nine boards of guardians were dissolved. This power was predominantly invoked against guardians who were deemed to have made insufficient effort in collecting the Poor Rates.[39]

The most controversial section of the Extension Act was the Quarter Acre or Gregory Clause. This clause was introduced by the M.P. for Dublin, William Gregory, and had the support of the majority of Irish M.P.s. It stipulated that a person who occupied more than a quarter of an acre of land could not receive relief either inside or outside the workhouse.[40] This regulation represented a significant restriction and new stringency in the terms by which entitlement to relief was defined. The substantial rise in evictions after 1847 was attributed largely to its introduction. The Quarter Acre Clause, however, was only one factor in a package of fiscal measures which accompanied the transfer to Poor Law relief, which were punitive both to indebted landlords and smallholders alike. The regressive nature of the Poor Law rating system meant that Poor Rates fell most heavily on areas where distress was most severe. Furthermore, since 1843, landlords had been liable for paying all rates on property valued at under £4, the tenant being exempt.[41] On a property where little rent had been paid since 1845, legislation provided an incentive to evict a tenant and pull down his cabin as a means of reducing the burden of Poor Rates.

The way in which the Quarter Acre Clause was interpreted by the local guardians varied greatly; many were confused as to what constituted a 'surrender' of land and whether relief could be provided in an emergency to either the occupier of land or his family. The central Commissioners sought a legal opinion on this issue, and, to their dismay, were advised that the families of a person who occupied more than a quarter of an acre of land should not be denied relief. This liberal interpretation was confirmed by a

116

second legal opinion.[42] The Home Secretary, alarmed by these opinions, warned the Commissioners that this interpretation should not be used to allow a more general liberalisation in the provision of relief as:

> It appears to the government that it would be obviously contrary to the spirit and intentions of the provisions of the law and tend to defeat the object with which it was enacted.[43]

The number of evictions continued to increase despite these rulings and, in 1849, recorded evictions doubled compared to 1848. The increase in evictions was welcomed by a number of members of the government who had become convinced that a draconian adherence to the provisions of the Poor Act was necessary if Ireland was to emerge from the Famine socially and economically stronger. One leading member explained this position unequivocally when he stated:

> It is useless to disguise the truth that any great improvement in the social system of Ireland must be founded upon an extensive change in the present state of agrarian occupation, and that this change necessarily implies a long, continued and systematic ejectment of small holders and of squatting cottiers.[44]

Within Ireland, however, there was increasing scepticism about the ability of the Poor Law alone to provide and finance relief. The government had designated twenty-two unions which would require external financial aid as 'Distressed', but as demand for relief rose after the autumn of 1847, it was apparent that this was an under-estimation. The local unions were expected to collect rates to the utmost of their ability, and to assist this, the rate collectors had been provided with considerable powers of distraint. To ensure that local effort was not undermined, the Treasury deliberately kept its financial contribution to a minimum and refused to release funds until they were convinced that starvation was the alternative. Consequently, the finances of the poorest unions remained precarious, whilst the relief provided was piece-meal and sparse. The impact of this policy on the poorest unions alarmed members of the Irish Executive and the Irish Poor Law Commission who were becoming overtly disillusioned with the system of relief that they were administering. The rise in mortality of people in receipt of relief in the winter of 1847–48, confirmed these fears. Twistleton was concerned that the risk of even more deaths was acceptable to the government because:

> It seemed to be a less evil to the Empire to encounter the risk than to continue the system of advances from the public purse.

He went on to warn the government:

> If the system pursued during the last four months is continued, there will be a continuance of the same risk.[45]

That the Poor Law was becoming an administration in crisis was indicated by the rise in excess mortality within the workhouses. Numbers in receipt of Poor Law relief rose steadily after autumn 1847. Outdoor relief peaked in July 1848 when over 800,000 persons were receiving it. At the beginning of 1849, almost one million people were in receipt of workhouse relief alone. This increase was facilitated by an expansion in temporary workhouse accommodation and the decision to increase the number of unions from 130 to 163. As a consequence, workhouse accommodation was almost ten times as high as had originally been envisaged. The much disliked order of the central Commissioners to clear the workhouses of young, infirm and old inmates in order to create more places for able-bodied paupers had little impact: in 1846, able-bodied paupers accounted for 4.9 per cent of workhouse inmates, and in 1848, had risen to 7.7 per cent. Fever patients, who had accounted for 0.9 per cent of workhouse inmates in 1846, had grown to 5.6 per cent two years later. In the fatal winter of 1846–47, workhouse mortality had reached over 2,500 deaths each week. In the winter of 1848–49, partly as the result of a cholera outbreak, mortality again reached this level. This represented a greater proportion of the population, however, as the total population had been falling since 1846. Subsequently, the level of mortality in workhouses decreased from a peak of 6.6 per thousand inmates per week in 1848, to 2.4 in 1852.⁴⁶ The numbers seeking workhouse relief also remained high long after the Famine had been declared officially over. In 1857, for example, the numbers of paupers in receipt of indoor relief was 269,800, and 35,432 persons were receiving outdoor relief, demonstrating the longevity of the increased demand for relief in Ireland.⁴⁷

ALTHOUGH THE TREASURY HOPED that all external financial assistance to the unions would end after the autumn of 1847, this was not possible. Pressure for relief continued to be high even after the harvest of 1848, and demand for Poor Law relief was higher in a number of unions in 1849 than it had been at any stage since 1845. In addition to current Poor Law expenditure, the Poor Rates also had to be used to repay earlier advances by the Treasury. Officials in England, however, had declared the Famine to be over since 1848, thus justifying their policy of minimum intervention.⁴⁸ In 1848, the British government subscribed only £156,000, and £114,000 in 1849 (over half of which was a loan) in aid of the Poor Rates. This was far less than the £4,848,000 advanced for the support of the public works in the months following the disastrous harvest of 1846.⁴⁹ Furthermore, by 1848 most of the external charitable assistance to Ireland had dried up, throwing the burden almost exclusively on the local rates. Despite this, the Treasury repeatedly reprimanded the Poor Law Commissioners for providing relief 'too liberally'. Increasingly, a split was apparent between the perception of the Famine by officials in Ireland and those in London. Twistleton's frustration with this policy was apparent and he rebuked the government because:

> The extent of the calamity which affects the Distressed Unions and the intensity of the distress in them, do not seem to be fully understood in England.⁵⁰

The Whig administration, however, was determined that the financial dependence of the Irish poor on British resources should finally be brought to an end. In May 1849, a new tax of 6d. in the pound, known as the Rate-in-Aid, was introduced on rateable property in Ireland.[51] The financial responsibility for Irish distress was no longer to be an imperial charge but transferred to the tax payers of Ireland, on the grounds that parts of Ireland had recovered from the Famine and could make a greater financial contribution to the poorest unions. The unions in the north-east of Ulster mounted a successful and vociferous propaganda campaign to discredit the new tax, arguing that the well-managed eastern unions were being forced to subsidise the lax administrations of the west thereby 'keeping up an army of beggars, fed out of the industry of Ulster'.[52] The table below demonstrates that the proportion of rates paid was higher in the western unions as a proportion of Poor Law valuation than in Ulster:

Table 2: Amount of Poor Rate collected by Province in 1848[53]

	Poor Rate Collected	Poor Law Valuation	Rate Collected as % of valuation
	£	£	
Ulster	100,462	3,264,205	3.1
Munster	241,682	3,808,905	6.3
Leinster	153,609	4,612,124	3.3
Connaught	103,278	1,391,065	7.4
Ireland	599,031	13,076,299	4.6

The strongest opposition to the Rate-in-Aid came from the official who was expected to administer it, Edward Twistleton, the Chief Poor Law Commissioner. Twistleton believed that in a period of such widespread and sustained distress, it was the duty of the empire to come to the assistance of its afflicted partner. He resigned on the grounds that he could not implement the legislation 'with honour'.[54] Following his resignation, Twistleton publicly and vigorously criticised the relief policies being pursued in Ireland, and denounced the government for bringing 'deep disgrace' on the country by refusing to finance adequately the Poor Law.[55] The continuation of high levels of distress and mortality in a number of western unions, notably those in Co. Clare, resulted in the introduction of a second Rate-in-Aid of 2d. in the pound in 1850.

In purely economic terms, the transfer to Poor Law relief in the autumn of 1847 had been a success, as the financial contribution of the Treasury to Irish distress fell markedly. In the eighteen months which followed this transfer, the total contribution from the Exchequer had been less than £300,000, much of which was a loan. In 1849, financial relationships had been reduced even further when the Rate-in-Aid threw the burden of relief onto Ireland and forced the wealthier Poor Law unions to come to the aid of local rates. In human terms, mortality, evictions, emigration, spiralling taxation and financial indebtedness increased in the local unions following the transfer to local responsibility. The Poor Law was viewed as an important tool in transforming the economy of Ireland and key members of the government and the Treasury were determined not to compromise this aspiration. The administrators most closely associated with the Poor Law were increasingly dubious about the relief policies which they were managing, culminating in the resignation of Edward Twistleton. George Nicholls, the individual responsible for framing and introducing a Poor Law to Ireland, recognised the fragile relationship between the Poor Law and a Famine:

> Although in one sense intimate, it is in other respects limited; for where the land has ceased to be reproductive, the necessary means of relief cannot be obtained from it, and a Poor Law will no longer be operative, or at least not operative to the extent adequate to meet such an emergency as then existed in Ireland.[56]

After 1847, ideological and fiscal concerns, combined with a zealous determination to use the calamity to bring about long-term improvements in the economy of Ireland, took priority over the immediate needs of the distressed poor. The consequence was a breakdown in the provision of relief in some unions, whilst the much desired economic transformation of Ireland continued to be elusive.

I would like to thank Seán Egan, Pat Brandwood and Arthur Luke for reading and commenting on an earlier draft of this article.

122

THE OPERATIONS OF FAMINE RELIEF, 1845–47

MARY E. DALY

ALL ACCOUNTS OF THE GREAT FAMINE devote considerable attention to the question of relief. Government efforts to relieve hunger and disease have generally been criticised for their inadequacy.[1] The high incidence of death and disease is proof of this fact, but we should beware of the omniscience of hindsight or of adopting a late-twentieth-century attitude of moral superiority. Any discussion of famine relief must take into account the extent of the crisis, the nature of Irish society in the 1840s and attitudes prevailing at the time towards poverty, charity and the role of the state. This paper focuses on relief during the years 1845–47, the first two seasons of the Great Famine, when a series of special government programmes were put in place to deal with the crisis. From the autumn of 1847, responsibility for famine relief rested almost entirely on the poor law and the contribution of private charities also dwindled.

Although the Great Famine of the 1840s was unique both in its extent and its duration, parts of Ireland, generally the western seaboard, were threatened with famine on several occasions during the previous thirty years. Every famine alert appears to have enlisted assistance from both government sources and private charities. During the years 1816–17 famine was common throughout much of Europe because a massive volcanic explosion in the Indian Ocean led to extremely cold weather conditions even in mid-summer.[2] Irish famine relief was the responsibility of the Irish Chief Secretary, a young politician called Sir Robert Peel. In 1816 he organised a shipment of oats to areas where famine was reported for sale at low prices, though apparently the quality of the grain was poor and there was some fraud in its distribution. When food shortages persisted during the following year he set up a commission to administer relief. They set up a programme of relief works which would enable the needy to earn money which they could use to buy food. The commission insisted on local contributions towards relief schemes, as a pre-condition for government assistance and depended on local committees to organise the actual relief. This pattern was replicated in 1822 when famine again threatened. A special commission was established to organise public works and local relief committees were again given a key role: their existence was viewed as proof that an area was suffering real distress and aid was again dependent on local contributions. Funds were also provided for the erection of fever hospitals and fever inspectors were appointed to report on conditions.[3] Several aspects of this story are relevant to the relief operations during the Great Famine: famine relief was to be handled by a special organisation, the government attached considerable importance both to local committees and to local contributions and they preferred to fund public works rather than supply food. Special committees were favoured because of a fear that funds for relief would become part of 'normal' government spending; public works were regarded as less pauperising than distributing food. Public works appear to have been an effective means of relieving distress, when the people were threatened with starvation due to a lack of entitlements – i.e., an inability to buy food, rather than a shortage of food *per se* and several modern experts on famine relief regard them as the best method for dealing with many modern famines.[4]

Government assistance was not ungenerous when faced with these earlier crises: approximately £500,000 was made available in 1816–17 and 1822. In 1822 a long-term programme of public works was set in train, which was designed, both to relieve immediate distress by creating employment, and to bring long-term improvements to remote areas where it had proved difficult to import food. From 1822 until the famine the government embarked on a programme of major road works, which were designed to open up remote and mountainous areas in Connemara and in Cork and Kerry. As a result wheeled vehicles appeared in many remote areas for the first time; some roads were routed through bogs and in the process land was drained. By opening up communications and making it possible to trade in food, it was hoped that long-term threats of famine would be removed. Further investment in piers, harbours and fisheries aimed at relieving poverty and generating new economic activity. Between 1817 and 1831 an estimated £1million was spent on public works, mostly in remote western areas. In 1832 control of these projects was transferred to the Irish Board of Works, which continued the programme of roads, harbours, and bridge-building. By the eve of the famine the Board had provided over £1million in loans and grants to local authorities for long-term development and relief of distress.[5]

By the autumn of 1845 therefore, when the blight first struck, causing a serious loss in the potato crop, the threat of famine was not a novelty, nor were government relief schemes. Reports of distress had reached Dublin Castle, mainly from western areas, in 1816–17, 1822, 1831, 1835, 1837 1839 and 1842. There is no evidence to suggest that significant numbers of people died as a result of famine during these years. The west of Ireland, the area worst affected also recorded the highest rate of population increase during these years. We can assume therefore, either that conditions were not as bleak as they were painted, or that the relief measures provided were adequate. In addition to government funds, the west of Ireland also benefited from a generous flow of charitable funds. In the years 1822, 1826 and 1831 a group of London businessmen, known as the London Tavern Committee provided substantial sums for seed potatoes, cheap food and yet more public works. These funds were again channelled through local committees consisting of Catholic and Protestant clergy and local gentry.[6] The momentum behind such voluntary efforts began to flag by the 1830s. Rising sectarian tensions following on the granting of Catholic emancipation and a new wave of proselytisation known as the Second Reformation made multi-denominational co-operation more difficult in Ireland,[7] while the London businessmen appear to have suffered what we would now term 'compassion fatigue'; they lost interest in the plight of the Irish poor. Recurrent calls for assistance were read both among private philanthropists and in the British government as evidence that there was something fundamentally rotten in the state of Ireland; in such circumstances, emergency aid was viewed as merely providing short-term palliatives which did nothing to resolve long-term problems.

The most common diagnosis suggested that Irish society as a whole was at fault, with landlords most to blame. They had tolerated rampant population growth and sub-division of holdings which had led to the creation of an impoverished class of cottiers and small farmers. Dependence on the potato, which was regarded as a morally inferior food, was seen as a symptom of this fundamental malaise. Relieving this situation would require radical surgery: the removal of many smallholding families from the land, either by emigration, or by turning them into landless labourers for whom work would be provided. In the meantime, if famine threatened, responsibility for relieving it should rest with the landlords, who were widely regarded as the authors of Ireland's misfortune because they had tolerated the population explosion and widespread sub-division.[8] This analysis was undoubtedly too bleak: although pre-famine Ireland was poor, it was less inefficient and socially irresponsible than many contemporary accounts suggest. Most of the population worked very hard to eke out a very basic living, contrary to the widely held belief that they were idle for most of the year.[9] Such views had gathered strength among the English elite by the 1840s, as had the belief that the invisible hand of the market economy reflected the working of divine providence which should not be thwarted. The logical conclusion of such views was that the Irish famine was God's will, an inevitable event, which should be permitted to take its course.[10]

WHEN THE POTATO CROP FAILED in the autumn of 1845, it was not immediately evident that an unprecedented disaster had occurred. Sir Robert Peel, by now, the British prime minister, put into action what could be described as the normal response to Irish famine. A relief commission was established in Dublin containing representatives of most government organisations which operated throughout Ireland: the army, coast guards, the Poor Law Commission, the Dublin Castle administration plus leading scientist Sir Robert Kane as token Catholic. Peel made arrangements to have maize bought secretly in the United States for shipment to Ireland where it would be sold from government depots, not to feed the people, but to dampen down the threat of rising food prices. Food was also sold to local relief committees for distribution, generally to those engaged on relief tasks which were organised by these committees. In order to enable the poor to buy food, relief works were set in train, both by the board of works and by grand juries, the ancestors to present-day county councils. In both cases all the immediate funds came from central government, though local authorities would ultimately be required to repay half the cost of board of works schemes and all the cost of schemes initiated by the grand juries. Time was on Peel's side. Although many areas lost up to forty per cent of their main potato crop, the overall yield had been high and the early crop was unaffected. Overall the county had about two-thirds of its normal crop. Some of the poorest areas such as Mayo appear to have escaped relatively lightly.[11] There was probably enough food in Ireland during the winter and spring of 1845–46 to feed the population. The quantity of food imported by Peel amounted to only two weeks' supply for one million people; approximately one-tenth of total maize imports during that season though the government depots were an important source of food for the west of Ireland.[12] Many local committees organised their own supplies of maize through private merchants and sold it at cost price in their locality. The government delayed the opening of food depots as late as possible; the first depot opened at the end of March, over six months after the blight was first reported, some did not open until June. Proposals for public works submitted by grand juries were scrutinised and approved by the board of works and the special famine relief works did not begin until March or April 1846 – six months or more after the potato crop failed. However the news that government funds were freely available brought an avalanche of applications: the barony of Moyarta in Co. Clare submitted a total of ninety-six road schemes, the neighbouring barony of Inchiquin, a total of 113. By the summer of 1846 approximately 100,000 were employed on relief works organised by the board of works with a further 30,000 on schemes controlled by grand juries.[13]

According to the Dublin newspaper, the *Freeman's Journal,* which was no friend to Sir Robert Peel, nobody died of starvation when he was prime minister and Peel has generally been given a good press in most accounts of the Irish famine.[14] However Peel used the failure of the potato in 1845 to justify his repeal of the Corn Laws, which was 'an essentially English question'.[15] Peel was also fortunate that the first year of the famine was very much a phoney famine and it is this, rather than Peel's relief measures which explains the apparent absence of famine deaths. The amount of food available both locally and from imports appears to have been adequate. Relief operations set in train in the autumn of 1845 provided food and work when both were needed in the spring and summer of 1846. Local communities were capable of raising money to fund local relief funds. Unfortunately the first year of famine sent false signals to those in authority; distress was real but manageable, in scale it was not dramatically worse than in earlier seasons. It is doubtful whether the relief funds went to those most in need. Grand juries were unelected bodies consisting of the largest property owners, mostly landowners, whose operations were a byword for corruption. Members of grand juries tended to favour their own areas when road works were being planned and to hire their tenants to carry out the contracts – so that they would be better able to pay their rents. Areas with

128

no representation on grand juries generally suffered from neglect. Local relief committees tended to be dominated by similar men. Board of works officials in Dublin complained that many of the localities which made the loudest demands were not suffering from serious distress and the Dublin-based commissioners held the view that most local commit-tees wished to off load the total cost of relief measures on the government, without any contribution from local landlords or other prosperous citizens. There was a strongly held belief in Dublin and at Westminster that the government had been unduly generous in 1845–46, with local property-owners evading their responsibilities and, that conditions in Ireland were not particularly acute.[16] Meanwhile at Westminster, Peel's Conservative government fell in the summer of 1846 and was replaced by a Liberal government, led by Lord John Russell, which was regarded as less disposed to approve of government intervention in the economy, though the differ-ence between Russell and Peel has been exaggerated; Peel's supporters did not criticise the relief measures adopted by their successors.[17]

Russell proposed that each local area would bear the full cost of further relief works in order to avoid the 1845 experi-ence of undue dependence on central government. In the short-run however all funds would come from government loans. Russell was less inclined to interfere in the food trade than Peel – for which he is often criticised. However Peel's purchase of maize had the element of surprise; by the autumn of 1846 Irish traders were threatening not to import grain unless given a commitment that the government would not spoil their market. In fact the government con-tinued to operate limited food depots in some remote areas, though they found it much more difficult to buy food than in the previous season, because the autumn/winter of 1846 was marked by widespread shortages of food throughout Europe.[18]

The greatest problem facing Ireland in the autumn/winter of 1846 was the scale of the Famine crisis. In August 1846 the potato crop, which was the main, often the sole food of the majority of the Irish people failed suddenly when blight swept through most of Ireland. Within six weeks a board of works engineer reported from Borris-in-Ossory that men working on relief schemes often had no food during the day. Food supplies within Ireland were grossly inadequate, approximately half the normal amount available, so prices began to soar.[19] Imports were slow to arrive; shipments from North America could take several months; by the time they reached Ireland in January/February 1847, it was too late. During the autumn of 1846 food was exported from Ireland because higher prices were available elsewhere. This food was exported not by landlords, but by merchants, who bought it from farmers. Had it remained in Ireland, food prices would have been somewhat lower and food supplies greater, but the policy of prohibiting imports would have totally contravened the prevailing free trade ideology of the time which was supported by the majority of English politicians. Retaining food exports within Ireland would not have prevented an acute famine, nor can we assume that the food would have reached those in need. It is highly probable that the exporters and large farmers denied their full profit would have resisted any restrictions. By the spring of 1847, food imports were considerably in excess of food exports and the Irish people benefited from free trade; in the autumn of 1846 however the question was less clear-cut.[20]

When the potato crop failed in 1846, the demand for employment on relief works escalated, despite the British government's decision to place the burden on local taxes. Cottiers who were contracted to work for farmers in return for land on which they grew potatoes abandoned their farmwork when the potato crop rotted in an effort to earn money to buy food for their family. As a result Irish farms may have been left without sufficient workers to carry out normal agricultural tasks. Piece-rates were introduced on public works to prevent labourers from idling. At the beginning wages were probably sufficient to enable workers to feed their families, however the retail price of maize roughly doubled between August and December 1846, so that a week's work bought less and less food. Workers, weakened because of lack of food, found their earnings declining and the quantity of food they could buy fell in turn. The government could have offered higher wages, but even the existing rates made it uncompetitive for many regular employers to hire workers; any further increase would only add to the labour-market disruption and would probably have caused further price inflation. The number of workers on relief works reached 750,000 by the spring of 1847. It was inevitable in the light of such numbers and the lack of time for organising works that there were many instances of incompetence, corruption and administrative problems. There was no time to plan for works offering long-term benefit to an area; any idea that famine relief funds could have been used to fund railway development as was suggested at the time took no account of the time-scale. It proved a major undertaking to organise payment in cash for such numbers in a country where there had previously been few weekly wage-earners and payroll robberies were common. Local committees determined who was eligible for employment on relief works and there were widespread allegations that undeserving large farmers were employed at the expense of labourers. High payments to farmers who supplied a horse were also resented. When a man was no longer able to work, pressure was often exerted to have his wife or son employed in his place in order that the family could earn some money. Applications for relief works relied on local initiative; thus an area with an active landlord, land agent or perhaps a clergyman was much more likely to offer extensive employment, whereas those which lacked a resident gentry – often the poorest areas – were left to fend for themselves. As a result the money spent on relief did not necessarily reach the neediest areas; it is no coincidence that Skibbereen, location of some of the most horrific accounts of famine deaths was wholly lacking in local relief organisations. Relief provided by charitable agencies suffered from a similar problem. Dr Murray, the Catholic archbishop of Dublin, channelled considerable sums which were sent to him by bishops in the United States, Britain and

Europe to priests who wrote seeking assistance. Yet Connacht had relatively few priests at this time relative to other parts of Ireland. Although the Society of Friends admitted that distress was much greater in Connacht than elsewhere they distributed proportionately more relief in Munster because the lack of community response in the west made it difficult to organise relief.[21]

No society could afford to withdraw up to three-quarters of a million workers – approximately thirty per cent of all males between the ages of fifteen and sixty-five, from their normal duties such as planting crops or saving turf. Relief works threatened to leave Ireland without food or fuel for the coming year – even if the blight did not recur. Board of Works officials pondered this problem and in December 1846, a commissioner, Sir Richard Griffith, issued a circular proposing that the state would pay labourers, farmers and their families a fixed sum, amounting to say a fortnight's wages, to carry out specified drainage work on their land. If they completed the work in less time, they could devote the remaining days to farm work. It is here that ideological issues impinge seriously on famine relief. The idea of paying men to farm their own land was anathema to the British prime minister and to the most senior civil servant, Sir Charles Trevelyan, a man who believed that for the typical Irish peasant:

A fortnight planting, a week or ten days digging and fourteen days turf cutting suffice for his subsistence. During the rest of the year he is at leisure to follow his own inclinations.

and the proposal was abandoned.[22]

Despite this rejection, the value of relief works was increasingly questioned. Deaths of workers on relief schemes, hostile verdicts at inquests, the graphic illustrations and descriptions in the *Illustrated London News*, plus the fact that appalling weather conditions during the winter of 1846 made work almost impossible, led to a decision to close down the public works and to supply cooked food.[23] Ironically, by the time that this decision was made in January 1847, food prices had begun to fall so that wages might have been sufficient to feed a family. By now, fever epidemics were well established and public works were spreading disease. If the decision to switch to food kitchens suggests that the government was responsive to public criticism, the change of policy was handled in an almost criminal manner. Relief works began to close in late March, yet most soup kitchens did not open before the middle of May. The government insisted on new committees and new applications to Dublin. During the hiatus the only assistance available came from either charities or the poor law. By mid-August 1846 soup kitchens were feeding up to three million people and in some parts of the west the whole population was being fed. Most accounts of the famine praise the soup kitchens and condemn public works out of hand. Yet by the summer of 1847 fever epidemics were widespread; any procedure which involved large sections of the population in regular queues for food was guaranteed to spread disease.

The late summer of 1847 brought a small but disease-free potato harvest. In the government's eyes the famine was at an end; the soup kitchens were closed, all special relief measures were terminated. Remaining cases of distress were regarded as part of 'normal' Irish distress, to be relieved by 'normal' mechanisms, i.e., the poor law. Charities and the British public also lost interest; the Society of Friends began scaling down its efforts. Yet famine did not end in the autumn of 1847; there was a major potato failure in 1848 and a lesser one in 1849.[24] If we wish to criticise government relief measures, their inaction after 1847 offers perhaps the most obvious target. By comparison the crisis in the autumn of 1846 was unexpected and unprecedented in scale; no government however humane and enlightened could have coped adequately. More could have done more to save lives during that terrible year, but responsibility does not lie solely with the government: greater humanity and activity on the part of landlords and land agents would have helped. Farmers should have shown greater sympathy to their starving cottiers; Catholic clergy could have been more proactive and grain traders less greedy. Politicians such as

O'Connell and Young Irelanders could have devoted less time to squabbling over political issues and more attention to the condition of the people.[25] It is easy to be wise after the event.

THE STIGMA OF
SOUPERISM

IRENE WHELAN

AMONG THE CATALOGUE OF GRIEVANCES accumulated by the Catholic Irish during the catastrophic years between 1845 and 1852, few attracted such odium as the phenomenon known as 'souperism', or the alleged attempts of evangelical missionaries to use hunger as an instrument to win converts to the Protestant faith. The bitterness of the 'souper' legacy became so deeply rooted that, even as recently as the past decade, the topic was still capable of arousing passionate controversy. In 1985 the Abbey Theatre's production of Eoghan Harris' play *Souper Sullivan* was followed by a spate of letters to the editor of *The Irish Times* as well as newspaper and radio interviews in which the author was forced to defend his claims and opinions in a way that few playwrights have been called to do in modern times.

The chief source of the controversy over *Souper Sullivan* was the implied innocence of the protagonist, the Rev. William Allen Fisher of Kilmoe parish in west Cork. The account of the Rev. Fisher's record during the famine years had appeared originally in Desmond Bowen's study of religious conflict in nineteenth-century Ireland.[1] Harris' interpretation of the event strongly reflected many of Bowen's sympathies, in so far as the Rev. Fisher was portrayed as a beneficent pastor who ministered to the Catholic population after their priest had fled the district during the height of the Famine. This may well have been the case, and the Rev. Fisher would hardly have been a singular example of a Church of Ireland pastor doing his utmost to relieve the afflictions of famine victims. The fact remains that the area of west Cork in which Rev. Fisher lived and worked was one in which evangelical missionaries had been operating both before and during the Famine, and his intentions, however benevolent, would have been associated by local people with this movement. What the audience did not see, in other words, what had been ignored completely in the play and dealt with in a cursory fashion in the book, was the vast institutional and ideological machinery that lay behind the drive to make Ireland a Protestant country. This included not only a massive system of private philanthropy which had been in operation since early in the century, but, more importantly, a fully developed political doctrine rooted in the belief that the source of Ireland's social and political problems was the Catholic religion, and that the country would never be prosperous and developed until Catholicism and all its influences were eradicated.

The question may be raised as to whether it is justified to describe anti-Catholicism as a political doctrine. If by 'political doctrine' we mean a developed idea or system of thought which is subscribed to by an intellectual and academic establishment and which professes a political agenda, then the anti-Catholicism of nineteenth-century Britain qualifies for the category as surely as the development of ideas on race which bore such remarkable fruit in the twentieth century.[2] British anti-Catholicism was as old as the Reformation, and was by no means a spent force in the eighteenth century, the scepticism and rationalism of the enlightenment notwithstanding.[3] During the early decades of the nineteenth century, however, it received a new lease of life because of political events in Europe as well as more immediate developments in Ireland.

The ascendancy of ideas on the necessity of spreading the Protestant faith worldwide was a feature of the 1790s and early 1800s in Britain, and coincided with the growth of the country's great power status, both politically and commercially.[4] This 'global imperative' was of particular significance in the case of Ireland, where the claims of the majority Catholic population posed an immediate and direct threat to the economic and political hegemony of the Protestant establishment. Following the Act of Union of 1800 it became an article of faith among evangelical Christians on both sides of the Irish sea that if the Catholic Irish could be 'brought over' to the Protestant faith, that the problems which bedevilled Irish society such as economic backwardness, lack of respect for the law, and hatred of the Protestant establishment would be eradicated. The demand among the common people for education and literacy in English, which was then at an all time high, was seen as providing an ideal conduit through which the desired moral reformation could be effected. A large number of voluntary societies devoted to scriptural education and bible distribution thus made their appearance during the early 1800s, and their object of evangelising the native Irish in the reformed faith soon made a battleground of the educational arena. When the moral crusade was intensified in the aftermath of the victory over Napoleon in 1815 (an event interpreted by evangelicals as a providential sign of the divine favour enjoyed by the Protestant cause), Catholic leaders began to unite in opposition to the claims of what had come to be known as the 'New' or 'Second' reformation.

I have argued elsewhere that it was this attempt at reformation that brought the Catholic hierarchy and clergy onto the political stage in the 1820s and united priests and people behind the popular campaign for emancipation organised by Daniel O'Connell and the Catholic Association.[5] The astonishing success of the tactics of peaceful mass mobilisation devised by O'Connell thwarted every attempt of the government to suppress the movement, and emancipation was conceded in 1829 in the face of the threat of civil war.[6] Two years later, the government made good its promise to act as a neutral force in the battle over education and introduced a national system of primary schools. Although funded from the public purse the national schools were managed by the clergy at the local level, which meant that in Catholic areas they were directly controlled by the priests.[7] This put an abrupt end to the evangelicals' ambition to effect a reformation through exploiting the educational needs of Catholic schoolchildren.

If the prospect for a national reformation was a lost cause by the mid-1830s, how do we explain the new phase of proselytism that began with the onset of the Famine in 1845–6? The consequences of the political and sectarian conflicts of the 1820s provide part of the answer. In response to the granting of emancipation and the government's decision to fund the national schools, the marriage between the intransigent ultra-Protestant political establishment and the promoters of the new reformation was cemented, and their anti-Catholic character became more, not less, intense. The years between 1828 and 1832 were ones of retrenchment and redefinition for the Irish evangelical movement generally, and certain trends began to take shape in this period that would bear fruit in the following decades. The most significant for our purposes was the trend towards the concentration of resources along the western seaboard. The impoverished condition of the western counties coupled with the continued dominance of Irish (as in Wales and Scotland, the use of the native language as an instrument of conversion had been in use in Ireland since early in the century) and, above all, the shortage of Catholic clerical manpower, all appeared to indicate that the area would be more conducive to evangelisation. Aligned with this shift westwards was the development of another novelty in the evangelical arsenal, the 'colony' or settlement which would function both as a refuge for converts and a base for missionary expansion. As part of this new offensive of the 1830s, and in response to what was seen as the government's endorsement of Catholic resurgence, an intensive propaganda campaign was simultaneously undertaken to alert the British public to the dangers that lay in store for the kingdom, and for the Protestants of Ireland in particular, from the threatened ascendancy of the Catholic establishment.[5]

The founding of the Protestant Colonisation Society in 1830 bore witness to the increasingly combative ambitions of the supporters of the evangelical crusade. Besides functioning as refuges for persecuted converts, the colonies were envisaged as economically self-sufficient communities which would demonstrate to the surrounding areas the benefits of the traditional Protestant virtues of cleanliness, industry, and good management. But their chief function was to operate as missionary centres from which the surrounding areas could be evangelised. During the early 1830s a small number of colonies were established in places like Aughkeely, Co. Donegal, and Kilmeague, Co. Kildare where one hundred families were said to have been settled before the Famine.[9] It was the experiments at Dingle and Achill, however, begun in 1831 and 1834 respectively, that really attracted the attention of the public. These were large-scale operations that planted deep roots and made a considerable impact on their respective localities.

The people behind the founding of the colonies, the Rev. Edward Nangle in Achill and the Rev. Charles Gayer in Dingle were connected with the evangelical wing of the Church of Ireland, and in both cases the critical factor in getting operations underway was the co-operation they were able to draw on from local clergymen and landlords. In the case of Dingle, certainly, key local support was provided to the Rev. Gayer by the Protestant rector of Dingle, the Rev. Thomas Chute Goodman, a fluent native speaker whose family was held in the highest regard by local Catholics.[10] The case of the Rev. Edward Nangle and the Achill Colony was even more striking, since Achill was part of the diocese currently presided over by the most staunch evangelical on the Episcopal bench of the Church of Ireland, the Rev. Power le Poer Trench of Tuam.[11]

Substantial material benefits rewarded those who joined the colonies and converts were said to enjoy comfortable homes, rent-free land, regular salaries if they were teachers, and career opportunities for their children. There was a great deal of dispute over who actually inhabited the colonies and local people repeatedly stressed to visitors that the occupants were not locals but converts brought in from different parts of Ireland. What most angered local people was the abundance of money the colony organisers appeared to have had access to, which allowed them to purchase the best available land and to provide, through regular employment and education, opportunities for advancement that were pitiably scarce in rural Ireland.[12] But people could take advantage of such opportunities only at the cost of complete ostracisation by their former neighbours, which was effected through the use of 'exclusive dealing', an early form of the boycott in which local people would refuse to buy from or sell to converts.

The source of the most bitter controversy associated with the colonies, however, was their capacity to provide material relief in times of dearth, a practice interpreted by critics as preying on the vulnerability of the starving and destitute. This was not a new phenomenon. At the height of the 'Second Reformation' in 1826–7 when mass conversions were being reported on the Farnham Estate in Co. Cavan, it was repeatedly charged that conversions took place because of the hardship and privation brought about by a localised economic depression.[13] The dispensing of relief, therefore, whether public or private, was second only to education as a weapon in the battle for the minds and hearts of the Irish poor. Following the passage of the emancipation bill, priests at the local level became increasingly combative in their efforts to prevent Protestants from dominating local committees entrusted with relief funds, particularly in areas where evangelical missions were entrenched.[14] To what degree were they justified in their fears? It was certainly an outbreak of famine and cholera that first attracted the attentions of the Rev. Edward Nangle to west Mayo in 1831. And it was during the same crisis in Dingle that the baneful term 'souper' first entered popular usage. It was said to have originated when a benevolent lady set up a soup kitchen and the local priest forbade his parishioners to have anything to do with it, referring to the dispensers of relief as 'Soupers'.[15]

By the 1840s the colonies at Achill and Dingle were permanent fixtures on the western landscape, with cottages, schools, dispensaries, and even, in the case of Achill, a hotel to accommodate tourists. Besides whatever advantages they brought to these remote districts in the form of employment and tourism, their presence heightened controversy of every kind. Seldom a month went by without reports in the local press of bible readers and preachers being attacked, or of persons being fined or bound to the peace because of sectarian incidents. Major law cases ensued when cases were taken against journalists and newspaper proprietors for allegedly libellous accounts of what was going on in the colonies. The evangelical press in Britain carried frequent accounts of the persecution suffered by converts because of exclusive dealing and the violence instigated against evangelical missionaries by the priests. Publicity and notoriety of this kind ensured that the colonies were a source of fascination for foreign visitors who came to observe what benefits the light of the Bible was bringing to the benighted inhabitants of the west of Ireland. Among the famous visitors to have left accounts of their visits to Achill, for example, were the travel writers Mr and Mrs Samuel Carter Hall, and the American philanthropist Mrs Asenath Nicholson.

As a result of the work underway at the colonies, the phenomenon of 'souperism' or the doling out of material advantages in exchange for the transfer of denominational allegiance was already a familiar one on the eve of the Famine. Shortly after the onset of the potato blight and the threat of widespread starvation in 1845–6, however, a new wave of proselytism was unleashed which involved a more explicit and intense campaign of evangelisation and the founding of a new organisation, the Society for the Irish Church Missions, which focused specifically on Connemara. What set the new operation apart from those already underway in the west was that fact that it was organised and funded from Britain. In terms of its choice of location and objectives, and the support and co-operation received from local clergymen and landlords, however, it actually differed little from what was going on in Dingle and Achill.

The choice of Connemara as a centre for the work of the Irish Church Missions was no accident. A remote and unknown region until the turn of the century, it had only recently been opened to the influences of the modern world. The years of the Napoleonic wars brought great prosperity to the area, however, and evidence of rapid modernisation could be seen in the appearance of new estates, roads, and villages, and even a 'capital' town in Clifden. Estate owners that might have scorned the bleak and impoverished west in the eighteenth century now rushed to take up residence in the currently fashionable romantic periphery, often equipped with the latest ideas on developing the rural economy and more often accompanied by wives even more ardently committed to the philosophy of improvement.[16] The Blakes of Renvyle, the D'Arcys of Clifden Castle, and the Martins of Ballinahinch, for example, all fall into this category. As early as 1824 the record of the Protestant gentry in Connemara was such that the area was described in the liberal *Dublin Evening Post* as being 'infected with the most virulent description of the biblical mania'.[17]

The source of the infection complained about in the *Dublin Evening Post* could be traced to the influence of 'improving' landlords' wives like Martha Louisa Blake of Renvyle, whose dispute with the local priest over the setting up of a school on her husband's estate had eventually ended up in the papers. The wives of John D'Arcy and Richard Martin similarly occupied themselves with education and philanthropy and introduced the schools of the Kildare Place Society and the London Hibernian Society to Clifden and Ballinahinch. What allowed or perhaps inspired these women to pursue their ambition to the degree they did was the support of local Church of Ireland clergymen sympathetic to the cause, and the prevalence of such clergymen in Connemara from the 1820s on was due directly to the influence of Archbishop Trench, who made it a policy to fill whatever clerical offices fell vacant in the Tuam diocese with men committed to spreading the reformation among the Catholic population. The joining of Killala and Achonry to the Tuam diocese in 1835 expanded the area of his influence in this regard, and his legacy was further strengthened when, on his death in 1839, he was succeeded by the Rev. Thomas Plunket, a churchman even more passionately and single-mindedly committed to the reformation crusade.[18]

By 1836 the results of Archbishop Trench's policy could be seen to good effect in Connemara in the work of three of his protégés, Rev. Anthony Thomas of Ballinakill, Rev. Mark A. Foster, and Rev. Brabazon Ellis. In 1836 these men, along with James and Hyacinth D'Arcy, the sons of John D'Arcy of Clifden Castle, and Colonel A. Thomson of Salruck, established the Connemara Christian Committee to advance the work of reformation. By 1839 there were plans underway to develop a colony. The trustees were already in possession of land to build a church and school, as well as houses for teachers and clergymen, and had been offered a lease of an additional 500 acres for further development.[19] By this stage, also, it is clear that they had attracted the attention and support of interested parties in Dublin. At a meeting of the Society for the Conversion of the Jews in Dublin in 1839, the Rev. Thomas was introduced to the Rev. Alexander Dallas, an English clergyman whose name would become synonymous with Connemara and the Society for the Irish Church Missions.[20]

The Rev. Alexander Dallas was rector of Wonston in Hampshire, and a subscriber to the particular strain of evangelical thought known as pre-millenialism. In brief, the adherents of this doctrine carried their literal interpretation of the Bible to the extreme that they believed the events of human history were to occur according to divine providence, and furthermore that the sequence of their occurrence was outlined in a coded form in the scriptures, particularly the *Book of Revelation*. The millenium would occur after certain conditions had been fulfilled, and foremost among these conditions were the conversion of the Jews and the heathens, and the destruction of the 'Anti-Christ' of the *Book of Revelation*, which was understood to be the Roman Catholic Church. The growth of this strain of religious thought had been on the increase since the 1790s, when the world-shaking events of the French revolution and the rise and fall of Napoleon provided abundant material for interpreters of 'signs of the times'. The vigorous revival of European Catholicism in the post-Napoleonic period, the resurgence of Irish Catholicism which fuelled the popular campaign for emancipation, the growth of political liberalism and the rise of the Tractarian movement in Britain during the 1830s were all prophetically interpreted as heralding the coming apocalypse.[21]

The most important theologian of pre-millenialism in Britain was the Rev. Edward Bickersteth of the Church Missionary Society, also resident in Wonston and a close friend of Alexander Dallas. Bickersteth had clearly been influenced in his thinking by men like Mortimer O'Sullivan and Robert McGhee who were products of the combative and embattled world of Irish Protestantism, and who had stridently and successfully carried their anti-Catholic polemics to Britain in the early and mid-1830s. In 1836 the Rev. Bickersteth had explicitly identified the Catholic church as the 'Babylon' of the *Book of Revelation*, and a clear convergence began to develop between the theology of English pre-millenialist evangelicals and the politics-driven anti-Catholicism of their Irish counterparts.[22] The consequence was a united effort to contain the threat of Catholicism, and particularly to undo the legislative measures which not only had granted political freedom, but were actually fostering the 'growth of popery' by providing public funds for the endowment of the Catholic seminary at Maynooth. What the pre-millenialists sought was nothing less than the complete extirpation of Catholic influence from any part of public life in Britain or Ireland, and the eradication of Catholicism as the religion of the majority population in Ireland on grounds that it was the cause of political subversion as well as economic backwardness.

When the liberal government decided to increase the Maynooth endowment in 1845, it appeared that the very rulers of the country were actively countenancing the triumph of the Anti-Christ. Evangelicals of every stripe united to oppose the plan and public opinion was consumed with the 'subject on which society appears to have gone mad', as Harriet Martineau described it. Given the disposition of pre-millenialist evangelicals like Dallas and Bickersteth to attach prophetical import to current events, it is small wonder that they interpreted the news coming out of Ireland in 1846 as yet another emphatic sign of divine providence in England's hour of peril. To this way of thinking, the Famine was nothing less than a punishment sent by God to chastise a sinful people.[23] The duty of the pre-millenial evangelical in this instance was clear: it was to use the opportunity to help fulfil God's plan for the universe by making Ireland part of his kingdom governed by the true religion of the Bible, on the one hand, and on the other to secure eternal salvation for the souls of the afflicted by wrenching them from the grasp of Rome before they finally abandoned the world.

Dallas' connections in Connemara and his ambitions to sponsor a mission there were already in existence when the first news about the failure of the potato began to break in the autumn of 1845. A gift of £3,000 from an English supporter allowed him to proceed with his plans, the first step of which was to use the new postal service to distribute 90,000 copies of a tract entitled *A Voice From Heaven to Ireland* in January, 1846. Similar tracts with titles such as *Irishmen's Rights* and *The Food of Man* were distributed in the same manner in the following months. After a visit to Ireland in August of the same year, he returned to Wonston and wrote letters to the *Morning Herald* calling for the setting up of a 'Special Fund for the Spiritual Exigencies of Ireland'. As funds accumulated in response to this appeal a committee was set up headed by the Duke of Manchester with Dallas and the Rev. Bickersteth as honorary secretaries.[24] These funds provided the financial backing for the missionary crusade that Dallas was now set to embark upon.

Dallas began his operations in Connemara in the district of Castlekerke near Oughterard where the usual combination of support from clergymen and a landlord's wife helped get him started. The urgency of his crusade was obvious from the beginning. As he wanted to get as many missionaries into the field as possible there was no time to develop colonies or settlements; instead his strategy revolved around the spread of 'mission stations' manned by individual clergymen or preachers entrusted with funds to advance the work of education and evangelisation. With the influence of landlords like Lord Roden and the Duke of Manchester behind him, the Rev. Dallas was in a particularly strong position to appeal for the support of the diocesan superior. Obligingly Bishop Thomas Plunket ordained two Irish-speaking converts, the Rev. J. B. O'Callaghan who had been in training for some time in Wonston, and the Rev. Roderick Ryder, a former Catholic priest. O'Callaghan shortly had a string of mission stations around Lough Corrib and into the mountains at Cornamona and Kilmilkin. Roderick Ryder was despatched back to his former parish of Rooveagh on the Errismore peninsula about ten miles south-west of Clifden. Between the work of these convert evangelists and resident gentry and clergymen like the D'Arcys and Rev. Thomas, Connemara was soon saturated with mission stations, schools, tract distributors and scripture readers, all funded from money raised in England by Dallas and Bickersteth. In the Clifden area alone in 1848, for example, there were mission stations at Errislannon and Errismore, Ballyconree and Ballinakill, and Sallerna and Rossadillisk near Cleggan, and in many of these locations Protestant service was available every Sunday.[25]

Most of the evidence concerning the proselytism of the famine years suggest that the new offensive began to gain serious momentum in the spring of 1848.[26] The speed with which Dallas had organised the Connemara missions created a momentum that spread all over Connaught and even farther afield, to the extent that the Rev. Edward Bickersteth was now devoting his entire fundraising efforts to the missionary cause in Ireland.[27] The infusion of money to set up schools and pay the salaries of teachers and bible readers had an immdiate effect on an area that was one of the worst hit in the country in terms of the effects of the Famine.[28] So successful was the first year of the campaign that a new organisation, the Society for the Irish Church Missions to the Roman Catholics, was established in March, 1849.[29] By 1850 the number of Protestant congregations in the area was such that the supporters of the mission were describing it as the breakthrough that evangelicals had been awaiting for decades. In explaining the rapid progess made in such a short period, it was claimed that the effects of the Famine had finally made people realise the errors of the Roman Catholic faith, and their disillusionment had finally served to break the traditional bonds with the priesthood.

The most convincing evidence of the true picture of conditions in the west at this time, the sufferings inflicted by disease and starvation as well as the workings of evangelical missionaries, comes, not surprisingly, from the letters of Catholic priests pleading for help from the relief committee organised by Dr Daniel Murray, the Catholic Archbishop of Dublin. It would be hard to draw a more intense picture of horror than that described by priests writing from remote districts of west Galway and Mayo in 1848 and 1849. The combined effects of starvation, disease, and mass evictions had reduced the west to a charnel house of death during these years. In one letter after another to the Archbishop's relief fund came accounts of the starving and the dispossessed wandering about like walking skeletons, 'without indoor or outdoor relief' as one correspondent noted.[30] Priests described the levelling of cottages by the hundred and deaths by the thousand in their individual parishes.[31] Several letters from the most stricken areas described the operations of proselytising agencies with money and food in abundance for distribution in schools or at Sunday service. Consider the evidence of a Fr Flannelly of Ballinakill (near Clifden) in 1849, for example, who admitted that 'not a mile of the public road can be travelled without seeing a dead body, as the poor are homeless and if they show any sign of sickness are thrown out of the poorhouses'. Fever and dysentry, he claimed, 'the sure precursors of cholera' were in every hut and cabin and there was no medical aid to be had in such a wild and extensive district. Half a pound of Indian meal per household per day was the sole food of the poor, and though men were offering to work a whole day for two pints of meal, there was no work to be had. In the midst of this situation Fr Flannelly said that proselytisers accompanied by apostate priests and lay people were going from cabin to cabin 'proffering food and money and clothing to the naked and starving on condition of their becoming members of their conventicles'.[32]

Echoing the opinion of Bishop Doyle of Kildare and Leighlin at the height of the Second Reformation in the 1820s, Fr Flannelly considered this situation more injurious and oppressive than the penal laws of the previous century. While this opinion enjoyed a wide consensus among fellow clerics in other parts of the west, few of them denied the claims of evangelical missionaries that their schools were full and their Sunday services well attended. A Fr Gallagher of Achill, for example, admitted that 'poverty has compelled the greatest number of the population to send their children to Nangle's proselytising villainous schools; he has at this moment one thousand children of the Catholics of the parish attending ... and so he can, for they have no other refuge. They are dying of hunger, and rather than die, they have submitted ...' [33] To the north of Achill, Fr Martin Hart of Ballycastle spoke of how his parishioners 'once honest and religious, are now the reverse', and that proselytising societies, 'with plenty of meal and money, have their agents busy in the area, trying to win the people from the faith, and when they give say, "I am not now fit to be their priest".'[34] What survived in the popular memory about the proselytising activities of the worst years of the famine corroborates the contemporary evidence of the priests. An elderly resident of Clifden interviewed by Stephen Gwynn in the early years of the twentieth century, for example, recalled how the expression 'Silver Monday' was used in Clifden to describe the shilling that was given out at the D'Arcy dower house at Glenown to those who had attended service at the Church of Ireland the day before. 'I saw them myself,' the old man recounted, 'blue with hunger in their houses and they had to go.'[35]

As there was no shortage of people willing to attend service or send their children to proselytising schools, neither did there appear to be a want of employees willing to work as bible readers, teachers, and tract distributors. A nun from the Presentation Convent in Galway, for example, spoke of the 600 pupils that were being prepared by proselytising agents in the national school in Rahoon to supply the workhouses of Connaught.[36] Similarly, the Presbyterian missionary, Edward Dill, in describing conditions in the west at this time referred to 'applications from the daughters of gentlemen, couched in terms enough to make the heart bleed, begging to be made teachers in our industrial schools at £20 a year'.[37] It was not only starving peasants, apparently, who relied on funds raised by missionary agencies during these terrible years.

If there were people who succumbed to the salaries and food provided by proselytising agencies, there were others like the parishioners of Fr Michael Enwright of Castletown-bere in west Cork, who were 'not yielding an inch, except when driven to it'.[38] But this was a rare voice, and the vast majority of the letters relating to this subject in the Murray papers claim that people were driven by starvation to 'take the soup' as the saying had it. From the evidence it appears that the years 1848–50 were those in which conversions occurred, but even the most supportive among those who investigated the phenomenon suggest that the numbers involved never amounted to more than several hundred in areas where missionary activity was most intense, as opposed to the wholesale capitulation of entire communities that was being heralded in the evangelical press. In 1852 John Forbes was told by a 'respectable local Catholic' of Clifden that three to four hundred adults had been converted in the town and the adjoining parishes of Omey and Ballindoon, an area listed on the census of the previous year as having a population of almost 11,000.[39] In his study of the Kilmoe parish of west Cork, where missionary agencies had been as active as they had been in Mayo, Galway, and Kerry during the Famine and indeed before, Fr Patrick Hickey, basing his evidence on the 1861 census, has estimated that there had been an absolute increase of 492 Protestants resident in the parish since 1834.[40] If the conversions were not at the floodtide level the apologists liked to claim, neither were they figments of the evangelical imagination as hostile Catholic critics like Archbishop MacHale of Tuam repeatedly observed.

After about 1850 when it appeared that the crisis years were finally at an end and the full scope of what the evangelicals had attempted in the west became obvious, there was a predictable backlash from the Catholic hierarchy and clergy. It was all the more intense because of the simultaneous uproar in England over the 'Papal Aggression' episode associated with the Ecclesiastical Titles Bill and the efforts of the papacy to re-establish the Catholic heirarchy in

Britain. What was happening in the west of Ireland was now seen as crucial to the great struggle between the forces of light and the 'Anti-Christ' of Popery, and the battle literally shifted to Connemara in 1851 with the arrival of Henry Wilberforce to head up the Catholic Defence Association and expose the fraudulent claims of the proselytisers. As the youngest son of William Wilberforce, the famous philanthropist and founding father of English evangelicalism, Henry Wilberforce was an unlikely candidate to end up in such a situation. His conversion to Catholicism as a result of his involvement in the Oxford movement speaks volumes about the seriousness with which religion was viewed in the heyday of Victorian Britain. Wilberforce set up his base of operations in Oughterard and made a point of investigating the colonies and the charges of bribery and intimidation associated with the evangelical missionary crusade. His condemnation of the entire movement was visceral; the granting of land and work to converts he dismissed as 'a demoralising system of wholesale bribery'.[41] He went further and charged that intimidation was regularly employed by agents and landlords who used their economic power to force parents to send children to evangelical schools, and to prevent the granting of sites for national schools on their estates.[42]

Valuable though it may have been in terms of the authors' family background and nationality, the evidence of Henry Wilberforce was hardly needed once the Catholic bishops began to take action to thwart the advances of the missions in the west. Outspoken bishops like John MacHale of Tuam and Edward Maginn of Derry did not hesitate to use the language of extermination to describe what had been attempted, and this attitude was quickly conveyed to the world of popular opinion by nationalist newspapers, especially the *Freeman's Journal*. When the returns of the 1851 census revealed that the population had declined by a million and three quarters the *Freeman's Journal* did not flinch from associating those who would eliminate Catholicism with the extermination of Catholics through hunger.[43]

Ridicule as much as outrage was the weapon of choice

that the *Freeman* wielded with deadly force against those whose stock in trade was the conversion of Catholics. In October of 1851 the paper carried an extensive account of a ceremony which took place in the Protestant church at Dromkeen, Co. Tipperary, where Bishop Robert Daly of Cashel confirmed a church full of converts assembled by a local clergyman, the Rev. Darby. The converts, it appeared, had shown up for the occasion as they had been promised new clothing in return. They received the clothing and went through with the ceremony as agreed. The following Sunday, however, they appeared at Mass at the Catholic chapels situated nearby (sporting the new clothes, naturally), and publicly claimed that hunger and cold was what made them engage in the fraud. The Rev. Darby set about taking legal action against the individuals involved with the intent of getting the clothes back, but the 'converts' would have none of it as they claimed they had fulfilled their part of the bargain and were entitled to their reward![44]

Ridicule of this kind no doubt provided for public entertainment, but ridicule and verbal condemnation were minor weapons in the Catholic arsenal when it came to preventing further inroads by the evangelicals in the 1850s. In fact the counter-attack of the Catholic Church, once it got underway in the west, bore all the hallmarks of a religious *blitzkrieg*: an initial bombardment in the form of episcopal tours in which massive numbers received the sacrament of confirmation, followed by parish missions organised by the Vincentian and Redemptorist preaching orders, and finally the founding of permanent establishment in the form of convents and monasteries in the larger towns of the west and sometimes even in villages. The combined impact of this 'counter-reformation' on the western counties has never received the attention is deserves, but Emmet Larkin's research on the role of parish missions in enshrining the 'devotional revolution' at the local level in the latter half of the nineteenth century gives some indication of the significance of what might justifiably be called an Irish counter-reformation.[45]

The effects of the proselytising campaign of the late

151

1840s and early 1850s on the Church of Ireland is more difficult to estimate. Unquestionably the reputation of the established church suffered because of the ambitions of evangelical sympathisers on the episcopal bench like Thomas
Plunket of Tuam and Robert Daly of Cashel. It was the
opinion of one observer in the west in 1854 that 'the Protestant establishment has been more fatally damaged by the
soup system than by all the attacks of Catholics and Radicals
put together'.[46] Nevertheless, when the disestablishment of
the Church of Ireland was finally effected in 1869, it was
more a consequence of events in the political world than the
particular anti-Protestant animus dredged up by the
evangelical crusade.

Surprisingly, given the bitterness of the famine years
and the strength of the Catholic backlash in the 1850s, the
evangelical crusade does not appear to have damaged
relations between Protestants and Catholics in the west of
Ireland. While the Irish Church Missions and the Achill and
Dingle colonies were still operating in the late 1850s and into
the 1860s the reports of court cases were still full of local
sectarian incidents involving violence against converts and
bible readers. Yet the more permanent and constructive
features introduced by the evangelicals often succeeded in
winning the respect and admiration of Catholics. It is quite
clear from the evidence of contemporaries that ordinary
people were capable of differentiating between genuinely
charitable evangelical Christians and the bitterness of
sectarian prejudice. The career of Dr Neason Adams of
Achill is a case in point. Adams was a medical doctor who
had joined the Rev. Nangle's colony soon after its foundation
and spent his whole life ministering to the health needs of
the local people, for which he was held in great esteem
locally. Similarly, the couple who ran the Ballyconree
Orphanage near Clifden in the late ninteenth and early
twentieth century, Dr and Mrs Purkis, were held in high
regard both as neighbours and philanthropists; a former
resident of the village who clearly remembered them described them in the most positive terms as 'lovely Protestant
people'.[47] The account of Allanah Heather of her youth in the

Errislannon Penisula outside Clifden clearly indicates that the most staunch evangelical principles of her two aunts, Jane and Edith, did not prevent them from having the warmest regard for their Catholic neighbours, a regard that was certainly returned in kind.[48] When Stephen Gwynn visited Connemara in 1909 he was told by a Protestant clergyman that, whatever sectarian violence had occurred in connection with conversions and 'souperism' that 'no Protestant was ever persecuted in Connemara as a Protestant'.[49]

The most damaging legacy of the evangelical crusade in the west was the poisoning of relations between the Catholic clergy and those Protestants, whether clerical or lay, who sought to involve themselves in improving social conditions. The work of philanthropists like James Ellis and James Hack Tuke was looked upon with suspicion by Catholic bishops, fearful that Protestant involvement in schemes like the setting up of light industry or assisted emigration in the west betokened an effort to usurp the authority of the Catholic clergy or to clear the countryside of Catholics. As a consequence of the proselytising missions, subversion was everywhere suspected, and was equally resorted to as a means of retaliation. When the estate that had been developed by James Ellis at Letterfrack came on the market in 1882 (with the express provision of the current owner, a virulent anti-Catholic, that it not fall into Catholic hands) it was purchased by an agent acting for the Archbishop of Tuam. It was then entrusted to the Christian Brothers of Artane to be developed as an industrial school.[50] What had been a showcase of Quaker philanthropy in the mid-nineteenth century, situated in the midst of the most glorious scenery of north Connemara, was thus transformed into an institution whose very name struck terror into the hearts of Irish children in the twentieth century and which occupies a place of its own in the literature of modern Ireland. The fate of Letterfrack is a fitting metaphor for the contribution of men like Alexander Dallas and Edward Nangle to the progress of events in the west of Ireland: in their attempts to destroy what they saw as Catholic tyranny they virtually brought it into creation. In the very recent past Letterfrack has undergone yet another

153

transformation and its buildings are now the centre of an impressive community development project as well as the Connemara National Park. The name commemorated on the community hall is that of the Quaker philanthropist, James Ellis.

MASS EVICTION AND THE GREAT FAMINE:
The Clearances Revisited

JAMES S. DONNELLY, JR

ANY SERIOUS STUDENT OF THE GREAT Famine soon becomes aware that contemporary voices speaking or writing
about this horrific experience could be strikingly discordant.
Just how discordant depended on such matters as political
and religious beliefs, social status, economic interests, practical experience, and physical distance from the events described or discussed. Thus government ministers could view
the mechanisms of the Irish poor-law system as expressions
of both economic rationality and Christian morality, whereas
a revolutionary nationalist like John Mitchel regarded those
same mechanisms as 'contrivances for slaughter'.[1] This dis-
cordance is perhaps greatest, and certainly very apparent, on
the highly charged subject of the mass evictions, or clearances, which will forever be associated with the experience
and memory of the Famine. It is the contention of this essay
that we can learn a great deal about the clearances in particular and the Famine in general by paying more careful attention than historians have previously done to the discordant languages or discourses of contemporary actors, observers, and commentators.

Before dissecting these discourses, let me make certain
preliminary remarks about the magnitude, timing, geographical incidence, and causes of the clearances. It is impossible to be certain about how many people were evicted during the years of the Famine and its immediate aftermath. The
police began to keep an official tally only in 1849, and they
recorded a total of nearly 250,000 persons as formally and
permanently evicted from their holdings between 1849 and
1854. Necessarily under the circumstances, this figure must

be an underestimate of the harsh reality. If we were to guess at the equivalent number for 1846–8 and to include the countless thousands pressured into involuntary surrenders during the whole period (1846–54), the resulting figure would almost certainly exceed half a million persons. Like several other aspects of the Famine, the geographical incidence of evictions varied enormously, with the most sweeping clearances in the years 1849–54 occurring in Clare, Mayo, Galway, and Kerry (in that order). These four counties alone were responsible for 33 per cent of all the permanent evictions officially recorded in Ireland during those years. Assessed temporally, the clearances began in earnest in 1847 under the spur of the notorious Gregory clause, a vicious amendment to the Irish poor law which will be discussed shortly; they reached a peak in 1849 and 1850, and then they fell steeply over the next four years, except in Mayo, where the eviction rate remained exceptionally high until at least 1853. Behind the clearances stood the widespread and long-standing landlord desire to modernise Irish agriculture, coupled with the virtual collapse of the tenant capacity for effective resistance to evictions and the extreme pressure which heavy poor rates and lost rents put on many landlords in districts of deep destitution.[2]

The vast majority of landlords and agents who engaged in clearances or numerous evictions appear to have found ways to relieve themselves of the charge of anything like gross inhumanity; some displayed not even the smallest sign of a troubled conscience. For a middleman tenant who evicted under-tenants, it was always tempting to shift the blame to the head landlord. Writing to the solicitor of the proprietor of certain lands in north Cork in August 1847, the middleman Dr John O'Neill observed, 'To the class of smallholders on the farm I have already made large allowances, and yet I feel they require further assistance, which I would willingly bestow on them if I had it in my power. Unless they are befriended by [the proprietor] Sir Riggs Falkiner, I fear they will go to the wall.'[3] By June 1850 these smallholders had become a 'wretched mass' of paupers

(236 of them receiving outdoor relief) and O'Neill excused their impending eviction by insisting that it was 'absolutely necessary to have the miserable sheds in which most of these unfortunates dwell done away with, so as to remove so heavy a burthen from the lands and induce the more than half-starved inmates to seek an asylum in the poorhouse'.[4] By making insignificant concessions at the time of the actual clearance early in 1851, such as the distribution of 'a few shillings' to the evicted tenants, O'Neill expressed the hope that 'we will part with all of the unnecessary folk, "over 200" in number, without causing any commotion in that district'.[5]

What some might have regarded as 'conscience money' clearance-minded landlords and agents saw as kind-hearted, if self-interested philanthropy. Joseph Kincaid, 'one of the most extensive land agents' in all of Ireland, with multiple agencies for different proprietors in various counties, ex-plained to a House of Lords committee in 1848 how he had removed about 150 families (probably 800 or 900 people) in the Kilglass district of Roscommon. To induce them to leave for England or Scotland, he gave these tenants £3 to £5 per family, or as little as 10s. to 18s. per head. No formal evictions were apparently necessary. Mortality around Kilglass was so great, claimed Kincaid, and 'the people were in that state of destitution that they entreated to have a few pounds to take them anywhere'.[6] Sir John Benn-Walsh took the same tack with similar attitudes on his extensive Kerry and Cork estates, which were 'very much weeded both of paupers & bad tenants'. As he noted in his diary in September 1851, in a tone of self-congratulation, 'This has been accomplished by [the agent] Matthew Gabbett without evictions, bringing in the sheriff, or any harsh measures. In fact, the paupers & little cottiers cannot keep their holdings without the potato &, for small sums of £1, £2, & £3, have given me peaceable possession in a great many cases, when the cabin is immediately levelled.'[7]

What some landlords perceived and justified as an eco-nomic opportunity that could be seized without inflicting any real hardship, many others justified as a financial necessity, given the way in which the poor law operated. What they had especially in mind was the provision of the poor law known as the £4-rating clause, which made landlords responsible for paying all the poor rates of all holdings valued at £4 or less. This gave landlords a strong incentive to rid themselves, by eviction or otherwise, of tenants in that category who were no longer able to pay rent. Recalling the Famine clearances in 1866, the Cork proprietor Sir Denham Jephson-Norreys insisted that the £4-rating clause 'almost forced the landlords to get rid of their poorer tenantry; in order that they should not have to pay for these small holdings, they destroyed the cottages in every direction'.[5]

Of all Irish landowners, those of Mayo were perhaps most likely to take refuge in this notion of compulsion. In that county a staggering 75 per cent of all occupiers had holdings valued at £4 or less, with the result that many landlords shouldered almost the entire burden of the rates – rates made extremely heavy by the coinciding mass of pauperism. With little rent coming in, and having had to borrow £1,500 even to pay his rates, the Marquis of Sligo described himself in October 1848 as being 'under the necessity of ejecting or being ejected'.[6] Betraying a guilty conscience in 1852 underneath his public face of reluctant necessity, he personally berated his cousin and fellow Galway landowner George Henry Moore, M.P., who had refused to carry out evictions during the Famine despite suffering lost rents. Lord Sligo told Moore that he would end up like Sir Samuel O'Malley, another Galway proprietor, on whose estate arrears of rent were allowed to accumulate to the point that its Court of Chancery managers decided to evict perhaps as many as three-quarters of the tenants. But by taking action in time and by evicting only 'the really idle and dishonest', Lord Sligo claimed that he would be dispossessing only about a quarter of his tenants. He concluded by blaming Moore and exonerating himself: 'In my heart's belief you and Sir Samuel do more [to] ruin and injure and persecute and exterminate your tenants than any man in Mayo. You will disagree in toto – time will show who saves most of his tenants and most of his rents ...'[10]

If Lord Sligo was reticent and felt guilty about clearances, some other landlords in Mayo and elsewhere seemed to relish them. In this category was the Earl of Lucan, perhaps the greatest depopulator in all of Mayo, who cleared some 2,000 people and destroyed 300 houses in Ballinrobe parish alone between 1846 and 1849. The cleared lands he converted to pasture and then either retained in his own hands or, more usually, transferred into those of large graziers, some of whom were Protestants from Scotland. Lucan publicly boasted that he 'would not breed paupers to pay priests', which partly explains why his greatest local antagonist was Fr Conway, the parish priest of Ballinrobe.[11] Lucan's outrageous remark was exceeded by the infamous declaration attributed in 1848 by the bishop and priests of the diocese of Derry to a certain Donegal landlord, who allegedly did not shrink from saying, 'The exuberance of the tree of Irish population must be immediately cut off by extermination or death'.[12]

Nothing facilitated clearances more than the quarter-acre or Gregory clause, named for William H. Gregory, M.P. for Dublin city, 1842–7, in the Conservative interest, future husband of Lady Gregory, and heir to a substantial Galway estate (he succeeded to it in 1847) which he largely dissipated by gambling debts on the turf in the late 1840s and early 1850s.[13] The Gregory clause was in effect a successful Tory amendment to the Whig poor-relief bill that authorised outdoor relief and became law early in June 1847.[14] The clause provided that no tenant holding more than a quarter-acre of land was eligible for public assistance either in the workhouse or outside it. To become eligible, he had to surrender the holding to his landlord. Although not all the consequences of the quarter-acre clause were fully appreciated in advance, its enormous potential as an estate-clearing device was widely recognised in parliament.[15] Defending his proposal in the Commons, where it initially stirred some controversy, Gregory used language that was dismissive and even contemptuous of the capacity of his amendment to in-

159

flict grievous injury. Many M.P.s, he declared, had 'insisted that the operation of a clause of this kind would destroy all the small farmers. If it could have such an effect [he said], he did not see of what use such small farmers could possibly be.'[16] Gregory's amendment carried by a vote of 117 to 7, and only a few Irish M.P.s (including William Sharman Crawford and William Smith O'Brien) were among the tiny band of dissentients.[17]

Throughout the rest of the Famine years the Gregory clause or 'Gregoryism' became a byword for the worst miseries of the disaster – eviction, exile, disease, and death. When in 1874 Canon John O'Rourke, the parish priest of Maynooth, came to publish his *History of the Great Irish Famine of 1847*, he declared of the Gregory clause, 'A more complete engine for the slaughter and expatriation of a people was never designed'. In case anyone might be inclined to forgive or forget (perhaps already there were a few revisionists about), O'Rourke insisted that 'Mr Gregory's words – the words of ... a pretended friend of the people – and Mr Gregory's clause are things that should be forever remembered by the descendants of the slaughtered and expatriated small farmers of Ireland'.[18]

Although the Whig government did not invent the infamous Gregory clause, Lord John Russell and his colleagues as well as relief officials in Ireland had to deal with its consequences and the associated public outcry. Two issues related to the clause which pressed themselves on the authorities were, first, whether poor-law relief could legally be given to the dependent wife or children of a tenant with more than a rood of land who refused to surrender his holding to his landlord; and second, whether landlords were entitled to insist that tenants wanting public assistance surrender their cabin and small garden, not simply their holding beyond a quarter-acre, to be eligible for relief. Obviously, smallholders would be less inclined to surrender their land if their starving or diseased wives and children could secure relief without their having to do so. But if dependants were refused relief in order to maintain pressure for surrenders, then

160

landlords, relief officials, and ultimately the government it-self could be accused of encouraging forced starvation. It was attempted evasion of the quarter-acre clause that prompted the Bandon board of guardians to complain bitter-ly in July 1847 of 'the very frequent and gross imposition practised on the union by several parents sending their chil-dren into the workhouse *as orphans*'.[19] Eventually, in May 1848, the poor-law commissioners in Dublin advised local boards of guardians around the country that dependants of men holding more than the stipulated rood of land could be relieved without infringing the law. The commissioners were careful to explain that they were not urging that indiscrim-inate or systematic relief be given to such persons, but rather that women and children must not be permitted 'to die of starvation or suffer extreme privation' because family heads had refused to make the surrenders necessary to qualify themselves for public assistance. Even after the central au-thorities delivered this advice, the local boards of guardians, usually dominated by landlords and their political allies, retained the flexibility to decide whether to pursue a fairly rigid or a more relaxed policy. Some boards did the one thing, and some the other.[20]

Even more consequential was the issue of whether to be eligible for poor relief, a tenant was required to surrender his house as well as his holding to his landlord. Strictly speak-ing, the law mandated that only the land in excess of the one rood be yielded up, but often when tenants took this ap-proach, the landlord or his agent refused to accept the partial surrender or declined to supply the certification of compli-ance with the law until both the house and all land had been given up. Eventually, the poor-law commissioners informed local guardians that the refusal of a landlord to accept a par-tial surrender could not be held to disqualify an otherwise eligible tenant from public assistance.[21]

But in the all-important matter of the disposition of the surrendering tenant's house, landlords and agents almost al-ways held the whip-hand. Tenants frequently unroofed their own cabins as part of a voluntary surrender in which they were graciously allowed to take away the timber and thatch of their former dwellings. But in many thousands of cases estate-clearing landlords and agents used physical force or heavy-handed pressure to bring about the destruction of cabins which they sought. Many pauper families had their houses burned, often quite illegally, while they were away in the workhouse. Many others were reportedly told when they sought admission that the law or at least the guardians required that their cabins be unroofed or levelled before they would be allowed entry, and so they went back and did the job themselves. Where tenants were formally evicted, it was usually the practice for the landlord's bailiffs – his specially hired 'crowbar brigade' – to level or burn the affected dwellings there and then, as soon as the tenants' effects had been removed, in the presence of a large party of soldiers or police who were likely to quell any thought of serious resistance.[22]

The gross illegality of some evictions, and the extreme hardship inherent in all clearances, prompted the raising of questions in parliament, not only about especially egregious cases of inhumanity but also about whether the government would intervene to restrict evictions and the wholesale destruction of houses on so many estates. Protesting M.P.s drew attention on several occasions to the large-scale evictions and house-levellings occurring in late 1847 and early 1848 on the Blake estate in Co. Galway, particularly to certain ejectments in the depth of winter which had led to the death of several dispossessed tenants from exposure. There were even demands that the government institute criminal proceedings for manslaughter in this case.[23] But the Home Secretary, Sir George Grey, saw no grounds for such action. Responding lamely to critics in March 1848, Grey admitted that 'it was impossible to read without feelings of considerable pain of the destruction of a great number of houses in the county of Galway'. He pointed out unhelpfully that a tenant unjustly treated by his landlord 'would have a right of civil action' against him, but he rejected the notion that house-destroying landlords 'were open to any criminal proceedings on the part of the government'.[24] When the matter was pressed again at a subsequent session, the attorney-general, as a critic bitingly noted, in effect 'declared on legal authority that the law did not reach outrages of this kind'.[25] The government's posture elicited a scathing public letter from Archbishop John MacHale of Tuam to Prime Minister Russell. Instead of hearing loud 'denunciations of oppression' or the announcement of 'any prospective measures which would check the repetition of such cruelties', declared MacHale,

> the people received only the chilling assurance that in those deaths, however numerous, there was nothing illegal or unconstitutional! It is, then, it seems, no matter what may be the amount of the people's sufferings, or what may be the number of those who fall victims to the Famine, provided that nothing illegal or unconstitutional is done in vindicating the rights of property.[26]

What is surprising is that Russell actually agreed with MacHale on the urgent need to curb ejectments and privately used language about evicting Irish landlords which sounded like that of a Whiteboy or a Rockite. As he told his cabinet colleague Lord Clarendon in March 1848, 'Of course, Irish proprietors would dislike such measures [i.e., curbs on evictions] very much; but the murders of poor cottier tenants are too horrible to bear, and if we put down assassins, we ought to put down the lynch law of the landlord'.[27] But Russell had to contend with two great Irish proprietors in his own cabinet – Lord Palmerston, the foreign secretary, and Lord Clanricarde, the postmaster-general – with hard-line views on the economic necessity of clearances. Palmerston told the cabinet in a memorandum of 31 March that 'it was useless to disguise the truth that any great improvement in the social system of Ireland must be founded upon an extensive change in the present state of agrarian occupation, and that this change necessarily implies a long continued and systematic ejectment of small-holders and of squatting cottiers'.[28] The cabinet was said to have exhibited a 'general shudder' when Lord Clanricarde made pronouncements as ruthless as Palmerston's.[29]

Opposed not only by these two Irish landlords but also by the 'moderates' in his cabinet, Russell was forced to water down his original proposals 'in favour of a bill which aimed merely to slow down and make ejectments more expensive to the proprietor'.[30] Even so, early in April Sir George Grey promised the Commons a bill which would not only prohibit evictions without proper notice to the local poor-law guardians but also 'prevent the pulling down of huts and homes of tenants, although a legal right to do so might exist'.[31] This sounded too good to be true, and in the end it was. Although Russell's bill quickly passed the Commons early in May, it came under fierce assault in the Lords, especially from Irish peers like Lord Monteagle, whose wrecking amendments further blunted the prime minister's measure.[32] The legislation that finally emerged reduced the advance notice required to be given to local relief officials in cases of eviction to as little as forty-eight hours, and its provisions relating to the destruction of houses had been shorn of nearly all of their protective features. The new law made it a misdemeanour to unroof, pull down, or otherwise demolish the dwelling house of a person whose tenancy had expired only if the tenant or members of his family were actually within the house at the time that the demolition took place. (In a concession of stunning magnanimity this law also prohibited evictions on Christmas day and Good Friday as well as before sunrise or after sunset.)[33] This outcome was all too typical of the general Irish record of Russell's ministry, as Peter Gray has shown in his recent and excellent Ph.D. dissertation. Instead of being the master of his cabinet, Russell presided weakly and sometimes powerlessly over a badly divided set of colleagues, and between cabinet divisions and parliamentary opposition the constructive side of Russell's legislative agenda, such as it was, frequently was neutered.[34]

Voices of opposition to clearances were not lacking in Ireland. In fact, what made it all the more necessary for landlords and government ministers to excuse, rationalise, and justify clearances was the persistent linkage made in the Irish press between mass evictions and mass death. The *Limerick and Clare Examiner*, whose special correspondent was chronicling the depopulation, protested vehemently in May 1848 that 'nothing, absolutely nothing, is done to save the lives of the people – they are swept out of their holdings, swept out of life, without an effort on the part of our rulers to stay the violent progress of human destruction'.[35] The huge clearances of the Earl of Lucan near Ballinrobe and elsewhere in Mayo were frequently depicted in this way. On one portion of his property close to Ballinrobe from mid-1847 to mid-1848, the clearance not only 'swept away' the houses of sixty-two families but also swept their former occupants (246 persons) into what one observer called 'the embraces of death'.[36] In a later report in the *Galway Vindicator*, which devoted two whole columns to a list of 187 families (913 people) whom Lord Lucan had dispossessed in the previous eighteen months, the following balance sheet was presented: out of this total of 913 evicted, while 478 persons were receiving public relief and another 170 had emigrated, as many as 265 were 'dead or left to shift about from place to place'.[37] The *Mayo Telegraph* drew attention in June 1848 to 'the shoals of peasantry crowding to the [Castlebar] workhouse in quest of relief', with many being turned away unaided. Declared the reporter: 'We afterwards, at the dead hour of the night, saw hundreds of those victims of landlordism and Gregoryism sinking on our flagways', some of them 'emitting green froth from their mouths, as if after masticating soft grass'.[38] Yet another newspaper, the *Tipperary Vindicator*, deploring early in July the wholesale ejectments in train in the northern part of the county, observed despairingly of the clearance system, 'More lives have been sacrificed to its blind fury than have fallen in all the wars that reddened the fields of Ireland'.[39] Writing of evictions in the Galtee mountains after having toured depopulated Kilrush union in west Clare, a correspondent of the *Limerick and Clare Examiner* protested that even 'the good landlords are going to the bad, and the bad are going to the worst extremities of cruelty and tyranny, while both are suffered by a truckling and heartless government to make a wilderness of the country and a waste of human life'.[40]

Probably no other poor-law union in the entire country in late 1847 and 1848 had a higher eviction rate than Kilrush in Clare, and the clearances there were considered instrumental in slashing the population from 82,000 to 60,000 souls in a period of only eighteen months. 'Of those who survive,' declared one expert in the *Limerick Chronicle* in September 1849, 'masses are plainly marked for the grave. Of the 32,000 people on the relief lists of Kilrush union, I shall be astonished if one-half live to see another summer ...' Elsewhere in the county the story was much the same, this writer claimed: 'Again, in the divisions of Moyarta and Breaghford one-third of the people have altogether disappeared, few or none by emigration, the great majority by eviction and the ever-miserable and mortal consequences that follow'.[41]

The most active and vociferous members of the anti-clearance lobby were Catholic priests and prelates. When their own parishioners were being evicted in droves, it is hardly surprising that local priests felt compelled to denounce the 'exterminating' landlords or agents whom they held responsible. Sometimes they hurled their denunciations from the altars of their own churches, but they were even more likely to use the press to expose clearances since they usually hoped to mobilise a wider public opinion against the guilty parties. A great deal of what we know about clearances in particular localities comes to us from the often detailed lists of evicted persons and accompanying commentary supplied to the national or provincial press by parish priests and curates.

From the language of these men, anchored deep in their communities but connected to the wider world, we can gain a vivid sense of how profound were the disruptions and how agonising were the wounds inflicted by the mass evictions. Writing from Causeway in north Kerry in April 1848, Father Mathias McMahon recited a dismal litany of completed or impending clearances from the estates of four different landlords in three surrounding parishes, the two largest in-

166

volving 650 persons on the property of a middleman named Mason and 120 persons on William Stoughton's estate. As to the claim of a third landlord, a middleman named Sandes, that 'he did not turn out anyone', Father McMahon heaped scorn on his denial: 'Not he, good man! He only applied to them the gentle pressure of rackrent, starvation, and threatened imprisonment.' Fired by a frustrated nationalism, McMahon concluded trenchantly: 'From the ruthless extermination now everywhere going on, it is clear that they [i.e., the landlords] are determined upon utterly exterminating the peasantry who constitute [Ireland's] main strength. Unless some stop be put to the murderous proceedings of these "thugs", it will soon be vain to look for materials for an Irish nation.' (Incidentally, the views of this strongly nationalist priest about the newly amended poor law were the same as those of John Mitchel: 'It places the poor man hopelessly and helplessly at the mercy of his destroyers; and with the true spirit of a British law, while it holds out relief, it inflicts death'.)[42]

Another priest who used only slightly less venomous language for the evicting landlords of his locality was the Rev. Dr Patrick Fogarty, the parish priest of Lismore, Co. Waterford, and since 1838 the vicar-general of the diocese. The sufferings of his parishioners he largely attributed to 'certain landlords in my parish who are utterly regardless of the deplorable condition of their famishing tenants', whose cabins they destroyed when dispossessing them. In a letter published in the *Waterford Chronicle* in April 1848, Fogarty declared:

Numbers of those poor creatures who were thus cruelly exterminated are now living in huts erected by them on the roadside, the victims of famine and fever. Hundreds of them have perished in these parishes during the last two years. The monstrous conduct of the landlords here and in every other locality throughout the country has considerably added to the extreme mass of human suffering.[43]

Besides the numerous protests of individual priests, there were also several remarkable collective clerical condemnations. In the diocese of Derry the coadjutor bishop, the Rev. Dr Edward Maginn, and ninety priests adopted a series of resolutions in July 1848 in which they addressed political as well as social issues. Embracing the causes of both Repeal and tenant right, they also handed out praise and blame to local landlords. Though they thanked Co. Derry's largest proprietors, the London companies, 'for the uniform humane treatment of the tenantry under them', they blasted the many evicting landlords in neighbouring Donegal as 'a disgrace to Christianity'. Every parish priest in the Derry diocese was enjoined to keep 'a register in which he will have inserted every act of [landlord] cruelty perpetrated within his jurisdiction ..., to be published yearly if deemed expedient or to be kept in the archives of the diocese for the benefit of the future statist [i.e., statistician] or historian'.⁴⁴

What the Derry clergy had to say about landlordism in the north-west appears almost mild beside the scathingly bitter and disrespectful address said to have been presented to Queen Victoria on her visit to Ireland in 1849 by the Catholic clergy and other 'inhabitants' of the barony of Upper Connello in Co. Limerick. In this document, signed by Archdeacon Fitzgerald, the parish priest of Ballingarry, and 'all the clergy ... of that district', the authors dwelled especially on the devastating clearances which had been carried out in the Kilrush union of Clare:

> Madam, in no other region of the habitable globe would it be permitted to two or three satraps, however specious the pretences of law or custom which they might allege, to unroof and demolish at their pleasure the homes of fifteen thousand human beings, and to turn out that multitude, in itself a nation, to die by the slow wasting of famine and disease.

The authors of this highly charged document did not blame Victoria herself for these 'incredible calamities', but they told her bluntly that 'thy royal name must be connected in future history with the astounding record of the extermination of our unhappy race', and they declared that an evil oligarchy 'hath snatched thy sceptre from thy grasp and converted it into a rod of iron and a whip of scorpions to torture, to crush, and to slay thy faithful people in Ireland'. Here was the genocide thesis unadorned, for the authors did not scruple to proclaim: 'If the bones of those who perished of want and misery in this land for the last eighteen months were disinterred and strewed at moderate intervals, they would form an appropriate footway for thy ministers from Cork to Dublin'.[45]

The prominence of priests as the avowed enemies of estate-clearing landlords and as the protectors of evicted tenants led to a heated controversy about their role in the pages of the English and Irish press. The initial focus for this controversy was whether a local priest's alleged altar denunciation of Major Denis Mahon in connection with a huge clearance on his Roscommon estate had led to his murder in November 1847.[46] It was later stated that Mahon, the only large landlord to suffer such a fate in all of the famine years, had ejected over 3,000 persons (605 families) before he was slain,[47] but in fact, what he did was to give the tenants a choice between eviction and assisted emigration to Canada, with the vast majority, not surprisingly, choosing the latter. Unfortunately for his reputation, and despite his heavy outlay on a lavish sea diet, as many as a quarter of his emigrants perished during the Atlantic crossing, and 'the medical officer at Quebec reported that the survivors were the most wretched and diseased he had ever seen'.[48] Thus the distressing tale of Major Mahon's clearance became a conspicuous part of the much larger and more dreadful story of the 'coffin ships' and the horrors of Grosse Isle, or as one contemporary called it, 'the great charnel house of victimised humanity'.[49]

These events set the stage for heavy journalistic skirmishing. In a public letter addressed to Archbishop MacHale of Tuam and given wide publicity in both the English and Irish press, the Earl of Shrewsbury, a prominent English Catholic, accused Father Michael McDermott, the parish priest of Strokestown, of having denounced Major Mahon from the altar on the Sunday before he was shot, and in effect demanded that MacHale discipline the offending priest for contributing to the landlord's murder. Adding insult to injury, Shrewsbury also observed in his letter that English public opinion held the Irish Catholic Church to be 'a conniver at injustice, an accessory to crime, [and] a pestilent sore in the commonwealth'. Father McDermott produced credible evidence that he had never publicly denounced Major Mahon at any time, but the furore soon broadened to embrace rival English and Irish religious and political stereotypes and clashing images of the Irish Catholic clergy in general. The *Nation* insisted early in January 1848 that 'every line that has been written in the English papers for the last two months' proved that 'the English charge the whole priesthood with instigations to murder'. It pointed out that the London *Spectator* had recently 'discovered that the prevalent sentiment in England was, "Hang a priest or two and all will be right"'.[50]

In a long and much quoted response to Shrewsbury, MacHale heaped bitterly ironic scorn on the calumniators of the clergy, as he saw them:

And what is the fate of the Irish priesthood [he asked] if they represent those scenes [of eviction] to call for the charity of the humane or the justice of the legislature? They are denounced as disturbers of the public peace who interfere with the sacred rights of property ... Their appeals are deemed importunate; their publications ... of the heart-rending evictions of the small tenantry are considered inconvenient; and like the prophet of old, they are stigmatised by an allied band of corrupt courtiers and apostate mercenaries as the 'troublers of Israel'.

It was in this context that MacHale displayed his adherence to the genocidal view of the Famine: 'How ungrateful of the Catholics of Ireland,' he remarked acidly to Shrewsbury, 'not to pour forth canticles of gratitude to the [Whig] ministers, who promised that none of them should perish and then suffered a million to starve'.[51] From this evidence and other statements discussed in this essay I would draw the following broad conclusion: at a fairly early stage of the Great Famine the government's abject failure to stop or even to slow down the clearances contributed in a major way to enshrining the idea of English state-sponsored genocide in the

Irish popular mind. Or perhaps one should just say in the Irish mind, for this was a notion that appealed to many educated and discriminating men and women, and not only to a revolutionary minority or the 'vulgar multitude'.

This shift in Irish attitudes, which was well advanced by early 1848, can also be detected in Irish responses to the language of Christian providentialism. Dr Peter Gray has shown that there was a widespread belief among the British political elite, especially its evangelical section, that the successive failures of the potato were a divine judgement against the traditional Irish agrarian economy and literally a heaven-sent opportunity to modernise it *à l'Anglaise*. It was usually taken for granted in Britain that the much desired economic transformation required clearances. Such providentialist beliefs influenced the thinking and policy prescriptions of several members of Russell's cabinet, including the chancellor, Sir Charles Wood, the home secretary, Sir George Grey, and the war secretary, Earl Grey, while outside the cabinet Sir Charles Trevelyan at the treasury was a firm, indeed remorseless, exponent of providentialism.[52] In this respect Trevelyan clearly showed his colours when in January 1848 he published what later became his egregiously complacent book *The Irish Crisis* in the *Edinburgh Review*.[53] In its crudest form this ideology degenerated into the view that through the Famine God himself was punishing the Catholic Irish for their stubborn attachment to all the superstitions of popery. After preaching a sermon on this theme in Liverpool in February 1847, the Rev. Hugh McNeile, the future Anglican Dean of Ripon, published it later that year as a tract under the title *The Famine a Rod of God: Its Provoking Cause, Its Merciful Design*.[54]

Whether in crude or sophisticated forms, this English providentialist perspective made a deep and lasting impression in Ireland. Almost sixty years later, in 1905, T. D. Sullivan, a native of Bantry who had seen the clearances and other horrors of the Famine at close quarters, vividly recalled what he considered the sinister influence of this phenomenon:

> There was only too much reason to believe that the [Whig] ministry regarded the situation as one that would eventuate in a mitigation of 'the Irish difficulty', and which therefore they need not be in a great hurry to ameliorate. Some of the British newspapers spoke out plainly in that sense, intimating their belief that the whole thing was an intervention of an all-wise Providence for England's benefit; while the extreme Protestant organs and some of their pulpit orators confidently declared that the Famine was a divine chastisement of the Irish people for their adherence to 'popery'.[55]

Initially, Catholic commentators had themselves adopted providentialist language to explain the coming of the Famine. Even Archbishop MacHale, in a vehement public letter of protest against Whig government policies in December 1846, had chosen to see the destruction of the potato as 'a great national chastisement', as 'one of those awful calamities with which Providence sometimes visits states and nations'. But for MacHale the Famine was God's judgement against rapacious Irish landlords and English misrule of Ireland under the Union, and out of the abyss into which the country had been plunged would come, at the hands of Providence, 'national regeneration' under a native legislature.[56] But by 1848 not only had Irish Catholic and nationalist commentators abandoned providentialist language and explanations themselves, but they had come to take deep offence at their use by others. In that year the *Nation* noted approvingly the declaration of Bishop John Hughes of New York that to identify Providence as the cause of the Famine was nothing less than blasphemy.

As Irish landlords and the British government were increasingly viewed as the human agents of misery, exile, and death, providentialism could only have seemed the cruellest of jokes to the victims and their advocates. From many different mouths all over Ireland in 1848 the fierce, piercing, unforgiving language of genocide was spilling out. Speaking before the Killarney board of guardians in January of that year, Denis Shine Lawlor suggested that Lord John Russell was a student of the poet Spenser, who had inhumanly calculated 'how far English colonisation and English policy might be most effectively carried out by Irish starvation'.[57] A

172

town councillor named Brady in Cork city declared to the cheers of his audience in the same month that the prime minister had 'violated every pledge previously made on arriving at place and power ... Yes [he insisted], a million and a half of Irish people perished, were smitten and offered up as a holocaust, whose blood ascended to the throne of God for redress ..., but the pity was that the minister was permitted to act so with impunity.'[58] The genocidal and anti-providential view was perhaps never put more succinctly than by an editorial writer in the *Nation*, who said with cold hatred on 1 April: 'It is evident to all men that our foreign government is but a club of grave-diggers ... It is not Providence but provincialism that plays the thief; we are decimated not by the will of God but by the will of Whigs.'[59] It could be objected that this was written by a revolutionary nationalist and could very easily have been written by John Mitchel himself. But it could be replied that the clearances and the gross inadequacies of government policy during the Famine would by themselves have given great currency to Mitchel's views had he never propagated them by speech or pen.

To conclude, in the historiography of the Famine so-called revisionist historians have tended to minimise the role of British government responsibility, in contrast to earlier nationalist historians and a long line of Irish revolutionaries who approvingly recalled John Mitchel's famous dictum, 'The Almighty indeed sent the potato blight, but the English created the Famine'.[60] This essay is deliberately intended as a challenge to the revisionist historiography of the Famine, in which Mitchel and other nationalist propagandists are dismissed as the creators of the baseless myth of genocide. My contention is that the idea of genocide had taken firm root in Irish political consciousness long before Mitchel published his most influential works on this subject.[61] And it is also my contention that while genocide was not in fact committed, what happened during and as a result of the clearances had the look of genocide to a great many Irish contemporaries.

FLIGHT FROM FAMINE

DAVID FITZPATRICK

'DEAR CATHARINE, YOU WILL let us Know what wages have you a year or how does that Country agree with you. As for our Country the potatoes all rot[t]ed this year in the ridges, and we are in the state of sta[r]ving'.[1] Letters like this cry for help from Roscommon, sent to Australia in April 1846, remind us that getting out of Famine-stricken Ireland was a matter of life or death. At the time of his marriage a few years earlier, the writer Thomas Burke had been quite comfortably off, with 'fifty Seven pounds in the Bank of Boyle and a good Cow and Heifer worth £20 when I marr'd Ann. So I am shook out of all By the Land and crop failing.' The Famine was not only a 'visitation' on the poor but a great leveller, undermining the gradations and hierarchies of Irish society. The survivors struggled to finds words to convey the horror in their appeals to friends and relations fortunate enough to have escaped Ireland. In May 1847, Thomas Burke wrote that 'they are Dying like the choler Pigs as fast as they can Bury them and Some of their Remains does not be Buri[e]d for ten or fifteen Days and the Dogs eating them some Buried in mats others in their clothes. So thanks be to God there is none of our Family Dying as yet.'[2] In similar phrases, a merchant in Co. Wexford told his son in Nova Scotia that the family remained in good health, but God 'knows not how long for the people the young and old are dying as fast as they can Bury them. The fever is rageing here at such a rate that them are in health in the morning knows not but in the Evening may have taken the infection. Its like a plague. The Caus they docters alledge is the kind of food that yellow Corn from america for last year the potatoes were all blasted.'[3] Listen to the stark imagery of the letters

174

from Ireland examined by the American historian, Kerby Miller: 'our fine country is abandoned by all the population'; 'one ile of our Chapel would hold our Congregation on Sunday at present'; 'there is nearly every door closed [and] the people can scarcely live in it'; 'I cant let you know how we are suffring unless you were in Starvation and want without freind or fellow to give you a Shilling'; 'we can only say, the scourge of God fell down in Ireland, in taking away the potatoes, they being the only support of the people'.⁴ Images like these, awkwardly inscribed in uncounted letters from home, haunted those who had fled from the Famine in search of a happier and longer life.

The scale of that flight was unprecedented in the history of international migration. Even in the period of heaviest Famine-induced mortality, emigration was equally important as a source of the decline in Ireland's population. About a million people left the country between 1846 and 1850, and emigration was still greater over the following five years. The total loss of over two million amounted to about a quarter of Ireland's highest recorded population of 8,175,000 in 1841. Yet the Famine 'exodus' was neither the beginning nor the end of large-scale emigration. Well before the Famine, many regions of Ireland, particularly in Ulster and the midlands, were already accustomed to sending steady streams of emigrants to Britain, North America and Australia. Networks of settlers had therefore developed overseas, providing some protection and assistance for future emigrants. The effect of the Famine was to extend massive emigration to every county and parish of Ireland. The habit spread with astonishing rapidity, so that the poorest counties of the western seaboard became the major sources of Famine emigration as well as mortality. The patterns established during the crisis were perpetuated, Connaught and Munster remaining the most important sources of emigration throughout the following century. Already in 1855, as the Poor Law Commissioner Edward Senior remarked with wonder, 'everybody has one leg over the Atlantic'.⁵

Who were the Famine emigrants? Many contemporaries lamented the departure of the 'better classes' of farmers and their children, by contrast with the predominance of landless labourers and servants in earlier migrations. Some, like Edward Senior in 1849, maintained that 'the very poorest classes, do not go in any way; parties, in fact, who are scarcely human, of whom there are great numbers, especially upon the sea-coast, whom everybody would be anxious to remove'.⁵ Yet the evidence about social class is contradictory. The reports of ruined farmers, sinking their remaining assets in a passage from Cork or Sligo to America, are matched by accounts of paupers and unemployed workers thronging the cattle boats from Dublin to Liverpool, hoping eventually to find money enough for the onward journey across the Atlantic. Choosing different itineraries according to their means, people of every social origin surged out of Ireland in search of a livelihood. Up to 1848, most of the long-distance movement out of Irish ports consisted of family groups or unmarried men. But the impulse soon proved strong enough to overwhelm the conventional aversion to emigration of young girls, an aversion reflected in the male domination of other migrations out of Europe. From the Famine onwards, male and female emigrants were quite evenly balanced. Boys and girls alike swarmed out of every parish, every social stratum, and almost every household, systematically thinning out the fabric of Irish society.

The majority of pre-Famine emigrants had settled in Britain, although increasing numbers had chosen the more expensive and dangerous option of the New World. The subsequent re-direction of most emigration from Britain to the United States was largely an accident of timing. A serious recession between 1847 and 1851 made Britain unattractive as a place of settlement, although hundreds of thousands of poor emigrants did their best to eke out a subsistence as unskilled workers, or paupers receiving relief in British towns. The Australian colonies were also in economic crisis, and did not regain their popularity until the discovery of gold in 1850. These factors increased the relative appeal of the United States, where prices were stable (if low) during the Famine period. For most of the emigrants, America's expanding industrial sector and receding frontier made it the desired destination. Even those who entered the New World through Canadian ports were celebrated for their determination to continue their journey southwards. In general, the process of migration was complex and prolonged, as the Irish moved from place to place, and job to job, in search of something worth settling down for. Further movement was commonplace between American states, and even between the continents of America and Australia in the era of gold-rushes. One country that seldom reappeared on the migratory itinerary was Ireland itself.

How was the Famine exodus organised? In the absence of extensive assistance from either public or philanthropic sources, the removal of over two million people in a decade, from an impoverished country, represents a miracle of private ingenuity and determination. There were numerous plans for state-subsidised 'colonisation', usually involving the removal of the 'surplus' population of a particular district to some uncleared tract of prairie in Canada or the United States. The advocates of colonisation included the Confederate leader William Smith O'Brien as well as Whig magnates such as the Earl of Fitzwilliam and Lord Monteagle, gaining some support in Lord John Russell's weak and divided administration. Like most grandiose schemes for social and moral betterment, these proposals foundered because of their great expense and uncertain outcome. 'New Erin' was not after all to be created, at public expense, by landlords or priests leading their grateful peasantry into the wilderness. Only a few thousand Famine emigrants received official subsidies, including tenants of derelict crown estates, workhouse inmates requiring supplements for pre-paid passages, and some crown witnesses or 'informers' who needed protection from enraged neighbours. The Australian colonies received a trickle of convicts, Smith O'Brien among them, and an increasing flow of assisted immigrants including 4,000 'female orphans' between 1848 and 1850. Some of these orphaned paupers turned out to be surprisingly sturdy, like the Clare girl weighing fifteen stone who had been reared 'on potatoes, and Indian meal porridge, slightly flavoured with onions. No animal food whatever.'[7]

Rather more emigrants received assistance from land-lords offering inducements to householders to surrender their holdings and so facilitate the consolidation of estates. But only the wealthiest landlords, such as Fitzwilliam and the Marquess of Lansdowne, could afford such strategic investment in a period of contracting rentals and mounting arrears. All told, less than 40,000 emigrants are known to have received subsidies from either landlords or the state between 1846 and 1850. In any case, both private and public schemes became largely redundant as unassisted emigration multiplied. The emigrants created their own informal mechanisms, and the opportunity for social engineering faded away.

The most effective agency for promoting emigration was the pre-paid passage or the 'American money'. The pioneer emigrants, of course, had been dependent on savings, loans, local lotteries or unrecorded gifts to help them out of Ireland. They took with them a strong sense of moral as well as financial indebtedness to those who had eased their path. By May 1849, the chairman of the Emigration Commissioners was marvelling at the rapidity with which the chains of human movement had been forged: 'Emigration begets emigration; almost the whole of the Irish emigration last year, certainly more than three-quarters of it, was paid for by the money sent home from America.'[8] In the following year about a million pounds was despatched in small remittances from North America alone, more than enough to transport the entire outflow from Ireland. The reverse flow of money offered a lifeline to those still in Ireland, and any faltering produced howls of anguish, and sometimes anger, from those relying on emigrant generosity. 'Dear brother, if you send any thing no matter what part of the year it is with the help of God nothing will stop me of goin to you'; 'for the honour of our lord Jasus christ and his Blessed Mother hurry and take us out of this'; 'if you don't endeavour to take us out of it, it will be the first news you will hear by some friend of me and my little family to be lost by hunger'.[9] In Australia, Catherine Burke was bombarded with requests for money enough to take her siblings 'to America out of this poor country', should they fail to get free passages to the colonies. Her mother in Roscommon enumerated the substantial sums sent home by former neighbours in the United States, adding pointedly that 'I Hope you Have the Kindness as well as them'.[10] The cumulative effect of these innumerable personal appeals was staggering, even though many emigrants presumably saved too little to provide a ticket, or simply evaded their duty. Hard-headed English economists were bewildered by the seemingly unforced generosity and good sense of a people whom they had so often chastised for their imprudence, indiscipline and irresponsibility.

Scarcely less astonishing was the success of shippers in getting most of the emigrants to their destinations, alive. The Famine exodus placed unprecedented pressure on the rickety and under-regulated passenger trade, and many steerage passengers endured disgusting and dangerous conditions on rudely converted cargo vessels. The perils of shipboard life were compounded by the weakness of many undernourished and diseased emigrants, and 'Famine fever' raged before, during and after the passage. The results were graphically recorded by the philanthropist Stephen de Vere, who described quarantine conditions at Grosse Isle, Quebec, in chilling terms: 'Water covered with beds cooking vessels &c of the dead. Ghastly appearance of boats full of sick going ashore never to return. Several died between ship and shore. Wives separated from husbands, children from parents.'[11] The fact that the horrors of the 'coffin ships' were virtually restricted to vessels making for Quebec, in 1847, provided little solace to the tens of thousands who perished after buying bargain tickets for as little as two pounds. Otherwise, however, few ships were wrecked, and shipboard mortality seldom exceeded one in fifty. The same applied to the even more hazardous and expensive voyage to Australia, which typically took three or four months. Because most Australian emigrants received state subsidies, shipboard conditions were far more closely supervised, by government inspectors and surgeons-superintendent. Even on the American routes, overcrowding and cross-infection were eventually curtailed by passenger legislation. If the passage from Ireland was scarcely a pleasure cruise, neither was it a death sentence.

The Famine exodus resulted in a startling redistribution of the surviving Irish population. By 1851 there were scarcely six and a half million people left in Ireland, while two million natives of Ireland were living elsewhere. In addition to nearly a million in the United States, there were three-quarters of a million in Britain, a quarter of a million in Canada, and about 70,000 in the Australian colonies. Others were scattered throughout the British colonies and to some extent in South and Central America, although the Irish were strongly inclined to choose English-speaking destinations. Few contemporaries imagined in 1851 that depopulation would continue indefinitely, or that the expatriate population would have grown by a further million within the next two decades. Nevertheless, there was widespread recognition that emigration was becoming an expected and even a desired episode in the Irish life-cycle. Indeed, Ireland's social structure became increasingly dependent on its perpetuation. The money sent home by emigrants had many functions apart from funding further movement. Small farmers often relied on remittances to pay the rent, buy livestock, supply dowries, or clear shop debts; the churches drew heavily upon emigrant purses to provide relief in periods of rural crisis; politicians and conspirators used American money to promote their campaigns.

The transition from a panic-driven expulsion to a calculated pursuit of economic betterment was already underway during the Famine, as emigrants reported their success in finding employment and marriage partners overseas. Admittedly, they faced formidable obstacles in securing a satisfactory livelihood. Lack of capital, education and skills restricted many of the Irish settlers in Britain and America to poorly paid menial employment and insanitary housing. Even in undeveloped Australia, where there was less competition from entrenched interests, the Irish often found prosperity elusive. Yet the fact that their success was modest by comparison with other nationalities in Britain, America or Australia seemed, at first, of little importance. Such resentments at relative deprivation were a luxury that became

180

affordable when Ireland had recovered sufficiently to offer counter-attractions. Meanwhile, unskilled labour seemed preferable to unemployment, sweet potatoes preferable to no potatoes, life preferable to death.

The scale and violence of the Famine exodus ensured that it would leave an ambiguous legacy in the memory of survivors. Had the emigrants been driven from home, or guided to the promised land? Bitterness and resentment were fostered by the harsh fact that most of them had no means of subsistence in Ireland, and therefore no acceptable alternative to departure. Nationalist politicians and historians often pictured the emigrants as victims of a conspiracy, whereby rapacious landlords (with official connivance) evicted their tenants and drove them into 'coffin ships', in order to solve Ireland's problem of over-population. The conspiracy model, though largely fanciful, provided a powerful metaphor for the still more horrifying reality of economic compulsion caused by natural disaster. By blaming human agents rather than impersonal forces, the nationalist interpretation made the tragedy more comprehensible. Yet the indignation arising from involuntary expulsion was balanced by gratitude for the opportunity to escape. Landlord assistance and government subsidies were eagerly accepted, the rigours of the voyage cheerfully overcome, and the attractions of other societies readily appreciated. Compulsion was transformed into opportunity.

Despite discordant notes, there is an oddly jaunty tone about many of the letters sent home by the so-called 'exiles'. Isabella Wyly had taken a free passage to Adelaide, as a steerage passenger aboard the *Navarino*, in 1851. Her father had been a public accountant in Dublin, descended from a wealthy Quaker family in Westmeath. But Isabella had fallen on hard times, as a result of her father's early death and the collapse of family fortunes during the 1840s. Most of the extended family went 'either to their long home, or to others Parts of the world', Isabella travelling alone to Adelaide. Five years later, in her first letter to Ireland, she recalled the loneliness and alienation of an exile: 'On my first arivel to Adelaide, I felt a stranger in a strange Land ... I new no one, nor had I a friend to take my hand.' Her subsequent experience was equally characteristic of the resilient survivors of the Famine. With the help of an introduction to a prominent colonial lady with Westmeath connections, she secured work as a draper's assistant, and soon found herself relishing life in the shop: 'I never felt more happy in my life than I do now that I am independent of everyone. There is no bread sweeter th[an] the bread you work for yourself. I should hav[e] been a long time in poor old Dublin before I should show so well as I hav[e] done here. I am very comfortable and happy, and have great re[a]son to be thankful.'[12] The transformation of Isabella from penniless orphan to successful settler was completed by joyful marriage to her employer, a devout Wesleyan from Co. Tyrone. Isabella never ceased to express gratitude to the merciful God who had delivered them from unhappy Ireland.

Another fascinating chronicle of the emigrant experience is provided by the letters of Michael Normile, a Clareman who left for New South Wales on the *Araminta* in 1854. Unlike the Wylys, the Normiles had survived the Famine period without total ruin, although Michael had joined most of the local population on the public relief works in early 1847. His father's small farm could not support a large family in post-Famine conditions, and Michael and many of his siblings joined the exodus to America and Australia. Michael and his sister Bridget secured assisted passages to New South Wales, through the intervention of the Protestant rector at Kilfenora. Michael's first letter was sent from the emigration depot at Birkenhead, and shows that he was full of excitement at the prospect of departure.

> My dear Father, I am to inform you that we left Dublin on the 26th. Instant for the ship Araminta and she is to Sail on Monday next. All the pasengers are a bord the vessel. We slept last night in it. There is about 300 Passengers on it and from 20 to 30 Sailors. It is a fine ship well regulated. They get good Provisions on Bread and tea for Breakfast potatoes and meat for dinner and the same as the first for supper. There is more Irish on it than any other Class of people.

His letter shows that emigration was already commonplace,

with whole parties of neighbours surging towards the New World:

> We came to the Depot. There we met our comerades, and you might think it was out of the heavens we Came to them. Michl. Gready Patt McGrath and Bridget Neylon were as glad as if we Gave them a thousand pound for we being along with them. I hope we will have luck please God. We had a good friend Dean Armstrong long may he live. He tried every Experiment to have us along with our Comerades and it did not fail him. What ever way the wind blows I am glad of being along with my Neighbours.

Once in New South Wales, Normile soon found steady employment as a carter and porter for a merchant in Maitland, where he became partial to the superb wines of the Hunter Valley. He married a neighbour from Clare and expressed contentment with his lot, despite his repudiation of the quick riches available to those venturing into the 'wild country to live and live there like wild cattle'. Normile chose to adopt Irish ways in Australia: 'I did not choose to go far away. I am near the priest and church and religion I have plenty as yet thank God.' Normile's ambivalence about his adopted land, and its uncivilised ways, coloured all his letters, and he never forgot that it was not by his own choice that he had gone 'far away' from Clare. Yet he took pains to reassure his father that life in New South Wales offered compensations. 'Don't ye be frightend about us. Although we had but a weak bigining we might be happy enough yet.'[13]

The twin themes of regret and satisfaction may also be found in ballads of the Famine period, such as 'A New Song Called the Emigrant's Farewell to Donegall':[14]

> So now my dear you need not fear
> The dangers of the rageing sea,
> If your mind is bent I am content
> So now prepare and come away.
> She says my dear if you'll agree
> To marry me, I'll quick prepare.
> We'll join our hands in wedlock's bands
> And we will stay no longer here.

It was in the year of '46
I was forced to leave my native land,
To old Ireland I bid a long adieu
And to my fond relations all.
But now I'm in America
No rents or taxes wee pay at all,
So now I bid a long farewell
To my native land old Donegall.

THE FAMINE IN THE
SKIBBEREEN UNION
(1845–51)

PATRICK HICKEY, C.C.

*Every civilised nation, aye, savage nation on earth is familiar with
Skull, the place of the Skulls.*

SOUTHERN REPORTER, 29 November 1847

By the memory of Schull and Skibbereen!

NATION 1847
[cited in *Cork Constitution*, 1 June]

THE RAPID SPREAD OF THE STRANGE potato disease in the
summer and autumn of 1845 caused great concern in west
Cork. Members of the Carbery Agricultural Society discussed it at the dinner held on the night of their show in
Skibbereen in October 1845. John Limerick, a landlord from
Schull, was pleased that butter was making more than £3 a
hundredweight in the Ballydehob market and felt confident
that the pit specially designed by his rector, Dr Traill, would
save the potato crop. But as these gentlemen headed home
that night their horses' hooves on the stony road rang the
death-knell of pre-Famine Ireland.

Skibbereen had always been a great potato-growing
district. A local landlord, J. H. Marmion, told how the markets of Cork and Waterford were 'principally supplied' from
here and that he himself had exported 2,000 tons of them in
one season. This he explained was due to the 'superabun-
dance of sea-manure'. The crop thus 'induced a superabun-
dance of population'. He added that 'however, when the
crop failed the labourers went hungry'. So when this disease
struck the potato crop again in 1846 it was no surprise that
the labourers went very hungry indeed.

185

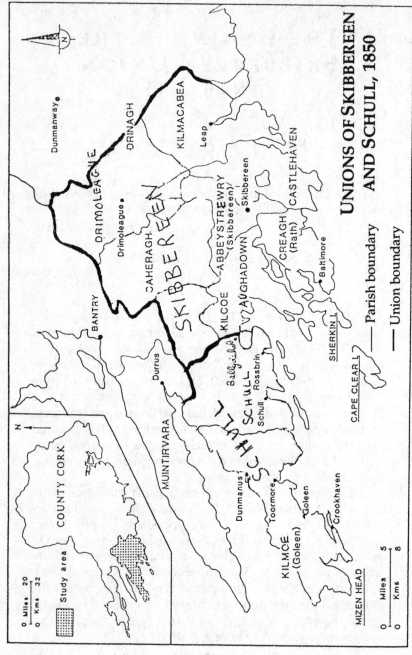

UNIONS OF SKIBBEREEN AND SCHULL, 1850

—— Parish boundary

—— Union boundary

CAPTAIN THOMAS OF COOSHEEN NEAR Schull, a Cornish miner, warned his employer, Ludlow Beamish, that 'small farmers are now as badly off as the poorest labourers'. Beamish forwarded the letter to Charles Trevelyan, assistant secretary to the Treasury. Beamish stated that in the city competition among the merchants would control prices but that in the towns the poor would be at the mercy of the covetous. Trevelyan replied that a reserved depot of Indian meal would be established at Schull but that he relied on the merchants of Cork to supply the eastern part of that county.

The labourers' main hope now was employment in the roads being made by the Board of Works. On 30 September 1846 about 1,000 men from Caheragh marched into Skibbereen with spades and shovels demanding food. Confrontation with the military was only barely avoided when the road workers were allowed to buy food by Col Hughes who was in charge of the government store. In October two road workers died. One named Denis M'Kennedy had not been paid for two weeks so the jury rather harshly declared that he had 'died of starvation, owing to the gross negligence of the Board of Works'.[1]

The chief refuge for the hungry people was the workhouse. At the end of November the previous year, 1845, there were only 277 poor in it but now in 1846 this had risen to 890. The previous year nobody had fever, now there were 176 cases. In the week ending 12 December thirty-eight persons died. In this period the previous year there were no deaths at all. The highest mortality for a workhouse similar to Skibbereen was in Carrick-on-Shannon, Co. Leitrim, where twenty-eight paupers died out of 803.[2]

The condition of the people around Skibbereen was so bad that Randolf Routh, Chairman of the Relief Commission in Dublin, sent Commissary Inglis from Limerick to help to organise the relief and as a result two more soup-kitchens were set up. The commissary for West Cork, Mr Bishop, informed Routh that from 5 November to 20 December 197 persons had died in the poorhouse and that almost half as many had been found dead in the back-lanes. He pointed out that mortality here was confined to labourers and beggars and that the country people generally never looked more healthy. He was told that they had provisions until May and were eating their own grain and paying no rents.[3]

Many of the country people were suffering too as a Cork magistrate, Nicholas Cummins, witnessed around the parish of Castlehaven and Myross. His open letter to the Duke of Wellington appeared in the newspapers and even in *The Times* on 24 December. A reporter from Cork described death and misery in Skibbereen but then announced:

> Greater misery was reserved for me in Ballydehob. Here they are in a deplorable state dying in all directions. The people are living on sea-weed and cattle they steal. On Sunday night they broke into the food-store and stole all that was in it. There were thirteen burials in Schull yesterday and not one of them had a coffin.

Major Parker, an Englishman and an inspector of the Board of Works, reported that Schull and Goleen were as badly off as Skibbereen, that 'a great number of people must inevitably be swept off by starvation and disease' because food was 'daily becoming scarcer and dearer'. He praised Dr Traill, for his soup-kitchens and concluded, 'but all will not do. Individual charity will not go far'. This letter was forwarded to Trevelyan who described it 'the most awful' he had yet seen and demanded to know from Randolf Routh what progress Mr Bishop was making as regards organising more soup-kitchens. Routh was annoyed at Parker's allegation about the scarcity of food. He claimed that there was plenty of it in the market in Skibbereen, that Swanton's two large mills were full of food for sale and that the government depot was also open. His explanation for the famine was that 'food is not lacking but rather the money to buy it'. This was a counter-attack on Parker's Board of Works which was supposed to provide employment and money. Routh also blamed the landlords of Schull and Skibbereen and produced a black list of the Skibbereen proprietors who had an annual income of £50,000. He then asked Trevelyan, 'Ought such destitution prevail with such resources?'

THE NEW YEAR WAS INDEED Black '47. The Skibbereen Board of Guardians announced that it had closed the workhouse. Deaths from 10 November 1846 to 7 January 1847 numbered 266 while for the same period previously they had been only ten. The house was 'full to suffocation', it had been built for 800 inmates but now there were 1,169 of whom 332 were in fever. There were 121 patients in forty beds. The union was in debt, the rates could not be collected as the land was deserted and the tenants destitute or dead or in the workhouse itself.

In the parish of Schull mortality was an average of twenty-five a day according to Dr Traill and in Goleen it was twelve a day.[4] R. B. Townsend, Vicar of Abbeystrewry, protested that 10,000 had already died out of the population of 100,000 in the union.[5] Bishop admitted to Routh that there was indeed misery in Skibbereen and added, 'but it is "famine" in the midst of plenty' as the town was 'sufficiently well conditioned to assist the starving portion of its population'.[6]

By the end of January soup-kitchens were set up by Bishop in the following locations: Skibbereen 1, Baltimore, Sherkin and Cape 3, Creagh, Baltimore 1, Castlehaven 2, Union Hall 1, Aughadown 2, Kilcoe 1, Schull 2, Ballydehob 1, Crookhaven 2, Caheragh 2, Drimoleague 1, Drinagh (proposed). Bishop admitted however that this relief was only '"a drop in the ocean". Hundreds are relieved, but thousands are in want.'[7]

Early in February the Skibbereen Soup Committee complained that local relief committees could not obtain sufficient provisions from Col Hughes in Skibbereen. This committee and Richard Notter of Goleen had each applied for ten tons of Indian meal but could obtain only two tons each. The price had been increased from £18 to £19.[8] Official records however reveal that there were 2,385 tons of meal in the store.[9] This can only be called sheer hoarding. It was the policy of Trevelyan that the 'resources' of the country should be 'drawn out'.[10]

The famine grew worse in February and its horrors were not only described but vividly portrayed by James Mahoney of *The Illustrated London News*. At Schull he saw a crowd of

189

about 350 women with money in their hands being doled out Indian meal in 'miserable quantities' at 'famine prices'. But there was not enough meal and some women had to go home disappointed. He sketched a forlorn boy and girl at Caheragh. Fr Creedon (a predecessor of mine) took him to see the famine-stricken village of Meenies which he also sketched. This village near Drimoleague disappeared in the disaster like many others.[11]

The rector of Caheragh, Francis Webb, received a frightful letter from a parishioner about children who had died and were left unburied. Rev. Webb published this account in the press and asked in disbelief, 'Are we living in a portion of the United Kingdom?' Bishop sent a copy of this piece to Trevelyan stating that the natural conclusion was 'food could not be found'. Bishop however also enclosed a letter from a Mr Swanton, a miller, informing him that he had from 100 to 200 tons of meal but that he had difficulty in disposing of it as the Skibbereen Relief Committee was selling meal *indiscriminately* for as little as 2s. 2d. a stone (1½p. a kilo).

The village of Meenies by James Mahoney

190

Boy and girl at Caheragh by James Mahoney

If the government bought it, the miller bargained, it would save him 'the freight of shipping it to another market'. Bishop pointed out to Trevelyan that all this meal was within *two* miles from Caheragh and asked indignantly if they could not conclude with the rector 'Are we living in a portion of the United Kingdom?' Swanton might have replied that he was only doing business according to the principles of free trade of that very kingdom. We are seeing how *laissez-faire* actually worked out in famine conditions. This price of meal was very high as a road worker earned only 8d a day (3½p.).

In mid-February Bishop reported to Trevelyan that 'fever, dysentery and consequent death' had increased around Schull and Goleen but added complacently that there was 'an ample supply of provisions in both places'. Once again food and famine are found side by side. No wonder Canon O'Rourke asked how they managed to die of starvation at Schull. The answer has been given by the artist, Mahoney; provisions were not adequate and were at inflated famine prices.[12] What provisions were actually there were not all distributed either. The records show that at the end of February 230 tons of Indian meal had been issued but that 410 tons still remained.[13]

Captain Caffin of the navy landed almost 100 tons of food at Schull and was shown the horrors of famine by Dr Traill who wrote that the captain was 'shocked beyond measure'. Caffin's letter was published in *The Times*. Trevelyan described it as 'awful' and wrote to the new chairman of the Relief Commission in Dublin, John Borgoyne, requesting some extra aid for Schull. Trevelyan granted however that relief could be carried out only to a limited extent and practically admitted defeat by telling Borgoyne, 'Let us save as many as we can'. Borgoyne refused to provide anything extra for Schull as accounts from other places were just as 'terrible'. A Treasury minute dated 23 February 1847 recognised 'the dreadful state of destitution in the parishes of Schull and Caheragh' and merely recommended that the local relief committees should do more for that district.

Captain Caffin continued to deliver food along the west

coast of Ireland. In March he wrote from Belmullet, Co. Mayo, describing the famine in Erris but concluded that 'starvation is getting worse as you go south, and at Schull and its neighbourhood the very climax of misery finds its resting-place'.

The urgent and efficient relief which the government failed to provide for the parishes of Schull and Goleen did indeed come but from another source, namely, the Church of Ireland curate of Cloughjordan, Co. Tipperary, Frederick F. Trench, who arrived in March. He immediately brought in eleven young men from Cloughjordan and a doctor from Dublin whom he called his 'agents'. On the vital question of the availability of food F. F. Trench observed:

> There is no want of food in any place but there is a most deplorable want of *available agencies, and a consequent want of suitable measures to bring the food and the medicine within the reach of the people.*

F. F. Trench was joined soon by his cousin, R. C. Trench, Professor of Divinity, King's College, London, (the next Archbishop of Dublin). He found that Skibbereen had 'the appearance of a flourishing place' compared to Schull and Ballydehob. These Trench cousins united forces with the local clergymen, Dr Traill and James Barry, P.P. of Schull. The result was that towards the end of April Professor Trench could claim that 'the mortality, though it had not ceased, yet it had been arrested'.[14]

Skibbereen was now fast becoming a byword for famine. In the week ending 27 March there were 106 deaths among the 1,170 inmates in the workhouse. In Ballina, Co. Mayo, there were only forty-five deaths in the house containing 1,002 poor. In Cork city 175 died out of 5,199. The mortality rate in the Skibbereen house was clearly the highest in the country, 106 deaths in a week when there had been only two the previous year.[15]

Conditions in the poorhouse only reflected the state of the union in general. This was vividly described by two visitors who came from Oxford, namely Lord Dufferin and G. F. Boyle. They told how fever patients in the workhouse lay three or four in a bed and the visitors also saw the pit at the Abbey.[16] There was another such trench at Drimoleague.[17] However undignified such pits were they prevented even worse, for example, a Rwanda-like scene of bodies floating down the Ilen river. Dufferin gave a subscription of £1,000 for relief.[18]

As the weather grew warmer fever spread more rapidly so fever hospitals or sheds were set up in Goleen, Schull, Ballydehob, Kilcoe, Baltimore, Leap, Caheragh and Drimoleague. By 1851 1,078 people had died in these places. Major Parker, Dr Traill and also a Dr Brady of the Caheragh hospital all died of fever. The Soup-Kitchen Act was efficiently introduced by an inspector named, J. J. Marshall in May. The road works were closed down, one such road at Castledonovan near Drimoleague was aptly called *Bóthairín na Déirce* or 'the little road of the alms'. Jeremiah O'Donovan Rossa's father died as a result of working on such a road near Rosscarbery. By June famine and fever were at last under some kind of control. The parish priest, James Barry, publicly expressed his deep gratitude to the Trench clergymen and their agents and also to J. J. Marshall. The hinged-coffin was being used no more. By September famine mortality was greatly reduced and the Soup-Kitchen Act phased out.[19]

QUITE A NUMBER OF EMIGRANTS sailed from West Cork in the 1830s, for example, the Harrigan ancestors of the singer, Bing Crosby, left Goleen. But when the potato rotted this stream turned into a river. John H. Swanton, a miller, offered free passages to people in his ships going to England. Dr Donovan, the workhouse physician, provided many of them with 'sea-stock'. Fever spread rapidly on board. One of the ships was detained in Newport in Wales for landing paupers and the doctor was accused of 'shovelling paupers' into England. Such was pauper panic emigration. Many people also tried to flee famine by leaving Baltimore, Crookhaven and Bantry. Most of them were reported to be 'snug farmers' using a few year's rent for passage money thus leaving 'the dregs' behind. A well-known emigrant ship, the *Dealy Brig* left Bantry in March for St John's, Canada, with 169 passengers. On arrival twenty-two had died at sea, forty were sick on landing and three soon died 'like fish out of the water'. This brig was something of a coffin-ship.

IN THE YEARS 1848 TO 1851 there were some deaths from famine and fever in the Skibbereen Union but conditions were not as bad as in other parts of the west for example Co. Clare.[20] The cholera of 1849 claimed many victims, thirty-one died around Crookhaven.[21] More accommodation was provided for the poor in order to avoid giving outdoor relief. An auxiliary workhouse was set up at Lowertown west of Schull and 600 paupers were transferred to it from Skibbereen.[22] This was closed when the new workhouse was opened in Schull in January 1850. Schull was now a separate union. It had also three auxiliary hospitals. The eastern part of Skibbereen Union was now cut off to form part of the new Clonakilty Union. Skibbereen still had as many as four auxiliary workhouses in or near the town and two others at Glandore and Union Hall.[23]

The number of people who died in the Famine has always been a disputed issue. Lord George Bentinck, leader of the Tories accused the Whig government of trying to cover up famine mortality but he himself insisted that it was at least one million for 1846-7.[24] Repealers seldom lost an opportunity to expose, exaggerate and even politicise this loss. The *Nation* declared that the Whigs should be opposed 'By the souls of the two million dead!' and 'by the memory of Schull and Skibbereen!'[25] Dr Donovan estimated that one million died and this is the figure which is accepted nowadays by historians.

The number of paupers who died in the Skibbereen workhouses, 'magnets for misery' from 1842 to 1851 was 4,346. Normal mortality is also included. In the Schull house 189 died in 1850–1. While figures are available for the people who died in institutions throughout the country no comprehensive count was ever made of the thousands who died in the ditches or cabins. As far as I know, the only exception is a census made by J. J. Marshall for the period September

1846 to September 1847 for six parishes in the Skibbereen Union namely Goleen or Kilmoe, Schull, Kilcoe, Caheragh, Drimoleague and Drinagh. There was nothing political about this census. It was accepted by the landlord, John Limerick, the parish priest, James Barry and the doctor, Daniel Donovan. Its purpose was to demonstrate the 'great mortality' which preceded the Soup-Kitchen Act and the 'equally great decrease' which followed its introduction. In the period May–September 1847 as many as 51,184 people out of a total population of 104,508 in the union were receiv-ing soup. This was in theory nearly half the 1841 population but in practice much more since by now many thousands had died or emigrated. About three million people in the whole country were on soup. This measure, of course, had nothing to do with proselytism. Many priests were thankful for it, for example, Fr Dore of Caheragh.

In 1841 the total population of the above mentioned parishes was 43,266 persons but 7,332 died or seventeen per cent from September 1846 to September 1847. The most terrible months were March and April 1847 when nearly half of these were lost. Mortality was highest, nineteen per cent, in Goleen, the most western and poorest parish. But it would be wrong to conclude that it was a case of the further west the worst the famine; the most eastern parish, Drinagh, near Dunmanway, had a mortality of eighteen per cent while Kilcoe near Skibbereen was only ten per cent. This census also gives the mortality according to gender; out of the 7,332 dead, men numbered 2,396 or thirty-three per cent, women 1,800 or twenty-four per cent, children 3,136 or forty-three per cent. In simple figures out of every nine persons who died, three were men, two were women and four were children. Child mortality was very high.

The causes of death are also presented. Fever took 3,191 or forty-four per cent, dysentery 1,626 or twenty-two per cent and starvation 2,515 or thirty-four per cent. Out of every nine who perished, three died of starvation, four of fever and two of dysentery. If fever and dysentery together designate famine fever then six died of famine fever and three of starvation.

196

This census also provides figures for emigration. For the 7,332 who died only 997 emigrated. The emigration rate 2.4 per cent was therefore very low while the mortality rate was very high, seventeen per cent. So out of every forty-two persons living in these parishes in 1841, more than seven died and only one emigrated. The destitute simply had not the means of emigrating. Rev. Webb remarked that the only escape for them was 'emigration to the next world without even the expense of a coffin'.

THERE WAS A CONTROVERSY ABOUT souperism centred about Rev. E. Spring in Baltimore and Cape Clear. A Protestant church was soon built on the island. W. A. Fisher, Rector of Kilmoe or Goleen also got involved in similar difficulties. He was extremely active in providing food for the people and actually built a church as a relief scheme. This was officially called *Teampall na mBocht*, or 'The Church of the Poor'. (It is also called the Altar Church.) According to the myth the parish priest, Fr Laurence O'Sullivan abandoned the people but there is solid evidence for his active presence among them at the height of the Famine. Dr Traill states that in the middle of February the priest told him at a relief committee meeting in Schull that every second one of his parishioners in Goleen had fever and that a thousand had already fallen. Rev. Fisher also made a large number of converts who were called 'soupers'. The Catholics accused him of abusing famine relief in order to proselytise. He denied this and maintained that the conversions were owing to the preaching of the Bible. Vincentian priests from Castleknock, Co. Dublin, who had preached in Dingle came in 1848. They were accompanied by Cork priest, John Murphy, known as the 'Black Eagle'. A conference of the Society of St Vincent de Paul was founded. Counter-charges of 'souperism' were made against the Catholics. Some of Rev. Fisher's converts returned to their former faith while others did not. It is impossible to know for certain how many converts were won back but by 1851 they still numbered about 400 around Toormore.[26] Why did these Catholics 'turn'? The fact that they 'turned' in a time and place of famine implies reasons of soup; the fact that some of them did not come back after the missions implies reasons of conscience. The unfortunate result of the whole controversy was that the heroic work of clergymen such as Dr Traill and the Trench cousins was overshadowed, distorted and at best forgotten. To Desmond Bowen's question 'souperism: myth or reality?', I answer 'both myth and reality but far more myth than reality'.[27]

THE FAMINE WAS A DEMOGRAPHIC disaster for the union. Fr Troy, parish priest of Aughadown, wrote on the baptismal register: 'A dreadful year of Famine, all dying of starvation, no baptisms'. In the parish of Schull in the 1820s the number of baptisms was in the 200s, in the 1830s in the 300s and in the 1840s in the 400s and almost reaching 500. In 1846 there were 494 baptisms but in 1847 only 194 and the number has been declining ever since. In the Church of Ireland parish of Caheragh there were four or five baptisms each year up to 1845 but in 1846 and 1847 there were none at all.[28]

Between 1841 and 1851 the total population of the union fell from 85,222 to 54,477 or thirty-six per cent which was the highest in the county of Cork. The workhouses contained large numbers of people. In Skibbereen there were 2,981 inmates in the workhouse where inhabitants of the town amounted to only 3,834 so inmates numbered seventy-eight per cent of the population of the town. In Schull there were 1,311 inmates in the workhouse while the total number of inhabitants of the villages of Crookhaven, Schull and Bally- dehob was only 1,505. In the Skibbereen Union the propor- tion of inmates to the general population was one to fourteen and in the Schull Union one to thirteen. Other unions however such as Dingle and Kenmare were even worse with a proportion of one to seven while in Ballymena, Co. Antrim it was as favourable as one to 200. For the country in general one out of every twenty-six persons was a pauper in the workhouse on 30 March 1851. It must be stated also that there had been even more paupers in these institutions in 1849.

IN THE AUTUMN OF 1847 the people of Ballydehob feared

that the coming winter would be like the previous one so they appealed to Lord John Russell for aid; he told them bluntly that:

> The owners of property in Ireland should feel the obligations of supporting the poor ... It is not just to expect the working classes of Great Britain should permanently support the burden of Irish pauperism.[29]

Since the government would not give very much more aid it meant that the rates on Irish property would have to increase. In October 1846 the rates for electoral divisions of the union ranged from 1s. 3d. (7p.) to as low as $2^1/_2$d. (1p.) but by December 1847 they had risen to 3s. 0d. (15p.) for each division.[30] Since the landlord had to pay the rates on holdings under £4 it would be in his interest to evict their occupiers if they would not pay the rent.

A Tenant Right meeting was called in Cork as early as January 1847, eight months earlier than Fintan Lalor's meeting at Holy Cross in Tipperary. In March Fr Barrett of Goleen appealed for Tenant Right.[31] Fr Sheehan of Leap protested that fifty-seven families had been evicted from one townland. In Gubeen near Schull 370 persons were also put out and they ended up in the workhouse in Skibbereen. Rev Webb now declared that he was in favour of Tenant Right and admitted that two years earlier he would have called it 'flat burglary'.[32] A Tenant Protective Society was formed in Skibbereen at the end of 1847. It was remarked that cattle were being driven to the pound and their owners to the poor-house.[33]

Such pauperism inevitably put pressure on property, some of it was already heavily encumbered. In October 1851, R. H. H. Becher of Hollybrook, Skibbereen, a resident and responsible landlord, sold his 17,000 acre estate under the Encumbered Estates Act. A year later Lord Audley, the epitome of an absentee negligent proprietor, also put his 5,676 acres under the hammer. This estate had been particularly notorious and provided many of the scenes described by N. Cummins in his letter to the Duke of Wellington. It was bought by an English miner, T. S. Cave, whose agent,

Thomas Scott, also English, condemned the 'higgeldy-piggeldy mixture of fields' so he 'consolidated' them into new farms. He introduced Italian rye grass seeds, mangolds, turnips, Peruvian guano and super-phosphate of lime. The tenants even agreed to pay a 50 per cent increase in rent and later gave him a gift of a gold watch costing £50 which was presented to him by the new parish priest, John Barry.

Scott urged the tenants to keep more cattle and grow more crops to feed them. 'Cattle signify manure, manure signifies crops, and crops signify income', he declared. He told them that they would be able to keep two cows to the acre if they were properly fed on hay, oats, mangolds and turnips. The whole purpose was to produce 'more and better butter'. In relation to their families, he exhorted them, 'you ought also send your sons and daughters out into the world and retain your farms unbroken, instead of trying, as you do now, on how small a spot of earth you can contrive to exist'. One can observe the new emphasis on the cow, butter and green crops. The farm was to be kept unbroken and passed on to only one son or daughter. The others would have to migrate or emigrate or if they stayed at home they would have to remain unmarried; the farm could not be divided to facilitate another marriage and family. Post-Famine Ireland is clearly emerging.

The Audley estate, however, was not the only place where improvements were being made in agriculture. For example the Griffith valuers found that Owen Hickey of Skeaghanore, (a great, great, grandfather of mine), had twelve acres of land which included 'superior pasture'.[34] No doubt he had some cows and sold the butter at the market in Ballydehob which had been started by Thomas Swanton, landlord and Gaelic scholar. The latter announced the *Margaidhe Muc, Caorach, Práthaidhe, Ime agus Éisc.*[35] The price of butter and livestock was steadily increasing. Owen Hickey was typical of the small farmers who survived the famine but only barely. There was now even a shortage of labourers as the 'hardy' ones were emigrating.

In relation to religion post-Famine Ireland was emerging too. Early in 1852 John Foley, the new parish priest of Kilmoe or Goleen, began to build a new parish church. Donations from emigrants were generous. This church is in the new Gothic style which contrasts with the vernacular style of the pre-Famine churches in Schull and Ballydehob.[36]

WHO WAS TO BLAME for the million dead in the Famine? It must be granted that it was an ecological disaster or the scourge of God as people like Dr Traill believed.[37] Some deaths were no doubt inevitable in the circumstances. But did there necessarily have to be as many as one million? Many commentators have been quite ready to make accusations but few thought of giving much credit to the men and women whose courageous efforts ensured that losses were not even worse. As many as 180 doctors died of fever in 1847; in addition to Dr Brady of Caheragh there was Dr Corbett of Innishannon and also his wife. Forty Church of Ireland clergymen died. Rev. R. B. Townsend, two of his servant maids and also the Rev. J. R. Cotter, Rector of Innishannon fell victims. It is not yet known how many priests perished but in the dioceses of Cork and Ross they numbered about eleven including P. Walsh of Sherkin Island, M. Ross of Castlehaven and D. McSwiney of Bandon. Workhouse staff and government officials such as Major Parker died at their posts. Fever or cholera swept off J. J. Marshall himself as well as fifteen other inspectors.[38]

As regards responsibility John Limerick bluntly told the people at a meeting that the landlords should not be blamed for the Famine but they themselves on account of their improvidence and idleness. His hearers loudly disagreed and would have naturally preferred to blame the landlords or the English. But the landlord was nearer to the truth than these people would have liked to admit. The strict population control exercised by the Irish people after the Famine reveals that in practice they did hold themselves responsible to a certain extent for the catastrophe. A.M. Sullivan who was involved in relief work in Bantry noticed that after this traumatic experience, 'Providence, forethought and economy are studied and valued as they never were before'.[39]

Cruelty was not confined to landlords or government

officials. Two women were robbed of food near Schull and killed. Two children near Leap tried to prevent a thief from stealing a cake and their throats were cut.[40] The Skibbereen solicitor, Timothy McCarthy Downing, said that the larger farmers 'dealt more hardy' with the labourers than the landlords did with themselves. Most of the larger farmers in Drinagh dismissed their labourers as indeed happened all over the country. The Skibbereen Soup Committee wrote that the farmers 'fearful for the condition of their own families were in no position to minister to the wants of others'. According to Boyle and Dufferin the farmers had alone 'flourished' from exporting corn and withholding the rent from the landlords. Such farmers might well have asked who would pay the rates for all the paupers in the workhouse. Lord John Russell need not have worried, it was not the English working class or any other which would bear the burden of Irish pauperism but the local ratepayers.

Fr Kelleher who succeeded James Barry as parish priest of Schull rebuked the local landlords: 'The disgrace and criminality are yours, but with two or three exceptions.' Among these exceptions must be John Limerick, R. H. H. Becher but certainly not Lord Bandon whom he condemned rather too severely for the high mortality on his hands near Ballydehob. There is ample evidence that Limerick, Becher and even Bandon did their duty as also did R. Notter and R. B. Hungerford of Goleen and also George Robinson of Drimoleague. But for many others there is far less evidence. Lionel Fleming of Newcourt, Skibbereen did indeed do his duty but in 'a cold and harsh' manner.[41] Apart from landlords altogether one can well ask why the east of the country failed to do more for the west. Why were there not some more people like the Trench cousins and their agents?

Irish nationalists of course violently censured England's role in the Famine. Yet there were others too who were severely critical for example Captain Thomas, the Cornish miner, who had established a fishery as a relief measure. He was scandalised to find that 'in a Christian country, in a time of profound peace' people should be left to live or die 'on political economy'. Fr Kelleher held that a 'great distinction'

202

should be made between the 'crimes and cruelties' of the Irish landlords and English statesmen on the one hand and on the other hand 'those generous hearted Britons who have made sacrifices to stay the steps of Famine'. Some were offended by the anti-Irish feelings of *The Times*. Rev. Webb was also grateful for English private generosity and exclaimed 'Thank God, England is not *The Times!*' Rev. R. B. Townsend protested that 'the principles of political economy have been carried out in practice to a murderous extent'. Thomas Swanton complained that 'murder' was going on for the benefit of English merchants. O'Donovan Rossa was sickened at the sight of 'the starved and the murdered of Schull and Skibbereen'.⁰ When the vicar, the landlord and the Fenian all use the vocabulary of murder it must be noted. As most of the Irish people grew increasingly nationalistic any sort of gratitude to any Briton on account of the Famine seemed absurd. The 'memory of Schull and Skibbereen' and 'the souls of the two millions dead' would soon raise the cry 'Revenge for Skibbereen!'

THE PERSISTENCE OF
FAMINE IN IRELAND

TIM P. O'NEILL

IN JUNE 1925, WILLIAM T. COSGRAVE, President of the Executive Council of the Irish Free State, received a telegram from the *New York Evening World* which read 'Reports here of widespread famine in west Ireland. Many dying, starving, freezing because of potatoe {sic} and fuel. Freezing. Would appreciate cable at once 500 words our expense on exact conditions. Is assistance needed? Editor.'[1] This and other telegrams were sent in response to widespread reports in America that the failure of the potato crop in Ireland was again threatening starvation in the west of Ireland.

In the seventy-five years after the Great Famine such reports were commonplace. Nor was this the first occasion the young leaders of the new Ireland had this experience. In March 1922 reports from the west of Ireland claimed people were dying from starvation and predicted famine. The Executive Council sent seed potatoes and other relief to the stricken areas. On that occasion Cosgrave had explained that relief could only have been avoided at the expense of famine which it was the duty of the government to prevent. The reaction of the government in 1925 was very different. The cabinet raised rigorous objections to reports of famine and in response to a telegram from the old Fenian John Devoy in America, the government pointed out that reports of distress were exaggerated and comparisons to Black '47 were absurd.[2]

The use of the word famine was commonplace in Ireland from the Great Famine down to 1925 but by then the new government had taken a firm decision to reject the validity of such claims. Ernest Blythe at finance argued that such reports would do great harm to the state's credit in every way unless they were immediately countered. A concerted campaign was mounted by a cabinet sub-committee to respond to reports of famine. Replies were carefully drafted denying starvation reports and the threat of famine. The Roman Catholic Primate, Dr O'Donnell joined the government in playing down famine reports.[3]

Before independence, letters to the press and to Dublin Castle from the early nineteenth century had regularly reported famine approaching and politicians in all periods rejected the word. Sir Robert Peel who had dealt with famine reports and letters from 1814 to 1846 scarcely ever used the word and substituted instead euphemisms such as scarcity, distress or food shortages.[4] Lord George Hill had wrestled with the distinctions between scarcity and famine as early as 1816.[5] Yet all had the same connotations of people in certain areas with no food, no money to buy food, insufficient local charity or employment and so the danger of starvation. Famine was a sensitive word which became a political rallying cry. In Ireland after 1850 the word had a new potency and was usually linked to comparisons with Black '47 as was done by Devoy in 1925. Henry Robinson, like Peel, a man with long experience of dealing with famine as head of the Local Government Board at the end of the last century, commenting on a telegram from the west which read 'send relief or coffins' wrote that no one took it seriously except the Irish Office in London.[6] In a dictionary definition, famine is described as an extreme scarcity of food in a district. If that is accepted there were many minor famines in the late nineteenth century. If widespread death from starvation is regarded as an essential ingredient of famine then there were few, if any famines in Ireland after the Great Famine. Deaths from starvation were always seen by politicians and administrators as the ultimate proof of the validity of famine reports. In 1862 over twenty reported deaths from starvation were investigated and all were returned as from natural causes.[7] This is not surprising as many were victims of famine related diseases and others were found to have either cash or food in their houses. There was a long tradition of

205

such investigation. In 1831 Gregory Haines had examined reported deaths for the government and in the same year Henry Hyatt of the Cornhill Relief Committee in London, while conceding great distress, reported, 'I have made it my business to search into some of these cases (of death by starvation) and have never been able to satisfy my mind of the fact in any one instance.'[8] After the Great Famine, investigation was even more urgent as the millions of Irish famine emigrants and their descendants overseas were prepared to believe the worst of the situation in Ireland. How justified were reports of deaths or indeed the threat of starvation after 1850?

In the post-Famine period the priests and increasingly the teachers on the west coast regularly sent alarming reports and there was no disputing the hardship experienced by many in the remote areas of Donegal, Mayo, Galway, Kerry and Cork. There is little doubt but that people died of starvation. One of the last recorded victims during a minor famine was a Mrs Flaherty on Garomna Island in Connemara in November 1897. English charity had aided twelve families on the island and the Flaherty family of four consisting of the parents and two children, had earlier been given a half a hundredweight of Indian meal by the relieving officer. After her death the police investigated. They searched the house and found no food and the police sergeant appealed to his men for aid for the surviving family members. The local curate, Fr Lavelle wrote to Gerard Balfour about this incident and complained that it was absurd for the Local Government Board to claim that not much distress existed.[9]

Cases like this were indisputable and encouraged both the government and private relief agencies to redouble their efforts. The level of destitution was such, in these areas, that significant excess mortality was only avoided during minor famines by timely injections of aid to prevent such fatalities. The small number of proven reports of death should not be mistaken for the absence of the threat of such deaths. In remote western parts of the country from Cork to Donegal where dependence on the potato remained high, where land was poor and pre-Famine conditions persisted, the fear of the return of a major crisis remained. Otherwise the rest of the country except for the urban slums, experienced more prosperous times. Distress and famine in the west was of enormous political importance because they were physical reminders of the general experience during the Great Famine. That 'living museum' aspect of the western counties was to be fully exploited by native politicians and had a major impact on political developments especially in 1879 and in 1898 when Davitt and William O'Brien saw problems in the west as a springboard for new political initiatives.

The first of the minor famines after the Great Famine began as early as June 1858 when storms destroyed crops on the Iniskea islands off Mayo.[10] That was to herald a period of distress in the west which was to affect not only Erris where 10,000 were distressed in 1860.[11] Drought in 1859 was followed in 1860, 1861 and 1862 by three of the wettest years in the nineteenth century except for 1846–7. These meteorological adversities led to heavy crop losses. Yields were down for a variety of crops and cattle disease allied with a fodder famine, saw the milch cow population drop from 1.6 million to 1.3 million. This was to have a general impact on the rural population but it was the failure of the potato crop which was to threaten famine in the western counties from Cork to Donegal. The potato crop was more than halved in 1861 and was only marginally better in 1862.[12]

The crisis was at its worst in 1862. In February the *Nation* carried an account of a meeting in Tuam where famine deaths were reported. Larcom at Dublin Castle had no difficulty in recognising the hand of Archbishop MacHale in the style of this report. On the margin of this news clipping he wrote, 'a growl from St. Jarleth's'. Nevertheless Larcom was sufficiently concerned to gather all the scraps of evidence he could find.[13] His superiors in Dublin and London, Carlisle and Peel were unsympathetic. Sir Robert Peel was compared unfavourably with his more famous father after he spoke of distress being caused by Irish character defects. It was in America that the reports drew the strongest response. The

Boston Globe carried reports of famine and called upon the priests to lead a rebellion to rid Ireland of a tyrannous government.[14] Irish America which had sent £11,000,000 in emigrants' remittances during the previous decade, saw Ireland through emigrants' eyes and was appalled by reports of the return of starvation. Aid was sent from emigrants world wide to relatives, to bishops and to prominent political leaders like William Smith O'Brien.[15]

In the spring of 1862 the traditional relief agencies swung into action. The Lord Mayor of Dublin called a meeting at the Mansion House at which a subscription list for relief was opened. This aid was distributed through local committees in the distressed districts.[16] Public opinion eventually forced the government to intervene. The Society of Friends also launched an appeal.[17] One estimate put the extent of private charity at £100,000. In a debate in the House of Commons some of the Irish members condemned the administration for its inactivity in the face of famine. Finally in the late spring of 1862, workhouse provision was extended, coal was sent to the west to replace waterlogged peat and Peel sent thirty spring carts, ordered earlier for Crimean War duty, to be sent to the west to transport the indigent to the workhouses. State aid was probably more limited than in any other crisis in the nineteenth century and the bulk of relief was from the private agencies.[18]

This was the most serious of the minor famines in post-Famine Ireland. As Professor Donnelly has noted, that without any approach to mass starvation, the Irish country people had passed through a longer and deeper crisis between 1859 and 1864 than even the more publicised and noted famine of 1879. There were fewer deaths than in the 1840s because relief agencies, including foreign charities were more sensitive to the threat of death, there was less eviction, cheap alternative sources of food were to be found and the new shops made credit available. Though shop credit could be a mixed blessing in the longer term it solved an immediate problem. Maize or yellow meal was to be of lasting benefit after Irish people overcame their dislike of it.

Imports of maize doubled between 1858 and 1864 and wheat imports were up by seventy-six per cent in the same period.[19]

If the government did its best to ignore this famine it was to attract the attention of journalists and commentators. Henry Coulter was to be one of the first of many journalists in the post-Famine period to file reports of famine in the west and later publish his reports in book form.[20] In learned journals the extent of distress was debated. D. Heron Caulfield, a caring Queen's Counsel, described the appalling scenes he had witnessed on the western circuit. There was controversy about the extent of distress and Randall McDonnell characterised the dispute as being between those who described western poverty with 'extravagant exaggeration' and their opponents who dismissed all reports with 'incredulity'. Caulfield attempted to reconcile the opposing views by saying that claims of death were exaggerated but denials of such deaths were equally unbelievable. He characterised distress on the west coast as 'recent, local and occasional'.[21] This general statement of the middle ground is probably accurate. But increasingly the gap between the different views was to grow in later famines. Every famine led to exaggerated claims of famine deaths and, as a ritual response, denials of any distress followed from the other side. Even as late as 1922 the White Cross accepted reports of famine deaths in Connemara but by 1925 Cosgrave's government was prepared to attempt to end this ritual war of words. But behind that war of words lay the reality of a section of the western poor living on the edge of starvation with the occasional casualty like Mrs Flaherty. Deaths such as hers gave validity to the exaggerators who saw their actions justified by the possibility of many following the few.

Perhaps the best known of the minor famines is that of 1879–80.[22] As in the earlier minor famine there was a widespread economic crisis allied with crop failure. Livestock and butter prices fell from 1876 and the market prices of Irish produce plummeted because of market conditions. Excessive rainfall in 1879 again threatened crops and the potato was badly affected by blight. The national yield was reduced by two-thirds. The potato was still the staple article of diet for many on the west coast and there the impact of poor yields and declining prices was a double blow.[23] As early as June 1879, 200 Roman Catholic priests warned of problems in Ireland from Wexford to Donegal.[24] The despair at the impending crisis felt by the half a million Irish people who would eventually be reduced to dependence on relief in the following year, gives an obvious reason for the zeal with which western tenant farmers embraced the newly founded Land League. Davitt's programme offered a panacea for all their ills. Some historians have seen the Land League in the context of the successful mobilisation of the tenant farmers by a new political elite. But there is little doubt that Davitt saw the value of famine as a rallying cry for political action and he was joined by other political forces in the New Departure in that year. This united political programme was set against a deteriorating situation in the west. Nineteen years later William O'Brien saw another famine in the west as an opportunity to again heal political divides following the Parnellite split and launch a new programme by founding the United Irish League.[25]

The full impact of the 1879 potato failure began to be felt in the new year. Journalists in search of famine stories were back in the west in January 1880. The *Daily Telegraph* reported that people were starving and in a 'relief or coffins' type letter, the parish priest of Carna warned of inquests if relief did not come. James Hack Tuke, the indefatigable Quaker philanthropist, was back in the west. He had been active during the Great Famine and by 1880 he had thirty years experience of relief work in Ireland. An enthusiast for assisted emigration he was confronted by people whom he claimed, begged him to 'send us anywhere, Your Honour, to get us out of our misery'.[26] Though not as serious a crisis as 1859–64, this minor famine excited much greater public interest. Clifden became a centre for English reporters who had a well worn itinerary which spread from Cork to Donegal.[27] Few travelled to the more remote areas of Erris, Connemara or Kerry and the route bears a remarkable similarity to the tourist route followed by travellers in the nineteenth century which crossed the distressed districts but increasingly by-passed the worst areas. The situation in Ireland was raised in the Queen's speech at the opening of parliament and in a subsequent debate it was claimed that 500,000 people were distressed in Ireland. Parnell and Dillon were in America where they collected £50,000 for relief.[28] Daily reports of distress in the press reflected a growing anxiety that this famine might indeed be the return to the 'Black '47' situation. One of the first moves to set up a relief committee was taken by the Lord Lieutenant's wife, the Duchess of Marlborough who organised her own fund. Later the Lord Mayor of Dublin was to establish another and the combined efforts of both were to raise over quarter of a million pounds for relief in the distressed districts. Though the Mansion House was regularly the venue for Lord Mayors' relief committees the records of these committees only survive for the one established in 1880. From its records we can see how Dublin workers contributed at the time. Guinness, Arnotts and other firms were well represented.[29] Telegrams were sent further afield to solicit aid. The Dominion of Canada donated $100,000. Appeals to India which had experienced regular and severe famine in the previous thirty years saw almost £7,000 sent from Madras.[30] In India, as in Ireland, British administrators had struggled to find a suitable response to famines and famine reports. Following the failure of famine prevention in India the Famine Commission Report was published in 1880 and it laid down guidelines to the local administration for the anticipation, recognition and relief of famines.[31] In Ireland the administration was moving towards the same conclusions. Curiously Irish and Indian famines, though the scale of the problems were different, presented administrators with the same difficulties in determining appropriate responses. By 1880 there was a greater readiness on the part of the state to accept responsibility and intervene. It was a memory of this shared history which persuaded the Irish government to give £100,000 to the Red Cross for relief in India in 1944 after a telegram from the Lord Mayor of Calcutta appealed for aid for Bengal.[32] Charity from overseas flowed into Ireland. Emigrants' remittances increased and charity funds in Europe, America, Australia and other places began to arrive. One estimate of aid sent directly to the distressed areas from overseas at £830,000 for the period between January and August 1880.[33] The *New York Herald* began its own fund as did other papers. In the west of Ireland there was a flurry of activity as relief workers moved into the distressed areas and food supplies began to move. Small and large relief committees had agents in Ireland and even the Duke of Edinburgh was here on a relief ship off the west coast until the death of his mother the Empress of Russia forced him to return home.

The government response following gloomy reports from its own agents was to introduce a loan scheme at favourable rates for public works and both landlords and public sanitary authorities were invited to apply. Temporary inspectors were appointed to the Local Government Board to monitor the situation and a seed potato scheme was introduced. A report prepared ten years later summarised the government's actions and expenditure. Grants £153,171; Loans £1,494,743; Seed loans £647,743. This estimate of expenditure shows roughly £2.3 million of state loans and grants, to which must be added the £267,000 British and Irish charities and the £830,000 from overseas.[34] Given the level of distress in 1879–80 the £2.3 million from the National Exchequer compares favourably with the £7,132,268 which was advanced in 1846–47 from the same source. A Relief Act was passed in March and the numbers on outdoor relief rose from 85,000 per week in September 1879 to 107,000 in February 1880. The arrival of Gladstone's government saw relief schemes extended and yet this whole programme was severely criticised later. It was argued that these schemes did not target the distressed and that both works and seed potatoes went to the undeserving and not the most needy. The schemes also ran on long after the distress had passed and so committed the government to further expenditure until 1884 though the 'necessity for it had ceased three years previously'. The schemes in the eyes of the Local Government Board were 'entirely disappointing'. Administrators saw some schemes as unnecessary and wasteful as the methods adopted did not direct aid to the most needy. The government scheme for the introduction of seed potatoes was an attempt to introduce better seed through a loan plan for the long term benefit of the tenant farmers. The Champion was to be the variety favoured for introduction into Ireland. As a percentage of the national crop it grew from thirty per cent in 1880 to sixty-three per cent in 1881 and it amounted to at least seventy per cent of the national crop for the next decade. In the same decade produce per acre from this variety, The Champion potatoes, gradually halved so the hope of long term improvement was frustrated.[35] Small wonder Arthur Balfour, the chief secretary, was to criticise the scheme ten years later.[36]

The private relief agencies claimed that this was 'a famine which must have swept away many thousands of the population' but which was stayed by the hand of private charity, and of private charity alone, until the bounty of the Almighty came to banish it altogether'.[37] Yet the level of state expenditure causes this statement to be questioned. The charities were impatient with the persistence of famine and increasingly called for radical reform.[38] The charities gave direct aid where many government schemes were for longer term improvements. At the height of the famine in July 1880 there were 92,619 persons on outdoor relief and 45,360 on relief works. On those figures more were given aid through the private charities but the state's role was crucial. Their combined efforts prevented deaths, carried people through a difficult period when credit was exhausted and prices had dropped. They saved people from death. When relief began it helped reduce mortality rates from 1.6 per 1,000 to 1 per 1,000 in excess of the rate for the corresponding quarter for the previous five years. While that was progress, Dr Sigerson who compiled the statistics observed that, 'many must have quietly succumbed to their suffering, and silently died out'. He further noted that for those who survived there was a return to a long period of privations, or of uniform and meagre diet, which predisposed the enfeebled bodies of many sufferers to disease. Government relief continued until 1886 and there were isolated pockets of distress.[39]

The next minor famine was in 1890 and was to be the first of three in the 1890s.[40] 20.9 inches of rain fell in the first nine months of 1890 and blight was a problem. The chief secretary directed the Land Commission staff to investigate and their returns were laid before parliament. The crop was almost normal in the country generally except for the western unions from Cork to Donegal where the estimated losses were from a half to a third of the average yield. In some of the most congested areas the yield was 'hardly one-fourth of the average'. Maps were prepared of the districts at risk in Dublin Castle in the early autumn. Reports of famine began in November but by then the administration had already decided on the introduction of relief works. Mindful of the wasteful nature of the earlier works in the 1880s, the new schemes were to be of a useful nature and to be of maximum benefit to the districts concerned with the least demoralisation of the population which inhabited those districts. The railway companies were encouraged to bring works forward. In other areas the royal engineers organised works which were supervised by the police. Roughly 24,000 persons were employed during the crisis period before the arrival of the new potato crop in the summer of 1891. A new seed potato scheme was introduced and 161 tonnes of potatoes were distributed free to the most distressed.

By 1890 the reaction of government was to anticipate famine rather than wait for a public outcry and representations in parliament to force it into action. In 1890 the government could see a crisis developing, studied it and made its plans before the reports of famine gathered momentum. Its guidelines for relief workers were prepared early and resemble the Indian famine codes of the 1880s. The state accepted its role in emergency relief though it still was anxious to restrict this as much as possible. It also wanted private relief to be organised and it was the Lord Lieutenant and

Balfour who took the initiative in starting a fund by a letter to *The Times* in January 1991. This fund raised £50,287 and distributed Indian meal to 50,641 persons. It also targeted children by providing school meals and distributing clothes through the schools. The extent of distress in 1890–91 was not nearly as extensive as in 1880 and an estimated 100,000 persons were assisted. Nor did this famine attract much attention from the politicians. The principal politicians were in America and were otherwise preoccupied with the O'Shea divorce issue which became public in November 1890. The crisis was of less impact in the traditionally distressed districts as emigration had begun to draw off the surplus population there in large numbers after 1880. Government's early reaction prevented the build up of criticism and proposals for new measures offered further hope of permanent improvements through the establishment of the Congested District's Board. Mick's, who had organised relief in Donegal in 1891 was to transfer to the new board and a new era for the west appeared to be dawning.[1] A short description of relief gives no idea of the activity in the local areas. Near Clonakilty in west Cork 108 men, seventeen women and fourteen boys were employed building a retaining wall at the Red Strand, constructing a boat slip at Ballycoyne Cove and improving approaches to the long strand. Closeby another 100 persons were making a road down the cliff to the strand at Simon's Cove and 136 were building a seaweed road near Mount Barry.[2] For many this type of emergency work was to supply them with the essential aid to enable them to survive.

Similar works were organised in 1895 following another potato failure in 1894. On that occasion 10,000 were employed but there is no evidence of any private subscription list being opened. The numbers in need of emergency aid was declining but a crop failure in 1897 was to herald the last of the nineteenth century minor famines and the last when the threat of starvation loomed. This was again caused by an exceptionally wet year and the situation was made worse by a fall in prices. Credit was difficult to obtain and for many there appeared to be a return of the old problems. Calls on the government to intervene were made as early as October 1897 and detailed reports of the situation in many areas were published in the press. On this occasion the government was slow to act and as a result there was a heightened political reaction to these reports. A works' scheme was organised through the Poor Law Unions and works began in March 1898. Yet another seed potato scheme was begun and seed from Scotland and the north-eastern counties was distributed in the west. Balfour could afford to delay because of the charitable reaction. A relief committee in Manchester began work in December 1897 and Daniel Tallon, the Lord Mayor of Dublin established another relief committee at the Mansion House in February 1898. Between them these two committees raised £31,000 for relief in Ireland. To this must be added the other funds which came to Ireland following the activities of the politicians. Maud Gonne made passionate speeches in Mayo and collected funds for aid, William O'Brien and Dillon were also involved and James Connolly visited Caherciveen and Valentia Island in Kerry where he witnessed at first hand famine conditions. Connolly saw the irony of what he described as the Home Rulers position when they demanded state intervention but who allied themselves with the Liberals who rejected that policy.[43] The public outcry helped to raise the issue in Britain and in America and funds were sent to individuals for distribution rather than through committees. It was at the start of this famine that Mrs Flaherty died and though the scale of famine was declining, it was still an important aspect of the realities of Irish life. The areas of distress were contracting and in the twentieth century were becoming more and more remote. There was great publicity for the plight of these poor. E. Keogh, the secretary of the Manchester Relief Fund described a typical congested, famine stricken district when he wrote about Gortumna, Co. Galway, in the *New Ireland Review* in June of 1898. In this he described the absolute poverty of the area, the impact of the potato failure, the indebtedness of the people and huge sums spent on relief over the years. Here old demographic patterns survived.

'The population of these districts is so dense,' he wrote, 'owing to large families, the result of early marriages, that it will be necessary to thin it out, and the fishing development must be supplemented by some scheme of migration.' Later in the same journal Charles Stevenson was to give an account of the Manchester Committee's activities.

In the early days of this century reports of distress continued and the west attracted more and more attention. The Countess of Aberdeen had set up the Irish Industries Association in 1887 for the encouragement of homespuns. She was one of the first to be attracted to the west and many were to follow. The Congested Districts Board also encouraged domestic industry and had a programme for land redistribution, home improvement and for the encouragement of better agricultural practices in the west. In 1904 there was another small crisis and in 1912 a localised crisis saw the Congested Districts Board criticised by many for its failure to rid the west of this problem. In the early years of the century the west came to be seen as a place apart, inhabited by the evicted tenants of the race who were seen as vastly superior to the urban poor in character, intellect and even physical beauty. For Pearse, Hyde, Stoppford Green and others it constituted the real Ireland where the language was preserved and true Gaelic values were to be found.[44] It had also developed a dependency culture which was an essential part of its survival but which was accepted as a necessary price for its preservation. Increasingly the rhetoric of condemning conditions in the west was divorced from general economic policies for the country at large. The distinctive features of the remote isolated districts mainly in the Gaeltacht in the present century made it easy to separate them from the general problem of poverty. It was for this reason Cosgrave reacted favourably to demands for aid in 1922 but by 1925 Cumann na nGael had a different view. By 1925 reports of death from starvation were viewed as a ploy to channel special aid to the west but by then the problem of urban poverty made it more difficult to justify.[45]

By 1925 the likelihood of death from starvation was even

more remote, the distressed districts had contracted, emigration had helped solve the problem of subsistence and a government attempting to restrict state expenditure was prepared to confront its critics on the question of western poverty in a way that no Westminster administration could have after 1850. The era of famine in Ireland had finally drawn to a close.

FOLK MEMORY AND THE FAMINE

CATHAL PÓIRTÉIR

I'VE BEEN STRUCK BY THE number of times I've heard Irish politicians, commentators and famine relief organisations refer to the 'folk memory' of the Great Famine as part explanation for the public's willingness to contribute generously to famine relief in other countries. But what is, or was, the folk memory of the Famine?

The material in this brief sampling of the English language folk memories of the Great Irish Famine is held in the Department of Irish Folklore in University College, Dublin.[1] It was collected systematically in two ways. About half of it in 1945 as the result of a questionnaire from the Irish Folklore Commission, the other half was collected from 1935 on by the Commission's full-time and part-time collectors who had expert local knowledge and understanding of the people, places and material they were dealing with.

Of the one thousand or so men and women who supplied this Famine folklore to the Irish Folklore Commission (later the Department of Irish Folklore, University College, Dublin) from 1935 on, a few were born in the 1840s and 1850s, but most were born after the Famine in the 1860s, 1870s and 1880s. So most of the material comes from the children and grandchildren of the generation who witnessed the Famine.

This oral history gives us a rare opportunity to hear about the Great Famine from the perspective of the people whose voice is usually lost or silenced by the passage of time. It comes to us in their words, with memories and images strongly linked to local places, individuals and events. These are the words of men and women who grew up surrounded by the physical and psychological legacy of the Famine. They echo what they heard from their parents and neighbours who experienced the reality of the Famine.

These testimonies have a simple emotional power that has carried them forward from one generation to the next. Here they have etched the intricate details of vivid human tragedy. It's not the type of statistical material you'll find in official documents. It's not an overview or analysis of the catastrophe in context, but a series of memories and interpretations from below.

As is the case with written accounts and sources, folk history is prone to errors of omission, distortion and bias. A sophisticated methodology or source criticism of oral history could add a fresh dimension to the study of history, giving a different perspective to that found in other document driven accounts. Certainly the attitudes, beliefs and feelings of the survivors of the Famine aren't central to most modern Famine histories. Therefore the shared memories of oral tradition may form part of the basis for a new understanding of how the common people related, and related to, the tragedy.

Indeed the folk material may throw up new facts or otherwise inaccessible details about the mental and material world of past communities and possibly act as a corrective to other sources. It certainly widens the range of historical evidence by offering an alternative and distinct perspective originating with the people themselves. The strengths of context and analysis that mainstream professional historians provide are mostly lacking in folk history, but to combine the strengths of all approaches may lead to a deeper and fuller understanding of the cultural context of the people, the period and the events in question.

The length of time between the Famine of the 1840s and the collection of the folk material in the 1930s, 1940s and 1950s means that inaccuracies and distortions may have developed in the retelling, as elements of the memories become embelished, forgotten or imagined.

It can also be argued that folklore studies have shown that the memories of many traditional storytellers were incredibly accurate over long periods and that a huge pride was taken in remaining faithful to the tradition as passed on within a community. A hundred years isn't a long time in folklore studies.

Even in those cases where selective memory, the transmission process or artistic licence may have confused chronology or other details, we can still find insights into the attitudes, feelings and psychology of the people which wouldn't be available from other sources.

SO LET'S LOOK BRIEFLY AT some elements of the folk history of the Great Famine.

Mr P. Foley, a farmer of Knockananna, Co. Wicklow was born around 1890, some forty years after the Famine. Nevertheless, his description of the coming of the blight could easily be that of an eyewitness:

> Next morning when they awoke and went out, to their consternation their lovely potato plants, which were in such bloom and showed such a promise of beautiful crops the day before, were all covered over with black spots and the leaves and stalks hanging down as if dead. The potato blight had appeared for the first time in Ireland. The awful smell and stench of the blight was everywhere.[2]

That style of account is found all over the country in descriptions of the blight. The government and scientists of Famine times didn't know the cause of the blight and neither did the people. The most widely found folk explanation runs along the same lines as this 1940s account from farmers around Mote, Co. Westmeath:

> So plentiful were they [potatoes] in pre-Famine years that it often happened that farmers filled them into sacks, took them into the markets at Moate, Athlone or Ballymahon, offered them for sale but nobody could be found to buy, so that on the return journey the farmers often emptied them into the ditch on the roadside for 'they wern't worth the sacks they were in'. Afterwards it was said that the Famine was a just retribution from God for the great waste of food. A local saying which may refer to this is 'A willful waste makes a woeful want'.[3]

Pádraig Sabhaois supplied this account from Moycullen, Co. Galway. A few words, a childhood memory, bring us back a

221

hundred years to the horror of starvation:

> The Parish Priest, Fr Kenny, who died in 1896 aged close to ninety years and who had charge of the parish long before the Famine, told me that on a certain Saturday on his way to the church to hear confessions he anointed nineteen on the roadside dying of starvation.
>
> On another occasion he pointed out to me a spot on the road just outside the church gate where he found a poor man sitting one Sunday morning. The man had a small loaf clutched in his hand and was making attempts to raise it to his mouth. He was so weakened from hunger and exhaustion that he had not sufficient strength to lift the bread to his mouth. Then he used to bend his head down, holding the loaf between his knees, to try to get a bite in that way, but the result was that he simply toppled over. The priest then anointed him and he died there tearing the dough with his nails.[4]

A similarly vivid eyewitness account passed on in oral tradition is one collected from Peter Clarke, of Usker, Bailiboro, Co. Cavan. Peter was born about 1860, when the majority of adults still recalled the stark Famine images of their youth:

> Doctor Adams, of Lower Knockhide, was a young man out of college at the time of the Famine, he was after finishing his medical course, and he got an appointment in the west of Ireland. He told me it was most terrifying to drive along the road and see a corpse lying here and a corpse lying there, and some of them seemed as if they had been trying to get as near as possible to the cemetery. Both sides of the road were strewn with them. He said that they died from starvation.
>
> When the Indian meal came out, some of them were so desperate from starvation that they didn't wait for it to be cooked properly, they ate it almost raw and that brought on intestine troubles that killed a lot of them that otherwise might have survived. They just gabbed it and swallowed it down almost raw.[5]

The effects of eating badly cooked relief food mentioned in that oral account is accepted as a medical and historical fact by nutritionists and doctors who have studied the events of the time. Another example, this time from Co. Cork, shows how aware the common people were of the results of this and how they were dealt with. This account was collected in 1945:

Jack Conell told me this tale or tales. He is eighty-four and he heard a lot of the tales of the Famine years from his own father who was a full grown man at that time, a labouring man. I knew him, Old Mick Conell.

When the people were so badly fed on greens and turnips, cabbage and certain kinds of weeds that, as they used to say, 'ran down through them', they were affected with a kind of fever and dysentery that was contagious or 'taking' as they used to say at that time, and all the people suffering in this way were put away in a place by themselves.

They built huts up against a sheltered ditch, poles were stood on the outside and a roof thrown across them to the ditch and they were thatched with brambles, briars and rushes. Here in those huts or 'scalpts' the afflicted people had to live, their own people or family shunning them. There were few of those scalpts, Jack Conell says, in the field now belonging to Willie Breen bounding the field now owned by Andrew Rahilly, Shanballa. The field or the port near the bounds ditch is a low and sheltered valley and was known as Park na Phooka. The sick poor had to have a vessel of their own and their friends would come now and again, a couple of times each day, and empty their own gallons containing milk or boiled potatoes or oatmeal porridge into them, taking care not to touch them at all as the mere act of touching the vessels used by the sick was suppose to bring on the sickness.[6]

The way in which the poor and hungry tried to find sustenance is the subject of hundreds of accounts, often startling in the detail given. Perhaps scarcity in later years helped make these accounts so real to those who retold them. Let's go back to Wicklow for this memory:

In crossing the hills they often saw groups of men cornering cattle which they would bleed by cutting a vein in the neck of the beast and extracting a few pints of blood, or whatever amount they could safely take, without endangering too much the life of the animal. When they would have sufficient blood extracted from a beast, they would fix up the wound to prevent further bleeding by putting a pin through the skin across the incision in the vein, then clapping a few hairs from the animal's tail around the pin to keep it in position. The men would carry the blood home in jars and other vessels slung across their shoulders, some of them having to travel many miles before reaching home.

When they would arrive their women folk would carefully salt the blood and some of it would be cooked by frying in a pan.[7]

William Doudigan (O'Dowd), Redbray, Tullaghan, Co. Leitrim was born in the 1860s. He supplied this account in 1945. While many tales of food stealing portray the thieves as blameless in the crisis, there are other accounts in the folk history of the hardship and anguish caused by the food stealing:

Pat Healy, Mullaghmore, Co. Sligo, now over ninety, and the only one around here who can speak Irish, having kept it up with his mother who could speak no English and lived to be over 100 ... told me a short time ago that all the potatoes around Malagh were killed except a few gardens. They had one which they dug and heaped out in the garden in front of the house and in view of it. They had other potatoes in the house which they used in the winter, but when they went to bring the potatoes into the house in the spring, as is still the custom in these parts, they had been all stolen, though the outward appearance of the heap remained undisturbed and the theft must have taken place by night. He says his father told him that they of the household cried in despair when they discovered the cruel wrong.[8]

Here's the other side of it, where the theft of food is seen as an act of heroism. It reminds us that folk history can take in more than one side of an event. It was with pride that Mrs Kavanagh of Knocknaskeagh, Co. Wicklow recalled a family tradition:

Her own grandfather went into a house of a well-to-do farmer in Slievenamoe and saw a leg of mutton boiling in a pot on the fire. His family were hungry so, despite being scalded, he took the meat out of the pot and brought it home.[9]

Central to many memories of the Famine is the relief the people got from various sources, including the government. While the quality and distribution of the food are often criticised, the welcome efforts to aid the starving were remembered in some detail a century later, as we see in this example from Rossport in Co. Mayo:

During the Famine years around 1847, there was a scheme of relief of distress and hunger operated by the Society of Friends, commonly known as the Quakers, instituted in north-west Erris. The scheme was administered by the local landlords and part of the procedure was the installation of large iron vats for the cooking of Indian meal porridge which was rationed out to the peasantry every day. Those huge vats or pots were known in each locality as 'the boiler', and a couple of paid men were always in attendance to minister to the cooking, distribution and supervision of the work of maintenance. One of these boilers was situated at Rossport and another at Rinroe. I cannot say definitely if there was one at Pollathomas, but the meal was distributed there by the landlords O'Donnell, and probably the boiler was in operation there too. Landlord Bournes was in charge of the boiler at Rossport and Landlord Knox at Rinroe. Of course, the work, especially the distribution, was in the hands of trusted servants of the 'big house'. The meal was imported by a ship which came regularly from Westport.[10]

It's worth making the point that the folk record, as collected in the 1930s and 1940s, often distinguishes between 'soup-kitchens', where relief was distributed, and 'souperism', were relief was linked with proselytism. For example, in this account from Emyvale in Co. Monaghan:

There was a food kitchen in the townland of Brackagh. Both broth and porridge were distributed. The meal was brought from Newry in carts and this took three days to go and three days to come back. It was usually a Protestant farmer's house was chosen for the distribution of porridge. A ladleful was given for every member of the family and it was distributed every day except Sunday, when two ladlefuls were given out on the previous Saturday. The people used to line up with their noggins for their share of the food.
There is no account of either souperism or proselytism in this district.[11]

A common feeling among the people who needed the relief food was that those entrusted with distributing it often didn't do so in an even-handed way. In Glenville, Co. Cork, the individual's name was still remembered a hundred years later:

Patrick Forde of Raheen gave out tickets to the poor to obtain Indian meal. Den Dunlea of Ballyvourisheen, Carrignavar was the distributor of the meal. When the poor went to him for meal he had none for them. He kept it to fatten pigs, and sold more of it dearly.[12]

Bill Powell, a pensioner of Enniskean, Co. Cork was born about 1870 and some of what he was told recalls the official efforts and policies of the Famine years:

It was the Indian meal sent here from America, and sent free on sea and every other way, there wasn't to be one penny of cost no matter what part of the country it was sent. It was that was given out as food. Even that would in some way save the people if it was distributed in any kind of a just way.

Pamphlets were distributed among the people by government orders giving instructions as to how the Indian meal should be cooked. I was told that most of these instructions were wrong or most misleading. Anyhow, the new meal at first caused widespread sickness and many deaths, I was told. Many people were afraid to use it except very sparingly until they found a method of boiling it to the proper degree.[13]

Other relief schemes are also remembered in detail. While public works were sometimes remembered as non-productive, others were seen as useful by the communities who carried them out. Those who organised them and worked on them are recalled by John Hanrahan of Inistioge, Co. Kilkenny in 1945:

Many relief schemes were started locally during and soon after the Famine. Hugh Green, landlord of Fiddaun, Cappa and Raheen carried out many relief schemes. He reclaimed all the land on his estate, clearing away existing fences, 'squaring' the fields, re-erecting much more modern fences thereby enclosing greater areas than previously, and draining the land.

A large number of people were employed in this scheme. Men came long distances to find employment, some coming even from Waterford. A man and his wife who lived in Garan, Tullagher parish, about seven miles from Inistioge, came to work on the draining of the land in Cappa every morning, returning home every night. Two other women from Inistioge, Mam Long and Nellie Whyte, worked for Green with shovels at this time also. They made drains just like the men. They were paid four pence per perch at the drain making. Out of this miserable wage they had to buy yellow meal, the only food they had to exist on. Not alone were they badly paid, but for quite a time they were wronged by a Scotch overseer who gave incorrect measurements when overseeing the work they had done. The balance due to them he kept for himself. When at last the landlord heard of the dishonesty, he had the Scotch man dismissed and appointed one of his own tenants, named Keefe from Cappa, as overseer.

The privations of the workers were very acute. When dinner-hour came each one washed his shovel, put some raw yellow meal on it and wet it from the water that fell into the drain and ate it. This was all they had for dinner.

Those who came a long distance from home to work stayed in one of Keefe's lofts in Cappa, and lived a sort of community life. The ration of meal that was left after the dinner was collected, each man giving his share. This was cooked for them by Keefe. They ate it on the loft where they slept.[14]

That type of rich and telling detail can also be found in this account from Co. Cavan. Unusually, an effort is made here to be specific about the number of people involved:

Old James Stafford, of Bailiboro, told me that he was a youth during the Famine, and that he remembered seeing a crowd of men walking down to the Workhouse every day for dinner. Free dinners were given in the Workhouse at that time. I think it was oaten porridge they got. I think the Indian meal only came in after that. They went twice a day to the Workhouse to get food. Bailiboro Workhouse was only built to accommodate 699 people, but at times during the Famine there would be over 1,000 people in it, between the Fever Hospital and the body of the house.

There were contractors for burying the people that died in the Workhouse and Fever Hospital, and an old man told me that the contractors would be working with lanterns till twelve o'clock at night, burying the people that died in both places.[15]

Kathleen Hurley, Corlock House, Ballymoe, Co. Galway supplied this incredibly detailed and vivid account from her memory of a conversation with Johnny Callaghan who was born about 1845:

My father who was also named Johnny Callaghan was a baker during the Famine years and for years after the Famine in the workhouse, Castlerea, Co. Roscommon. And I as a young lad assisted my father at the baking trade. I distinctly remember the Famine and every time I think of it I shiver all over. In the bakehouse in the workhouse my father and I were engaged all day baking. My father was always nervous to appear in public with flour dust on his clothes, so ravenous were some people he feared they would attack him and kill him. There was one large pot resting on stones in the Workhouse yard and in this huge pot was made gruel to be distributed to a constant stream of starving people. The people came by every road to the work-house for their measure of gruel. Another large pot was erected on stones at the back of the present National Bank. This pot was fed with water running in the demesne outside the town. There was a third pot erected and in the three pots gruel was boiled for the starving people.

Seeing people die of hunger was awful but it could not equal seeing them die of the cholera that set in. On the road leading from Ballymoe to the workhouse a son was wheeling his dying father (dying of cholera) on a wheel barrow. On reaching the workhouse the father was dead and the son collapsed and died in a few hours time.

The workhouse was full with sick people. When a person was near death, he or she was removed from other parts of the workhouse to a large room at the other gable-end of the workhouse (the gable nearest the town of Castlerea). This room was called 'The Black Room' and the gable the 'Black Gable' for in this room the sick person was allowed to die. Sometimes there were up to seven persons in this room. From the window in this room there were a few boards slanting down to the earth and beneath was a huge grave or pit. When a death occurred the corpse was allowed to slide down the boards into the pit beneath and 'lime' was put over the corpse, along the boards and along the wall of the gable. This caused the wall to get black and gave the name to the 'Black Gable'. This black gable was to be seen up to a few years ago.[16]

John Doyle who was born at Craffle, Ballyteigue, Aughrim, Co. Wicklow supplied the horrific account:

There were so many deaths that they opened big trenches through the graveyards and when they were full of dead they filled them in. His father worked at the opening of these trenches and he was paid by the Government.

No one was allowed into the graveyards except the men hired to cover the graves. Two guards were always on to keep the people out and there were many rows with people trying to get in. They dug graves twelve foot deep and put seven or eight bodies into each grave. They never put coffins on them at all. Some of the bodies used to swell up and when they would be dropped into the grave they would burst and the gravediggers would have to run until the smell would ease. Often they would get the disease.[17]

Graphic tales of death and burial are to be found in the folk memory from all over the country. Many of them echo the eyewitness accounts that have survived in written sources of the time. Here's a typical account from Ballina, Co. Mayo:

Most of the dead were buried in fields or along the roads. The corpse was frequently wrapped with straw ropes and buried in this way without a coffin. Corpses were sometimes carried to the graveyard on donkey's backs.

Tombstones were not erected as it was difficult to find men with the strength to make the graves. Sometimes a large stone or flag was placed at the head or foot of the grave to mark it out. This practice still continues in the absence of a tombstone.

Bodies actually lay unburied by hedges for rats soon devoured the flesh and only the skeleton remained. There is an instance of a family being found dead with their skeletons only remaining and the neighbours' efforts failed to frighten away the rats which were feeding on the flesh.[18]

Another staple of Famine folklore is the evictions which took place during and after the Famine. While it's impossible to accurately date many of these oral accounts to distinguish them from post-Famine evictions, it's fair to accept them as carrying similar and relevant atmosphere and detail.

Michael Gildea, Dromore, Ballintra, Co. Donegal was born about 1860. He heard the following from his father and other older people who remembered the Famine:

The year 1849 was chiefly noted for the large number of evictions which took place in the parts of Drumholme parish. Many farmers were from two to three years in arrears, with no immediate hope of clearing them off.

On the Knox estate, which includes the southern half of the village of Ballintra and runs in a north-westerly direction towards the coast, there were dozens of people put out of their homes. There were several families in the townlands of Foyagh and Birrah in 1845 who vanished root and branch before the decade came to a close.

The usual procedure after an eviction was to burn the thatched roof to prevent the tenant from entering the house again after the bailiff and his assistants had left the scene.

A man named Diver who lived in this townland was among those who were evicted out of their homes.

The landlord himself was present on this occasion and he offered the sum of one pound to anybody who would set fire to the house.

Diver, who was standing out on the street with a number of neighbours, stepped forward and said he would earn the money. He thereupon stepped into the kitchen where some turf was still smouldering on the hearth, brought them out on a shovel and placed them among the thatch of the roof. In a few moments it was ablaze, fanned by a strong south-westerly breeze and in a short time his home was gone.

His neighbours were so amazed that they could say nothing, and they made no effort to prevent him when he climbed onto the roof, scooped out a hole, and in a short time had reduced what was once the home of himself, his father and grandfather, to nothing but a few fire-scarred walls.

When the landlord tendered Diver the money which he had thus so strangely earned, he coolly put it in his pocket, turned on his heel, nodded to the neighbours and disappeared from the scene.

He lived alone and left nobody to mourn his departure. The few pieces of furniture were left to rot in the ditch, as the rest of the people around said they would not soil their hands by touching them.[19]

Another example will help show that the landlords were not held solely to blame for the evictions. Often those who got the land of evicted neighbours were seen as the real culprits, having taken advantage of 'their own'. Here's a typical account form Co. Cork in 1945:

In my young day I used to hear old people discuss the awful cruelty practised by farmers who were fairly well off against the poorer and less comfortable neighbours. The people who were old when I was young, I'm sixty-six, were never tired of discussing how some of those, taking advantage of the poverty of their neighbours, used to offer the rent of their farms to the landlord, the rent which the owners could not pay, and grab their farms adding some to their own farms.

Several people would be glad if the Famine times were altogether forgotten so that the cruel doings of their forebears would not be again renewed and talked about by the neighbours.[20]

The memories of emigration often feature the destinations of those who left. Although this process had already started before the Famine, the size and speed of emigration during and after the Famine left a strong memory of it as being the start of mass emigration. In this Kerry account, the memory is vivid:

Many of the local families went to America. Often they moved in one night, selling most of their possessions to the neighbours and carrying with them enough to supply them with food during the voyage. They left by night so the landlord could not interfere with their goods.

The voyage usually took from three to nine months. The food was cooked in communal pots. A number of people's food was thrown in together and cooked. The strongest sometimes came out better than the others because of this. Lots died of disease on these voyages. Some of the ships had water oozing in between the planks.

The Poor Law Guardian had the power of getting places for a certain number on these voyages to America. He usually gave them to his friends who needed to go.[21]

From Dromore West, Co. Sligo, we get a view of what happened the emigrants when they left Ireland and the Famine behind:

> The depopulation of this district during the 1845–1855 or so, according to what I can gather, is almost unbelievable. The depopulation was caused far more by emigration than by deaths caused by hunger, although hunger took its toll in every district here, and indeed in every townland.
>
> I was told that most people who could muster sufficient money to pay the passage to America went, father, mother, children, young and old. All sailed from Sligo and the voyage, I was told, took sixteen weeks. One voyage to Quebec was given to me very accurately in one instance as sixteen weeks and three days.
>
> When the emigrants landed in Quebec, if there was no one to meet them there, a thing that rarely happened, they wandered round until they could find work. I was told that employers from states in the Middle West who needed help on farms, etc. came into Quebec, met emigrants and engaged them and took them home with them. Irish emigrants often had to wander around for weeks before getting employment.
>
> The emigrants paid their passages without any outside help. Later came the 'Free Emigration' when emigrants were transported free without payment from Sligo to Quebec. The British sponsored and paid the fares of these emigrants.
>
> In regard to food each person brought a supply of oaten cakes, baked three times, baked in the ordinary way first, then allowed to cool, then baked again until each large cake was hard as a stone. Even bags of potatoes and any other items of food available for which the individual had a taste, but the oatcakes always, potatoes generally and ordinary oatmeal raw.[22]

As yet, in Ireland no acceptable methodology has been arrived at between folklorists and historians to evaluate folk material as an historical source, although both the wealth of that tradition and its systematic collection in Ireland is very highly regarded by folklorists and ethnologists world-wide. Until an acceptable system of evaluation is arrived at, I hope that this necessarily brief sampling[23] of the folklore of the Famine has given a taste of the richness of detail available, an idea of the variety of experience recorded and the very human way in which it has been remembered since the Great Famine of the 1840s.[24]

IRISH FAMINE IN LITERATURE

DR MARGARET KELLEHER

IN WILLIAM CARLETON'S FAMINE NOVEL, *The Black Prophet*, the narrator hesitates before the task of describing a famine victim with the exclamation, 'But how shall we describe it?'[1] Such a question recurs throughout Irish famine literature: can the experience of famine be expressed; is language adequate to a description of famine's horrors? Fears as to language's adequacy in face of overwhelming events also appear in other literary contexts, most famously in writings concerning the Holocaust by George Steiner and others. Steiner's work expresses a further anxiety as to whether such representations should even be attempted: 'The world of Auschwitz lies outside speech as it lies outside reason. To speak of the *unspeakable* is to risk the survivance of language as creator and bearer of humane, rational truth'.[2]

Analogies between famine and the Holocaust, while suggestive, are limited; but significant comments on the role of literature have emerged in response to Steiner's challenge. Critics such as Laurence Langer and Paul Ricoeur emphasise literature's distinctive power to 'make present' the historical experience, thus *'making* such reality "possible" for the imagination'[3] in what Ricoeur has called the 'quasi-intuitiveness of fiction'.[4] In Irish famine literature, questions about language's competence give way to a detailed attempt at representation. Nineteenth and twentieth-century literary works thus reveal both the difficulties encountered and the strategies necessary in making the events of famine imaginatively accessible for their readers.

Carleton's novel *The Black Prophet* is one of the earliest and most famous of Irish famine novels. First published in *The Dublin University Magazine* in 1846 in eight parts, and set 'some twenty and odd years ago', its story employs details from the famines of 1817 and 1822. The first instalments, beginning in May 1846 after the partial failure of the potato crop, had themselves a prophetic quality in their anticipation of a further recurrence of famine; by December when the final chapters were published, the contemporary significance of this 'Tale of Irish famine' had become acutely clear: 'The sufferings of that year of famine we have endeavoured to bring before those who may have the power in their hands of assuaging the similar horrors which have revisited our country in this.' Carleton's novel has an explicit interventionist role, seeking, as he explained in the preface to the single-volume edition of February 1847, 'to awaken those who legislate for us into something like a humane perception of a calamity that has been almost perennial in this country' and to stir readers' 'sympathy' into 'benevolence'. In addition, Carleton's preface characterises the very purchase of the novel by the reader – inevitably a member of 'the higher and wealthier classes' – as equivalent to a charitable act, this some 150 years before the 'pioneering' Band-aid appeal!

The Black Prophet exemplifies many of the difficulties faced by novels in representing the event of famine, its causation, progress and effects. Famine constitutes only one of its plots, along with a conventional love story and murder mystery. References to famine include a number of strong indictments of the legislature for its history of 'illiberal legislation and unjustifiable neglect', and its failure to provide a 'better and more comfortable provision of food for the indigent and the poor'. This neglect, Carleton argues, has allowed 'provision-dealers of all kinds, mealmongers, forestallers, butchers, bakers and huxters' to 'combine together and sustain such a general monopoly of food, as is at variance with the spirit of all law and humanity' constituting 'a kind of artificial famine in the country'. These comments contrast sharply with definitions of government responsibility held by many of Carleton's contemporaries, while his identification of an 'artificial famine', created by monopoly rather than food shortage, anticipates recent work on the significance of food distribution and entitlements. The progressive nature of this analysis initially carries over into a sympathetic depiction of famine victims, people 'impelled by hunger and general misery'. Carleton's representation of famine crowds, however, becomes increasingly ambivalent, as evidenced in a profusion of oxymorons and other dualisms: 'dull but frantic tumult', 'wolfish and frightful gluttony on the part of the starving people', who possess an 'expression which seemed partly the wild excitement of temporary frenzy, and partly the dull, hopeless apathy of fatuity'. This ambivalence seems to originate in the author's fear of the activity and potential violence of those who are starving. In these passages, the starving poor appear less as victims of a neglectful legislature and more as creatures dangerously misguided, now 'victims of a quick and powerful contagion which spread the insane spirit of violence' rather than victims of disease and starvation. Carleton's characterisation of famine victims thus works against some of the implications of his political analyses. In addition, the differing, even competing, requirements, of story and famine analysis become clear as the novel ends: one family, the chief characters in the story, has its land and fortune restored as the story draws neatly to a close; the fortunes of the other 'starving people' are ignored.

The difficulties in combining famine material with conventional fictional plots can also be seen in Anthony Trollope's novel, *Castle Richmond*.[5] Trollope had lived in Ireland from 1841 to 1850, and intermittently in the 1850s. Written in 1859, on the eve of Trollope's final departure from Ireland, *Castle Richmond* is set in the south of Ireland, in counties Cork and Kerry, and covers what the author calls the 'Famine year' of 1846–7. The majority of the novel consists of a sentimental love story, with familiar nineteenth-century ingredients of illegitimacy and blackmail; the curious presence of famine material in the background led an early reviewer to declare that 'the milk and the water really should be in separate pails'.[6] One of the functions of *Castle Richmond*'s famine references is to assert the heroic status and attractiveness of Herbert, the chief character, in the face of the reader's quite likely view to the contrary; Herbert's work in famine relief seems, at least partly, intended to counteract the threat of the reader's growing dislike. Trollope's more detailed treatment of famine occurs through a series of encounters between upper class characters and the starving poor. These episodes allow the author to discourse on political economy and the dangers of 'promiscuous charity', especially in light of the apathy of the poor, and are intended to illustrate the operations of a power which was to Trollope 'prompt, wise and beneficent'. The characterisation of famine victims in *Castle Richmond* employs gender terms which recur throughout famine representations: male characters, though apathetic and idle, are situated on relief works, while females seek charity or remain within the domestic scene. In addition, female victims receive a physical scrutiny and inspection unparalleled in male representations. In contrast to Trollope's intention, the manner of his depiction of famine victims, the anxiety released by the encounter between the upper class and the starving, threatens to uncover very different power-relations.

While Carleton and Trollope's works constitute the two most famous nineteenth-century Famine novels, many other fictional treatments exist, a majority of which were written by women.

In 1851, Mary Anne Hoare published *Shamrock Leaves*, a collection of tales and sketches gathered 'from the famine-stricken fields of my native country', in which she argues that the horrors of Ugolino's dungeon, as depicted by Dante, 'fade into nothingness before the everyday tragedies of our Irish cabins'.[7] Controversial famine issues make an early appearance in famine fiction: Mary Anne Sadlier's *New Lights* (1853) strongly condemns the evils of prosleytism in the context of famine while Elizabeth Hely Walshe's *Golden Hills* (1865) depicts agrarian outrages and attempted assassinations by 'a lawless Riband tribunal.'[8] Other novels link the 1840s Famine to the events of 1848, as in Annie Keary's *Castle Daly: the Story of an Irish Home Thirty Years Ago.*[9] Annie Keary was the English daughter of an Irish-born clergyman; her novel, deemed by John O'Leary, Rosa Mulholland and others to be the best Irish novel of its time, was based on memories of conversations with her father and a total of two weeks spent in Ireland!

Other famine stories, such as 'The Hungry Death' by Rosa Mulholland and *Rose O'Connor* by Emily Fox, concern famines or periods of distress later than the 1840s.[10] Late nineteenth-century novels such as Margaret Brew's *The Chronicles of Castle Cloyne* [11] and Louisa Field's *Denis*[12] directly engage with contested issues in famine historiography such as the role of the landowning class, Brew emphasising that for the landed proprietors, 'with very few exceptions, the ruin, if it had come more slowly, did not come the less surely or pitilessly'. Given the extent of fictional writing about famine, it is not surprising that, in 1875, a writer in *The Saturday Review* noted that Irish events in the 1840s, including the Famine, compared to the French Revolution in providing writers with 'an inexhaustible mine of stirring incident', 'a mass of kaleidoscopic material that may be thrown together a thousand times'.[13]

A central question with regard to nineteenth-century famine literature is its role in preserving and shaping the memory of famine for succeeding generations. The majority of famine fiction was published either in London or jointly in Dublin and London, though a few novels were published in North America. This suggests that these narratives possessed a particularly significant function in terms of a British audience, a view supported by reviews of and prefaces to the novels. Famine stories were sometimes welcomed as explanations of the 'abiding Irish difficulty' for those 'perplexed by the contradictory versions of the present state of Ireland'; other reviewers were less sympathetic, seeing them as proof of the intractability of the Irish.[14] In the preface to her novel *Denis*, Louisa Field strongly emphasised the contemporary role of a famine story in throwing 'some light on circumstances and characteristics too often unknown and ignored, which yet are vital factors in that vast and ever-recurring problem, the Irish Question'.

The difficulties of representing famine included, for many writers, fears of being charged with exaggeration; frequently the defence employed involves an interesting configuration of issues of 'imaginative truth' and 'historical fact'. As early as 1847 Carleton argues that events in the 'present time' prove 'how far the strongest imagery of fiction is frequently transcended by the terrible realities of Truth'. Thus, as Mary Anne Hoare notes, the 'inventions of fiction' are rivalled, even surpassed, by 'matters of fact'. Similarly in 1865, Elizabeth Walshe defends her novel against charges of being overdrawn or exaggerated by bidding her readers to study the historical record: 'Let the files of contemporary journals, or the reports made to parliament be examined, and it will be found that the reality was far more terrible than anything which has been told in the "Golden Hills".' Ironically some years earlier, in 1850, in a letter to *The Examiner*, Anthony Trollope had refuted angrily the veracity of such reports in contemporary journals, declaring their accounts to be 'horrid novels'.[15] Nineteenth-century famine writings produce striking inversions of literary fiction and historical fact – where imaginative fictions are deemed more credible than 'the terrible realities of Truth'.

Nineteenth-century literature also includes a substantial amount of famine poetry, much of which was published contemporaneously with the 1840s Famine in periodicals such as *The Dublin University Magazine*, *The Nation*, and the short-lived journals *The Cork Magazine* (1847–8), *The Irishman* (1849–50) and *The United Irishman* (February–May 1848). As Chris Morash, editor of *The Hungry Voice*, an anthology of Irish famine poetry, notes: 'these contributors were by and large professionals from the middle class' – lawyers, doctors as well as journalists.[16] Nineteenth-century famine poetry varies from the fiery, apocalyptic visions of James Clarence Mangan, Jane Wilde and Richard D'Alton Williams, with their images of 'Revolution's red abyss' and the avenging 'Angel of the Trumpet', to more individualised, lyrical ballads such as Rosa Muholland's Wordsworthian 'A Lay of the Irish Famine' (1900). Poems such as 'The Famine Year' by Jane Wilde ('Speranza'), first published in *The Nation* on 23 January 1847 and later frequently anthologised, played an important role in nationalist famine historiography:

237

Weary men, what reap ye? – Golden corn for the stranger.
What sow ye? – Human corses that wait for the avenger.
Fainting forms, hunger-stricken, what see you in the offing?
Stately ships to bear our food away, amid the stranger's
   scoffing.

In many poetic treatments, famine is retold as part of the story of eviction, starvation and emigration, as in the famous 'Lament of the Irish Emigrant' ('I'm sitting on the stile, Mary') by Helena Dufferin (1807–1867), or Jane Wilde's 'The Exodus' (1864) :

'A million a decade!' Count ten by ten,
   Column and line of the record fair;
Each unit stands for ten thousand men,
   Staring with blank, dead eyeballs there;
      Strewn like blasted trees on the sod,
      Men that were made in the image of God ...

'A million a decade!' What does it mean?
   A Nation dying of inner decay –
A churchyard silence where life has been –
   The base of the pyramid crumbling away –
      A drift of men gone over the sea,
      A drift of the dead where men should be.

Motifs which recur in famine poetry include images of an infant at the 'clay-cold breast' of its mother (Matthew Ma-Grath's 'One of Many', 1849) or the mother's lament, often delivered at the grave of her child. 'The Dying Mother's Lament' by John Keegan (1809–1849) constitutes one of the most frequently-anthologised famine poems, appearing in Daniel Connolly's American-published *The Household Library of Ireland's Poets* with Wilde's 'The Voice of the Poor', Dufferin's 'The Irish Emigrant's Lament' and 'The Black Forty-six' by Alfred Perceval Graves.[17] The popular *Gill's Irish Reciter*, first published in 1907 and selling four thousand copies within little more than six months of publication, also reproduced Keegan's lament.[18] Frequently, within depictions of famine mothers, analogies are drawn with Mary, the mother of Christ, as in Keegan's lament, while other poems present horrific images of mothers, closer to Medea than the Madonna, as in the anonymous 'Thanatos, 1849':

The mother-love was warm and true; the Want was long withstood –
Strength failed at last; she gorged the flesh – the offspring of her blood.

As may be seen throughout famine representations, female images are chosen to represent famine's worst consequences, in characterisations ranging from heroic self-sacrifice to 'monstrous' perversions of 'Nature'.

One of the most striking of famine poets is James Clarence Mangan (1803–1849), of whom Richard D'Alton Williams, in his 'Lament for Clarence Mangan' (1849), wrote:

Thou wert a voice of God on earth – of those prophetic souls
Who hear the fearful thunder in the Future's womb that rolls.

Mangan's work had indeed a prophetic quality; his 'Warning Voice' published in *The Nation*, 21 February 1846, prophesied that 'A day is at hand/Of trial and trouble/And woe in the land!'

The chronology of famine was to prove tragically linked with Mangan's own life; his poem 'The Famine' appeared in *The Irishman* on 9 June 1849, eleven days before his death of malnutrition, during a cholera epidemic in Dublin.[19] This interweaving of Mangan's personal fate and that of the land in general becomes explicit in his poem 'Siberia' (1846) with its portrait of a landscape of 'blight and death':

And the exile there
Is one with those;
They are part, and he is part,
For the sands are in his heart,
And the killing snows.

Similarly, Mangan's poem 'The Funerals' (1849) creates a terrifying vision of 'endless Funerals' sweeping onward, over an 'Earth' which has become 'one groanful grave', a vision both surreal and mercilessly real, of overwhelming power:

It was as though my Life were gone
With what I saw!
Here were the FUNERALS of my thoughts as well!

239

> The Dead and I at last were One!
> An ecstasy of chilling awe
>   Mastered my spirit as a spell.

Mangan's work contains powerful tensions between his determination to represent the contemporary horrors and his fear of language's inadequacy; thus in 'A Voice of Encouragement – A New Year's Lay', published in *The Nation* on 1 January 1848, the poet exhorts himself to

> Follow your destiny up! Work! Write! Preach to arouse and
> Warn, and watch, and encourage! Dangers, no doubt, surround
>   you –
> But for Ten threatening you now, you will soon be appalled by
>   a Thousand
> If you forsake the course to which Virtue and Honour have
>   bound you!

Yet his poems also record Mangan's fear that the experience cannot be conveyed:

> But oh! No horror overdarks
> The stanzas of my gloomsome verse
>   Like that which then weighed down my soul!
>   ('The Funerals')

The 'Voice of Encouragement' concludes with the 'mission unspoken', recognising that the 'Impending Era' will enter 'the secret heart', silently:

> Cloaked in the Hall, the Envoy stands, his mission unspoken,
> While the pale, banquetless guests await in trembling to hear
>   it.

In 1910, in the preface to her novel, *The Hunger*, Mildred Darby ('Andrew Merry') noted that 'Few people of the present generation know more of the appalling catastrophe than its broad outlines, gathered from some attenuated volume of Irish History';[20] fictions such as Darby's were to play an important part in constructing and preserving a famine memory. Twentieth-century literary representations were to encounter further difficulties since famine was now a historical event no longer verifiable by personal testimony and also a

240

central and increasingly controversial event in the national chronology. As Paul Ricoeur has noted, 'As soon as a story is well known – and such is the case with most traditional and popular narratives as well as with the national chronicles of the founding events of a given community – retelling takes the place of telling.'[21] The 'Great Famine' has received a number of twentieth-century retellings, in fiction, poetry and drama, each situating it within the 'national chronicle' but in very different ways.

Liam O'Flaherty's novel, *Famine* is the most famous of Irish Famine stories; translated into French, Spanish, Portuguese, Dutch and German, it remains in print.[22] In one of the earliest reviews of the novel, Seán O'Faoláin declared: 'It is tremendous. It is biblical. It is the best Irish historical novel to date.'[23] First published in 1937, *Famine* emerged while the new state was still in the process of self-definition and as a particular version of the 'national chronicle', the Irish Constitution, was being written. The novel's powerful immediacy, from its detailed opening chapters to the quiet tragedy of Brian Kilmartin's death makes it, for this reader, the most successful Famine narrative; as the *Irish Book Lover* reviewer in 1937 noted: 'there are moments in it that have the heroic quality of sudden piercing lines in an old saga.'[24] Much of the novel's historical detail comes from Canon John O'Rourke's *The History of the Great Irish Famine of 1847 with Notices of Earlier Irish Famines*, first published in 1874; in terms of causation, O'Flaherty shares O'Rourke's interpretation that the famine demonstrated England's ability and unwillingness to 'save the lives of five million of her own subjects'.[25] The novel displays some difficulty in combining historical explanation with individualised characterisation; some of the historical comment is introduced quite awkwardly while the centre of investigation increasingly moves to the dilemmas and horrors experienced by female victims such as abandonment of children, prostitution and infanticide; thus a domestic sphere deflects political and socio-economic analysis.

Both the challenges faced by famine representations and O'Flaherty's particular successes may be seen in his memorable final chapter which tells of the death of Brian Kilmartin in quiet yet piercing detail:

> He clutched the handle of the spade, leaned forward, threat-
> ened the frosty earth with the point, and raised his foot. There
> was a deep, gurgling sound in his throat and he fell forward
> headlong. The spade skidded away over the frost and rolled
> into a hollow. The old man lay still with his arms stretched out.

In stark contrast to other characterisations of famine victims,
O'Flaherty presents a victim who has a name, a voice, a
family, a past, an individual identity. As a confrontation
between the individual and inexorable circumstance, Brian's
death is tragic; this tragedy, however, occurs as a force
associated more with Nature and the inevitable than the
politics of starvation. The novel's political comment is to be
found instead in the context of its other ending, Mary and
Martin's departure for America. In an image repeated
throughout nationalist historiography, sacks of grain are
taken abroad for transport to England as ships are loaded
with people bound for America. The reference to emigrants'
'cries of future vengeance' invokes events in Irish history
from the story's end in 1847 to the time of its publication in
1937 and underlines O'Flaherty's own myth-making activity.
The 1840s Famine proved part of the charter-myth of Irish-
America, a community which was and continues to be a significant part of O'Flaherty's audience. *Famine*'s first reviewers recognised its mythic aspect, suggesting that O'Flaherty
had 'in some sort fulfilled a destiny by writing this book', as
well as its function as history: 'it is not only a story but a
history told in terms of men and women'.[26]

References to the 1840s Famine recur within twentieth-
century Big House literature. Novelists such as Edith Somerville and Martin Ross and William Trevor depict famine as a
significant event in the family history of their characters with
implications for the identity of their wider political community. In these Ascendancy or Anglo-Irish chronicles, famine
is both a glorious and sorrowful event, a time in which representatives of the family, usually a woman, sacrificed their
lives in order to aid the starving Irish. In *The Big House of
Inver*, Somerville and Ross's novel, first published in 1925,

the famine relief performed by a female ancestor forms a central episode in the family genealogy; the woman's famine work is compared with the colonial service of her son in India and valued as 'fought against heavier odds than her son had to face':[27]

> In the end of the trouble, when the storm had to some extent died down and the shadow was lifting a little, she, who had come safe through the worst of the bad times, went down with the Famine-fever that still loitered on in 'backwards places'. A beggar-woman brought it in her rags to Inver, and Madam Prendeville died of it, with the tears wet on her cheeks for the son whom she would not see again.

Madam Prendeville's sacrifice possesses a clear political significance, proving that 'things were suffered by the people of all classes during the years of the Famine of 1845', including the owners of 'ancient properties' or Big Houses. These 'martyrdoms, heroisms' and 'devotion' have now passed into 'oblivion', a 'forgetting' which Somerville bitterly muses to be 'better so, perhaps' since 'it might only intensify the embittering of a now outcast class to be reminded of what things it suffered and sacrificed doing what it held to be its duty'. The context within which these famine events are recalled and retold is particularly significant; writing in 1925 in the knowledge that the descendants of the famine benefactor are 'now outcast' from the newly-created Irish state, Somerville tells the story of famine as a time of suffering and victimisation in which her class has shared.

A similar exchange in which the ancestor donates food and charity and receives famine fever is remembered in John Hewitt's poem 'The Scar' (1971); Hewitt views the consequences of her death with ambivalence:

> and that chance meeting, that brief confrontation
> conscribed me of the Irishry for ever.[28]

This cameo scene recurs within the fiction of William Trevor; in *Fools of Fortune* the death of a female ancestor because of her kindness to the starving poor parallels the fate of a later generation who, during the War of Independence, are deem-

243

ed 'outcast' and 'traitors' to their class.[29] Trevor's work displays increasing ambivalence towards the famine role of the Ascendancy: 'The News from Ireland' (1986) records the construction of a famine road 'leading nowhere, without a real purpose', and suggests that the relief project is both an absurd folly and vitally necessary in terms of the employment it provides for the famine poor.[30] In *Silence in the Garden* famine is only one episode in the chronology of a family who had come to Ireland in the middle of the seventeenth century 'with slaughter in their wake'.[31] Writing sixty years after Somerville and Ross, Trevor retells the story of famine and the acts of benevolence performed with a clearer knowledge that they form part of a dying, soon to be 'silent' chronicle.

Twentieth-century famine writing also produces its own reversals of fiction and history; if O'Flaherty's novel was deemed history, Cecil Woodham's Smith's historical treatment *The Great Hunger* was deemed by one historian to be 'a great novel'.[32] Woodham-Smith's history, however, proved to be an important impetus for an expansion in Irish famine literature in the 1960s, most famously Seamus Heaney's famine poems in *Death of a Naturalist* and Tom Murphy's play *Famine* (1968). Heaney's poem, 'At a Potato-Digging' begins with a contemporary rural scene in which the 'live skulls, blind-eyed' of the potatoes become the living skulls of famine victims 'balanced on/wild higgledy skeletons':

> Stinking potatoes fouled the land,
> pits turned pus into filthy mounds:
> and where potato-diggers are
> you still smell the running sore.[33]

The cultural memory of famine receives its most famous poetic treatment in the work of Patrick Kavanagh; in poems such as *The Great Hunger* and *Lough Derg*, the consequences of famine are still legible in the pysche and the landscape:

> The middle of the island looked like the memory
> Of some village evicted by the Famine,
> Some corner of a field beside a well
> Old stumps of walls where a stunted boortree is growing.[34]

Questions concerning famine and its significance for the present also underlie its most famous dramatic treatment, Tom Murphy's *Famine*.[35] Among his historical and literary influences, Murphy cites Woodham-Smith's *The Great Hunger* and Carleton's writings, as well as accounts of other famines, including contemporary scenes of starvation. In an introduction to his plays, he writes: 'there are three broad approaches from which one can look at *Famine* and its genesis': historical, autobiographical and thirdly, dramatic; 'It has, as a play, a life of its own and, tired of history, tired of me, it continues its own process and discovery to its own conclusions'.[36] First produced in the Peacock Theatre by Tomás MacAnna in 1968, *Famine* has received a number of productions, one of the most recent being Garry Hynes' anniversary production in the Abbey Theatre, in October 1993.

Murphy's *Famine* has much potential dramatic power though aspects of the play, in particular its multiplicity of scenes, pose severe challenges to productions. The central opposition of the drama rests on the differing definitions of 'right' offered by John Connor and 'the mother', John's wife. While John becomes obsessed with political meetings and definitions, his wife is disturbingly pragmatic, suggesting the construction of coffins to earn money, favouring emigration, willing to renounce her religion for food, stealing turf from others to preserve her family. She dismisses his claim that 'It's only by right that we can hope at all', with the powerful questions 'What's right? What's right in a country when the land goes sour? Where is a woman with children when nature lets her down?' Yet the mother's words, with all their dramatic force, reinforce equations of famine and natural disaster; while the characterisation of the mother as apolitical, or perhaps, more correctly, anti-political, affirms women's separation from the political sphere. Famine emerges as an enclosed event, definable only within the realm of women, children and 'nature', in which the victims prey on one another to survive. The mother, addressing John, acknowledges that she can only 'withhold' herself by attacking his strength while John 'protects himself' and his family's 'right' by killing their mother. The survival of the community here, as in many other famine texts, requires a sacrificial death, that of the mother; a problematic dimension of Murphy's play is the suggestion that this is also her moment of freedom, the protection of her 'right'.

Famine has continued to provide material for popular historical novels such as Walter Macken's *The Silent People* (1962), Elizabeth Byrd's *The Famished Land* (1972) and Michael Mullen's *The Hungry Land* (1986). John Banville's 1973 novel *Birchwood* contains some intriguing references to famine in a metafictional narrative which comments on the very act of representing famine.[37] *Birchwood* exploits many of the conventions of the Big House novel, its chief character Gabriel is the surviving member of a Protestant landed family. Most obviously, it parodies the usual linear progression of novels; while much of the novel suggests a setting in the late nineteenth to early twentieth century, anachronistic elements, mainly concerning the 1840s famine, disrupt the chronology. Famine enters the novel through the use of recognisable motifs: people eating grass, children 'gobbling fistfuls of clay', even cannibalism; a reality worse than any invented story, with an 'eerie malevolent silence'. Underlying the narrative is the fear expressed by George Steiner and others that some secrets should and must remain silent: 'Anyway some secrets are not to be disclosed under pain of who knows what retribution, and whereof I cannot speak, thereof I must be silent.' Banville further explores the strategies deployed in order to evade such silence:

> I hardly dare to voice the notion which, if it did not come to me then comes to me now, the insane notion that perhaps it was on her, on Sybil, our bright bitch, that the sorrow of the country, of those baffled people in the rotting fields, of the stricken eyes staring out of hovels, was visited against her will and even without her knowledge, so that tears might be shed and the inexpressible expressed. Does that seem a ridiculous suggestion?

Hardly, as Banville highlights what is prevalent in famine literature – the characterisation of the sorrows and horrors of famines through female forms – and, more rarely, acknowledges their function: 'so that tears might be shed and the inexpressible expressed'. Why female images predominate in famine representations is a significant question, one which requires further exploration; undoubtedly, recent literature continues to provide striking examples. In Eavan Boland's 'The Making of an Irish Goddess' (1990), the woman's body bears the traces of earlier 'wounds': in her

> must be
>
> an accurate inscription
> of that agony:
>
> the failed harvests,
> the fields rotting to the horizon,
>
> the children devoured by their mothers
> whose souls, they would have said,
> went straight to hell,
> followed by their own.[38]

From the middle of the nineteenth century, the story of famine has found various literary forms and remains part of our literary and historical imagination. If the literary map of famine is marked by gaps and absences, and the feared impossibility of representation, it also retains the power to 'make present'. Famine roads will not be found in the 'map of the island':

> the line which says woodland and cries hunger
> and gives out among sweet pine and cypress,
> and finds no horizon
>
> will not be there.[39]

Yet their 'lines' are retraced, memorably, in Boland's own.

THE GREAT FAMINE AND TODAY'S FAMINES

CORMAC Ó GRÁDA

MANY IRISH PEOPLE TODAY, FROM President Mary Robinson down, are given to drawing analogies between the horrors endured by Irish Famine victims in the 1840s and the plight of the Third World poor in our own times. And, indeed, it is tempting to see a link between the generosity of ordinary Irish people towards the victims of disasters such as Biafra in the early 1970s, Ethiopia in the 1970s and 1980s, or Somalia in the 1990s, and Ireland's own sad past. This generosity must be set in perspective, however. The numbers suggest that we Irish really have little to crow about when it comes to overseas development aid. Ireland comes close to being bottom in western Europe in terms of such aid as a percentage of GNP (though it must also be said that the percentage these days is rising, against a general European trend). What is distinctive about Irish overseas aid is the high share of non-governmental agencies, and the generous and spontaneous response of the public to Third World disasters. Nor, despite the seemingly endless run of demands, is that generosity showing signs of slackening; so far Irish people have contributed several million pounds to relief in Rwanda in again mainly through non-governmental agencies.

Are we in some sense repaying the generosity of those who were good to Ireland in the 1840s – Irish expatriates, the Society of Friends, and the Catholic Church worldwide? Or are we somehow exorcising our own past, vicariously making amends for those who died for the lack of help at home long ago? The link is not lost on the creators of the fine new Famine Museum at Strokestown, County Roscommon, one section of which is devoted to the problem of malnutrition and famine in the Third World. President Robinson reminded the large crowd invited to the opening of the Strokestown museum last May that 'the past gave Ireland a moral viewpoint and an historically informed compassion on some of the events happening now'.

However, if we consider this historically, the link between the 1840s and today is not obvious or unbroken. The record suggests that the Irish Famine was relegated to being a slogan and a taboo for generations. It is curious that a tragedy which is so much in the news today was hardly commemorated at all in the 1940s, surely a far more appropriate anniversary than the 1990s. Indeed it might be argued that the more we have distanced ourselves from our own past and the more we have forgotten what really happened in the 1840s, the more generous we have become in the face of Third World disasters.

A more plausible historical link between history and Third World giving may be the Irish tradition of missionary activity far afield, particularly in sub-Saharan Africa. Such activity grew in tandem with the growing self-confidence of the Irish Church in the last century, particularly after the Famine. Ordinary Irish people have long respected missionaries and supported the missions, be it through buying *The Far East* and *The Word* or contributing to those collection boxes you see in retail outlets everywhere. Famine giving is arguably more in that tradition.[1] Historians have largely neglected Irish missionary endeavour, but for a century or more most Irish people (Catholic or Protestant) have had a close blood relation or a neighbour who ended up as a missionary in Africa or Asia. And to be honest, are not some of those ubiquitous billboard stereotypes of Third World children, smiling or crying, really the 'black babies' of old in another guise?

I believe that if the sufferings of half-forgotten, wretched Irish Famine victims can inspire greater concern for the Third World today, then they may not have died entirely in vain. Yet history never quite repeats itself, and the contexts of Ireland's Famine and those modern African famines that I have mentioned are quite different. Superficially, of course, all famines are alike; contemporary accounts of *les années de misère* at the end of Louis XIV's reign[2] and of Ireland's Great Hunger might well, *mutatis mutandis*, describe the horrors of Biafra or Ethiopia. But the differences are worth reflecting on.

First of all, today's famines, proportionately at least, are less murderous than the Great Famine. About a million people died directly as a result of the potato failures in the 1840s. By comparison, the official death toll in Bangladesh in 1974 was twenty-six thousand out of a population of over sixty million. Even if the real cost in lives was considerably greater, the point of the comparison still stands. Another well-known famine of the 1970s, the Sahel Famine of 1973, killed perhaps one hundred thousand people in an area inhabited by twenty-five million. Again, in Ethiopia in 1972–4 about two hundred thousand are held to have died out of a population of twenty-seven million. It is true that Stalin's Ukraine Famine of the 1930s, the Great Bengali Famine of the 1940s, and the Chinese Great Leap Forward Famine of the late 1950s killed far more people, but the reference populations were also proportionately greater.[3] Ireland's Famine, then, was a 'great' Famine.

Secondly, unlike Biafra in the 1970s or Somalia and the Sudan in the 1990s, Ireland faced no civil war or major unrest in the 1840s. Indeed some contemporary observers spoke of a delusive calm in Ireland on the eve of the Famine. Faction-fighting and rural strife, so common in the 1820s and 1830s, had been quelled by an alliance of police and priests. Ordinary crime was also in decline. So disrupted communications and military distractions were not a factor in Ireland during the Famine. The roads were quite good, and bad weather in the guise of flooding or frost was no excuse for not getting relief to the people. Since the 1840s, improvements in transport, particularly the railway, have lessened the impact of local harvest failures in many parts of the world, notably in India. Yet even today, poor communications are also seen as exacerbating famine, giving rise to market fragmentation, as, for example, in Bangladesh and in Wollo in the 1970s.[4]

250

A third difference is that in today's famine-stricken areas, neighbouring regions or countries tend to be nearly as poor as the region directly affected. We need think only of famine-afflicted Ethiopia or southern Sudan. But one of the remarkable things about the Irish Famine of the 1840s is its geographical setting: it occurred in the back-yard of that prosperous region which Prince Albert would soon dub 'the workshop of the world'. This is not to overlook the harsh conditions faced by the British poor at the time.

Nor, fourthly, is the philosophical context the same to-day as in the 1840s. This is an important point. During the Irish Famine, the first editor of *The Economist*, James Wilson, answered Irish pleas for public assistance with the claim that 'it is no man's business to provide for another'. He asserted that official intervention would shift resources from the more to the less deserving, since 'if left to the natural law of distribution, those who deserved more would obtain it'. Wilson may have agonised in private about the inevitability of deaths in Ireland, but what really mattered is that in print the tone of *The Economist* was dogmatic and pitiless. In the same vein, economist Nassau William Senior calmly defend-ed policies that were reducing the Irish to starvation, re-marking that they would provide 'illustrations valuable to a political economist'. Irish novelist Maria Edgeworth, by then an old woman, rightly accused people like Senior and Wil-son of having 'a heart of iron – a nature from which the natural instinct of sympathy or pity have been destroyed'. They were not alone. Even the most Thatcherite of European politicians today would be deemed 'wet' if compared to some of those with power and influence in Westminster dur-ing the Famine. There is some truth, then, in John Mitchel's claim that in the 1840s 'Ireland died of political economy'.[5]

Still, it is important not to make nationalist hay out of this. Some of those who peddled this kind of ideology may also have heartily despised the Irish poor, and may have been religious bigots. But in the Netherlands in the 1840s, many died too, and the attitude of government officials to-wards the starving poor was just as mean and doctrinaire as Chancellor Charles Wood's or under-secretary Charles Trevelyan's. There it was a case of Dutchman against Dutch-man.[6] Thus attitudes sometimes described as 'racist' were really as much about class as race. Nor should our rejection of dogmatism in the matter of relief blind us to the dangers of dependence on hand-outs outlasting the crisis itself – as, it is sometimes argued, happened in rural Ireland after the Famine.

While the attitude to relief is less harsh today, ideology can still exacerbate crises or the risk of crises. For example, the structural adjustment package imposed on Somalia in the 1980s by the World Bank and the International Monetary Fund is held to have destabilised that country and weakened its resistance to crisis. Similarly, the insistence that Zimbabwe's grain marketing board balance its budget each year prompted the board to sell off its surplus in 1991, even though a food crisis threatened in 1992, a crisis averted only by record food imports. But if ideology can exacerbate famines, how can bureaucracy relieve them? History suggests that 'good' government can help avert famines. This seems to have happened in Kenya in 1984, when the timely importation of yellow maize, which was promptly disposed of, averted a potential disaster. The maize, or 'yellow male' (echoes of Ireland), was sold mostly through ordinary market channels. The same has happened in Botswana. Again in Bangladesh, following the famine of 1974, rapid intervention and food rationing by the government averted a repeat in 1979 and 1984. The ambitious public works programme set up in Maharashtra in India in the early 1970s is another well-known case in point. Now, in these instances, the institutional infrastructure was there to begin with. The same could not be said of Ethiopia in the 1970s or the Sudan in the 1980s.[7] However, in this respect Ireland in the 1840s was at no disadvantage. The mandarins of Whitehall and Dublin Castle and their representatives were less corrupt and more sophisticated than most Third World bureaucracies today. In Ireland police monitoring and newspaper accounts of the second harvest failure in the summer of 1846 offered an 'early warning system' of looming disaster. The bureaucratic delays so often a feature of African administrations were hardly a constraint in the Irish context. In Ireland the problem was less institutional than ideological.

It is often said of modern famines that they are less the product of food shortages or poor harvests *per se* than a lack of purchasing power. In particular, Harvard economist Amartya Sen has pointed to famines in his native Bengal in the 1940s and in Ethiopia in the 1970s as products of a reduction in what he terms the 'entitlements' of the landless. Sen instances the Bengal Famine as a 'boom' famine, brought on by war-time inflation and precautionary and speculative hoarding of foodstuffs. In Ethiopia in 1973, he argues, 'famine took place with no abnormal reduction in food output, and consumption of food per head at the height of the famine was fairly normal for Ethiopia as a whole'.[8] Such claims have not gone uncontested,[9] but they have some resonance for Ireland in the 1840s also. One of the most evocative images of the Irish Famine is of a people being left to starve while their corn was being shipped off under police and military protection to pay rents. Poverty in the midst of plenty, crudely put.

The Famine replicated and magnified graphically the hardships and exploitations at the heart of Irish society. However, this enduring, populist image of the Famine as starvation when there was enough food to go around oversimplifies. It ignores the sheer gravity of the potato failure, which produced a shortfall of one-third or so in calorie production three years in a row.[10] Dwelling on the exported grain ignores the reality that during the Famine grain exports were dwarfed by imports of cheaper grain, mainly maize. Moreover, the exported corn belonged not to the landless or near-landless masses, but Ireland's half a million farmers. Those farmers did not escape the crisis unscathed, but few of them perished; and they certainly would not have welcomed the lower prices that an export embargo would have brought in its train. Though generations of neglect and injustice may have produced conditions more likely to lead to Famine, this is not to deny that it was also a classic case of food shortage.

Mass emigration is another legacy of the Great Famine,

and one that also distinguishes it from modern Third World famines. All famines induce people to move in search of food and in order to escape disease; there is much movement from rural areas into the towns. But a distinction must be made between local movements from more to less afflicted areas and permanent long-distance migration. For many of the Irish poor in the 1840s, unlike the Somali or Sudanese poor today, emigration provided a welcome safety-valve. Estimates of Irish Famine-induced emigration can be only approximate for two reasons. First, the outflow was imperfectly enumerated at the time. Second, a significant share of the actual movement would have occurred in any case. Emigration during the early 1840s had been 50,000–100,000 a year. But Famine emigrants surely numbered half or more of those who emigrated between the mid-1840s and the early 1850s. The Famine emigration was different to what had gone on before; probably the poorest of the poor died, lacking the funds and the knowledge to emigrate, while many of those who could scrape together the funds, or who were compensated for giving up their smallholdings, left.[11]

Much has been written about the terrible conditions endured by these 'economic refugees' and the high mortality on 'coffin-ships'; indeed, half of those participating in a landlord-funded emigration scheme from the Strokestown estate, which surrounded the present museum, died in transit to the New World.[12] That was not the norm, however. Now, ignorance nearly always leads to exploitation, and it is hardly surprising that some desperate emigrants in Queenstown, Liverpool and elsewhere were cheated out of the little they had. But the fundamental comparative point to make here is that surely many of today's famine-stricken poor would give up every penny they have in return for manual jobs and poor accommodation in North America, Japan, or western Europe. The journey may have taken longer than it would today, but most of Ireland's 'boat people' eventually reached their destinations in North America or in Britain.

Perhaps it is because emigration was so important during and immediately after the Famine that Irish nationalists have had an ambiguous attitude towards emigration ever since. Yet reflecting on the alternative offered by Third World experience tells us that the Irish were 'lucky' to emigrate, and that many more would have died had this safety-valve not existed.

Another important feature of the Irish Famine, which of course makes it difficult to fit into any neat commemorative schedule, is that it was a very long-drawn out affair. Beginning in the summer of 1846 with the second and near-total failure of the potato crop, in Whitehall Lord John Russell's Whig administration declared it over in summer 1847. Responsibility for relieving those affected was then turned over to Ireland. But this was rather like adopting the strategy of Senator George Aiken of Vermont, who, on becoming fed up with the Vietnam War, is supposed to have exclaimed, 'let us declare victory, and get the hell out of there!', or words to that effect. The notion, it must be said, still has some resonance today. A recurring critique of the international aid community, to quote Trócaire emergency officer Niall Tobin, is that it 'goes in with emergency relief, declares early victory and leaves'.

The crisis sparked off in Ireland by the potato blight did not end in summer of 1847. Famine conditions lasted for a long time after, particularly in western counties such as Clare and Mayo. At the level of macro-economic indicators such as bank note circulation or company profits, the recovery took a long time to occur. The number of inmates in Ireland's bleak workhouses, a more immediate proxy for deprivation, remained high long after 1847. In 1852 they still numbered 166,821 or 2.6 per cent of the population; the total dropped to 129,401 in 1853 and 95,190 in 1854, and then fell off more gradually to 40,380 in 1859.

Because there was a population census in 1851, Irish historians are inclined to deal with the Famine as a five year block (1846–51). The ploy has its historical validity too. There is plenty of evidence, both statistical and narrative, for excess mortality in 1849 and 1850, and some would go so far as extend the Famine into the 1850s. The Great Famine therefore had more in common with the Pharaoh's seven lean years than the better-known famines of the 1980s and 1990s. Perhaps this meant that what is called today 'famine fatigue' was more of a problem in Ireland's case. This is implicit in the well-known efforts of the Society of Friends, who threw in the towel quite early on, exasperated at the unfeeling attitude of officialdom, and refusing to heed government proddings to do more. It is also seen in the more modest efforts of local charities such as the Society of Sick and Indigent Room keepers in Dublin.

By contrast, the Finnish Famine of the 1860s, another major catastrophe, lasted just one awful year. The latest verdict on the better-known Ukrainian famine of 1932–3, based on newly-available data, suggests that it too lasted a year at most. However, the Great Bengali Famine of the 1940s approximates the Irish experience in this respect. There excess mortality also continued high for several years, the product of famine-induced epidemics such as dysentery, cholera, and diarrhoea; indeed, though standard accounts today refer to the Bengal famine of 1943, substantially more than half the excess deaths occurred after 1943.[13]

Ireland's catastrophe was the product of three factors: a backward economy, bad luck, and the ideology briefly mentioned above. Those countless lazy beds that people carved out of wet, stony hillsides are a reminder that backwardness was compounded by land hunger. This raises the question, how poor was Ireland in the 1840s compared with, say, Ethiopia or Somalia today? Only the crudest answer is possible. However, we know that in the 1840s average income in Ireland was about two-fifths that of Great Britain, and that incomes in Britain have increased eight or tenfold in the meantime. Today, moreover, average incomes in Ethiopia are about three per cent of Great Britain's, and in Somalia about seven per cent. Taken together, these numbers indicate that Irish living standards on the eve of the Great Famine lay somewhere between Ethiopia's and Somalia's today.

As for bad luck, traditional accounts explained the Famine as the inevitable product of over-population. However, the best recent analysis of the failure of the potato crop in 1845 deems it an ecological fluke, something (as Peter Solar has put it) 'far out of the range of actual or likely European

256

experience'.[14] The Irish poor themselves, deeply religious and bewildered by what had hit them, were sometimes inclined to see the failure as God's revenge for earlier improvidence. In folk memory potatoes were particularly bountiful on the eve of the Famine, and in north Wexford, for example, 'people thought the blight was a visitation from God because of the careless way they treated the potatoes'. In the words of an East Cork song, *'ba mhaith é an práta, dob fhial is dob fhair-sing é, chun é roinnt ar bhochtaibh Dé'*. Yet those potatoes could not have been stored from one year to another in any case. It would be the stern historian indeed who would impose on an impoverished and largely illiterate people the degree of foresight needed to allow for three years of shortfall in succession.

I mentioned amnesia a few moments ago. Half a century ago, useful second-hand reminiscences of the Famine might still be had from old people throughout Ireland, particularly from Irish speakers in the worst-affected areas in the south and west. Unfortunately, not enough people, least of all historians, wanted to listen and record. Local memories are now much vaguer, and physical evidence of the Famine's ravages is scarce. The resulting amnesia has rid the Irish psyche of what was most troubling and traumatic about the 1840s: neighbours and relations being buried hurriedly and without ceremony, clearances and house-burnings, thieving on a massive scale, and strife about the scant food supply.[15] Modern reports of corruption and cruelty in famine areas in the Third World remind us of what it must have been like in Ireland. Unless these horrors of the 1840s are given their due, a more tourism-friendly, heroic, and sanitised version of that ugly chapter in Irish history is on the cards.

Finally, if the Irish attitudes to Third World famines are to be informed by our own Famine, what can the Third World tell us about the Great Famine? One message, per-haps, is that though aid can achieve much, how difficult it would have been to avoid all mortality in the 1840s. Yet the efficacy of the timely purchase and distribution of cheap food by the authorities is also a reminder that more could have been done along these lines for Ireland in late 1846 and early 1847 by buying up and re-distributing domestic stocks, before large quantities of grain could be obtained from abroad and processed for consumption. Another message is the amount of anti-social and often vicious behaviour which hardship provokes. Given the scenes of thieving and looting in Somalia and Rwanda depicted in the media, stories of robbers, cattle rustlers, and high death rates in bulging prisons in Ireland in the 1840s are hardly surprising. Finally, today's famines are a reminder of the pain endured by our own Irish poor in the 1840s, a pain sometimes downplayed in, or left out of, historical accounts.

I wish to thank Andy Storey (Trócaire), and Frank Barry and Brendan Walsh (University College, Dublin) for their helpful comments and suggestions on an earlier draft.

NOTES

THE OTHER GREAT IRISH FAMINE

1 The inscription on the Killiney obelisk can still be deciphered: 'Last year being hard with the poor, the wall around these hills and this was erected by John Mapas Esq. June 1742': F. E. Ball, *A History of County Dublin* (Dublin, 1902), I, pp. 53–7; cf. Desmond Guinness and the Knight of Glin, 'The Conolly Folly', in *Quarterly Bulletin of the Irish Georgian Society*, VI, 4 (October–December 1963), p. 63.

2 This estimate represents a reworking of the list of famines in L. A. Clarkson, 'Conclusion: Famine and Irish history', in E. M. Crawford, ed. *Famine: The Irish experience* (Edinburgh, 1989), pp. 220–26.

3 Sir William Petty, *Tracts; Chiefly Relating to Ireland* (Dublin, 1769), pp. 312–4. Note that there are internal inconsistencies in Petty's back-of-the envelope calculations. This plague pandemic, which seems to have been imported from Spain, killed around a million people in the western Mediterranean: R. A. Stradling, *The Spanish monarchy and Irish mercenaries 1618–68*, (Dublin, 1994), p. 78.

4 *The census of Ireland for ... 1851*, part V, Tables of death, I (British Parliamentary Papers, 1856, XXIX), pp. 108–110; James Hardiman, *The History of the Town ... of Galway ...* (Galway, 1926), p. 139; T. W. Moody et al., eds, *A New History of Ireland: III, 534–1691* (Oxford, 1976), p. 389; Raymond Gillespie, *The Transformation of the Irish Economy 1550–1700* (Dundalk, 1991), p. 16; Stradling, *Spanish monarchy*, p. 78.

5 David Dickson, *New foundations: Ireland 1660–1800* (Dublin, 1987), p. 40; James Kelly, 'Harvests and hardship: Famine and scarcity in Ireland in the late 1720s', in *Studia Hibernica*, XXVI (1991–2), p. 66.

6 K. H. Connell, *The population of Ireland 1750–1845* (Oxford, 1950), pp. 223–4; David Dickson, Cormac Ó Gráda & Stuart Daultrey, 'Hearth tax, household size and Irish population change 1672–1821', in *Proceedings of the Royal Irish Academy* LXXXII, C (1982), p. 164; Kelly, 'Harvests and hardship', pp. 65–105.

7 Dickson, et al., 'Hearth tax', pp. 156–64; Dickson, *New foundations*, p. 96.

8 Kelly, 'Harvests and hardship', p. 87.

9 Dickson, et al., 'Hearth tax', p. 164; Dickson, 'In search of the old Irish poor law', in Rosalind Mitchison and Peter Roebuck, eds, *Economy and Society in Scotland and Ireland 1500–1939* (Edinburgh, 1988), p. 153; Kelly, 'Harvests and hardship', pp. 73, 78, 82–3, 87, 92–3.

10 Translation by Nessa Doran in Robert McKay, *An Anthology of the Potato* (Dublin, 1961), p. 45.

11 Michael Drake, 'The Irish demographic crisis of 1740–41', in T. W. Moody, ed., *Historical Studies* VI (Dublin, 1968), pp. 101–24; John D. Post, *Food Shortage, Climatic Variability, and Epidemic Disease in Pre-Industrial Europe: The Mortality Peak in the Early 1740s* (Ithaca and London, 1985), *passim*.

12 Drake, 'Demographic crisis', pp. 116–7, 121.

13 *Ibid.*, pp. 121–2; Dickson, et al., 'Hearth tax', pp. 165–8; Post, *Food Shortage*, pp. 37–8, 96–7, 174–8, 264–6.

14 If the distinctly north-western harvest failure of 1744–45 is included in the comparison, then the duration of the two crises is comparable. But only a few counties, such as Roscommon and Sligo, seem to have been drastically

affected in both 1740–41 and 1744–45: Dickson, *et al.*, 'Hearth tax', pp. 168–9.
15 Dickson, 'An economic history of the Cork region in the eighteenth century' (unpublished Ph. D. thesis, University of Dublin, 1977), pp. 630–4.
16 *Ibid.*, p. 632; Post, *Food Shortage*, pp. 177, 185, 244.
17 Dickson, 'Poor law', pp. 151–9.
18 Drake, 'Demographic crisis', pp. 113, 116.
19 Dickson, 'Poor law', p. 155. The precedent for organised voluntary action in Dublin was 1729; in May of that year over 3,600 people were relieved, not it seems by food but by cash doles: Kelly, 'Harvests and hardship', pp. 90–1.
20 Timothy P. O'Neill, 'The state, poverty and distress in Ireland 1815–45' (unpublished Ph. D. thesis, National University of Ireland (University College, Dublin) 1971), especially pp. 82–8; Dickson, 'Poor law', pp. 155–7. On the harvest crises between 1750 and 1820 see Dickson, 'The gap in famines: A useful myth?', in Crawford, *Famine*, pp. 96–111; Ó Gráda, *Ireland: A New Economic History 1780–1939* (Oxford, 1994), pp. 4–5,12, 73.
21 Post, *Food Shortage*, chapter 7.
22 *The Census of Ireland for ... 1851*, part V, Tables of death, I (British Parliamentary Papers, 1856, XXIX), p. 128.

FOOD AND FAMINE
1 *Illustrated London News*, vol. 9, 1846, p. 134.
2 *Sixth Annual Report of the Poor Law Commissioners*, British Parliamentary Papers, 1840 (245) XVII, Appendix (D).
3 *Twelfth Annual Report of the Poor Law Commissioners*, British Parliamentary Papers, 1846 [745] XIX, Appendix A, No. 17, p. 91.
4 Minute Book of the South Dublin Union, 1845.
5 See P. Solar, 'The Great Famine was No Ordinary Subsistence Crisis', in E. Margaret Crawford [ed.], *Famine: the Irish Experience 900–1900* (Edinburgh, 1989), p. 114.
6 C. Woodham-Smith, *The Great Hunger* (London, 1962), p. 50.
7 G.V. Sampson, *Statistical Survey of the County of Londonderry* (Dublin, 1802), p. 316.
8 W. J. Green, *A Concise History of Lisburn and Neighbourhood* (Belfast, 1906), p. 23.
9 S. J. McGrath, ed., *The Diary of Humphrey O'Sullivan*, vol. 1 (London, 1936), p. 79.
10 Woodham-Smith, *The Great Hunger*, p. 73.
11 William Wilde, 'The Food of the Irish', *Dublin University Magazine*, xliii (1854), p. 138.
12 *Correspondence relating to the Measures adopted by Her Majesty's Government for the relief of Distress arising from the Failure of the Potato Crop in Ireland*, British Parliamentary Papers, 1846 [735] XXXVII, p. 89.
13 Woodham-Smith, *The Great Hunger*, p. 73.
14 P. Solar, 'The Great Famine was No Ordinary Subsistence Crisis', p. 125-6.
15 William Edward Forster from Galway on 25 January 1847, report in *Transactions of the Central Relief Committee of the Society of Friends during the Famine in Ireland 1846 and 1847* (Dublin, 1852), Appendix III, p. 158.
16 *Ibid.*, p. 167.
17 *Correspondence relating to the Measures Adopted for the Relief of the Distress in Ireland*, Commissariat Series, British Parliamentary Papers, [761] 1847, p. 26.

18 *Census of Ireland for the year 1851*, Part V, Tables of Deaths, vol. I, British Parliamentary Papers, 1856 [2087–I], XXIX, p. 283.

19 See John O'Rourke, *The Great Irish Famine*, abridged version (Dublin, 1989), p. 194. Original version first published in 1874.

20 R. J. McHugh, 'The Famine in Irish Oral Tradition', in R. D. Edwards and T. D. Williams, [eds], *The Great Famine* (Dublin, 1956), pp. 389–9.

21 A. T. Lucas, 'Nettles and Charlock as Famine Food', *Breifne*, vol. 1, No. 2 (1959), p. 139.

22 S. Godolphin Osborne, *Gleanings in the West of Ireland* (London, 1850), p. 34.

23 *Transactions of the Central Relief Committee of the Society of Friends during the Famine in Ireland 1846 and 1847*, p. 359.

24 *Illustrated London News*, vol. 10 (1847), p. 44.

25 *Transactions of the Central Relief Committee of the Society of Friends during the Famine in Ireland 1846 and 1847*, pp. 53–4.

26 Cited in Woodham-Smith, *The Great Hunger*, p. 178.

27 *Correspondence Relating to the Measures Adopted for the Relief of Distress in Ireland* (Commissariat Series), First Part, British Parliamentary Papers, 1847 [761] LI p. 437.

28 See John O'Rourke, *The Great Irish Famine*, p. 218. Also in Woodham-Smith, *The Great Hunger*, p. 294.

29 *Correspondence Relating to the Measures Adopted for the Relief of Distress in Ireland* (Commissariat Series), First Part, British Parliamentary Papers, 1847 [761] LI, p. 480.

30 *Ibid.*, pp 482–90.

31 *Papers relating to Proceedings for the Relief of the Distress and State of Unions and Workhouses in Ireland*, Sixth Series, British Parliamentary Papers, 1847–8 [955] LVI, p. 59.

32 Woodham-Smith, *The Great Hunger*, p. 178.

33 Woodham-Smith, *The Great Hunger*, p. 178.

34 C. Kinealy, *This Great Calamity: The Irish Famine 1845–52* (Dublin, 1994), p. 121.

35 John O'Rourke, *The Great Irish Famine*, p. 222.

36 *The Times*, 8 February 1847.

37 John O'Rourke, *The Great Irish Famine*, p. 222.

38 W. R. Aykroyd, 'Definition of Different Degrees of Starvation', in G. Blix [ed.] *Famine: A symposium dealing with Nutrition and Relief Operations in Times of Disaster*, Symposia of the Swedish Nutrition Foundation, 9, (1971), p. 18. See also E. Margaret Crawford, 'Subsistence Crises and Famines in Ireland: A Nutritionist's View', in E. Margaret Crawford, [ed.], *Famine: The Irish Experience* (Edinburgh, 1989), p. 200.

39 Minute Book of the Antrim Poor Law Union 1845, Public Records Office, Northern Ireland, BG1/A/1.

40 *Returns from the Several County Gaols and Workhouses in Ireland, of the Daily Diet allowed to an Able-bodied Man*, British Parliamentary Papers, 1847–8 (486) LIII.

41 *Correspondence relating to the state of Union Workhouses in Ireland*, First Series, British Parliamentary Papers, 1847 (766) LV, p. 51.

42 *Correspondence relating to the state of Union Workhouses in Ireland*, Third Series, British Parliamentary Papers 1847 (863) LV (Irish University Press edition), p. 211.

43 *Report of the Committee appointed to inquire into the Dietaries of County and*

Borough Gaols in Ireland, British Parliamentary Papers, 1867–8 [3981] XXXV, p. 13.

44 *Returns from the Several County Gaols and Workhouses in Ireland, of the Daily Diet allowed to an Able-bodied Man*, British Parliamentary Papers, 1847–8 (486) LIII.

45 J. D. O'Brien, 'Symptoms produced by eating Diseased Potatoes', *Dublin Hospital Gazette*, 15 January, 1846), p. 166.

46 M. J. McCormick, 'A Case of Land Scurvy produced by eating Diseased Potatoes', *Dublin Hospital Gazette*, 15 April, 1846), p. 263.

47 J. O. Curran, 'On Scurvy', *Dublin Quarterly Journal of Medical Science*, vol. 4 (1847), p. 100.

48 *Third Annual Report of the Commissioners for Administering of the Laws for Relief of the Poor in Ireland*, British Parliamentary Papers, 1850 [1243] XXVII.

49 For a more detailed analysis of the disease see E. Margaret Crawford, 'Scurvy in Ireland during the Great Famine', *The Journal of the Society for the Social History of Medicine*, vol. 1, No. 3 (1988), pp. 281–300.

50 'Dearth, Diet and Disease in Ireland 1850: A Case Study of Nutritional Deficiency', *Medical History*, vol. 28, No. 2 (1984), pp. 151–161.

51 *The Census of Ireland for the Year 1851*, Table of Deaths, vol. I, British Parliamentary Papers, 1856 [2087–I] IXXIX, p. 439.

52 *Fourth Annual Report of the Commissioners for Administering the Laws for Relief of the Poor in Ireland* 1851, pp. 130–151; *Fifth Annual Report of the Commissioners for Administering the Laws for Relief of the Poor in Ireland* 1852, p. 14; W. R. Wilde, *Observations on the Epidemic Ophthalmia which had prevailed in the Workhouses and Schools of the Tipperary and Athlone Unions* (Dublin, 1851).

53 *Fourth Annual Report of the Commissioners for Administering the Laws for Relief of the Poor in Ireland*, p. 137.

54 *Ibid*.

55 *Ibid.*, p. 145.

56 See E. Margaret Crawford, 'Dearth, Diet, and Disease in Ireland 1850: A Case Study of Nutritional Deficiency', *Medical History*, 28 (1984), p. 159.

57 *Recommended Daily Amounts of Food Energy and Nutrients for Groups of People in the United Kingdom*, Report on Health and Social Subjects No. 15. Department of Health and Social Security (London, 1979).

58 *Ibid*.

59 *Fourth Annual Report of the Commissioners for Administering the Laws for Relief of the Poor in Ireland*, p. 145.

FAMINE, FEVER AND THE BLOODY FLUX

1 *The census of Ireland for the year 1851*, Part V, Tables of deaths, vol. 1, British Parliamentary Papers, 1856 [2087–1], xxix, p. 246.

2 *Poor inquiry (Ireland). First Report from his Majesty's Commissioners for Inquiring into the Condition of the Poorer Classes in Ireland, with Appendix (A) and supplement*, British Parliamentary Papers, 1835 (369) xxxii, appendix (A), p. 322.

3 D. J. Corrigan, *On Famine and Fever as Cause and Effect in Ireland; with Observations on Hospital Location, and the dispensation in Outdoor Relief of Food and Medicine* (Dublin: J. Fannin, 1846), p. 4.

4 Henry Kennedy, *Observations on the Connexion between Famine and Fever in Ireland, and Elsewhere* (Dublin: Hodges and Smith, 1847), pp. 1–50; Robert James Graves, *A System of Clinical Medicine* (Dublin: Fannin, 1843), pp. 41–2, 45.

5 William A. R. Thomson, ed., *Black's Medical Dictionary* (London: Adam and Charles Black, thirty-fourth ed., 1984), pp. 758–9, 920; William P. Mac-Arthur, 'Medical history of the famine', in R. Dudley Edwards and T. Desmond Williams, eds, *The Great Famine: Studies in Irish History, 1845–52* (New York: New York University Press, 1957; reprinted Dublin: Lilliput Press, 1994), pp. 265–8; William O'Brien, 'The fevers of the great famine', *Journal of the Irish Colleges of Physicians and Surgeons,* 10 (July 1980), pp. 46–9; John D. Post, *Food Shortage, Climatic Variability, and Epidemic Disease in Pre-Industrial Europe. The Mortality Peak in the Early 1740s* (Ithaca and London: Cornell University Press, 1985), pp. 228–233.

6 Post, *Food shortage,* pp. 26–7, 270–4

7 Kennedy, *Observations on the Connexion between Famine and Fever in Ireland,* pp. 36–7.

8 John O'Brien, *Observations on the Acute and Chronic Dysentery of Ireland; Containing a Historical View of the Progress of the Disease in Ireland, with an Enquiry into its Causes, and an Account of its Symptoms and Mode of Treatment; with a Report of Selected Cases* (Dublin: Hodges and McArthur, 1822), p. 6.

9 *Black's Medical Dictionary,* pp. 290–2; MacArthur, 'Medical history of the famine', pp. 268–9.

10 E. Margaret Crawford, 'Subsistence crises and famines in Ireland', in E. Margaret Crawford, ed., *Famine: the Irish Experience, 900–1900. Subsistence Crises and Famines in Ireland* (Edinburgh: John Donald, 1989), p. 205; Kennedy, *Observations on the Connexion between Famine and Fever in Ireland,* p. 37.

11 *The Groans of Ireland in a Letter to a Member of Parliament* (Dublin, 1741), quoted in Michael Drake, 'The Irish demographic crisis of 1740–41', in T. W. Moody, ed., *Historical Studies, vi* (London: Routledge and Keegan Paul, 1968), p. 103.

12 *Ibid.,* pp. 101–124; David Dickson, 'The gap in famines: a useful myth', in Crawford, ed., *Famine,* pp. 97–8.

13 F. Barker and J. Cheyne, *An Account of the Rise, Progress, and Decline of the Fever lately Epidemical in Ireland, together with Communications from Physicians in the Provinces, and Various Official Documents* (Dublin: Hodges and McArthur, 2 vols., 1821).

14 William Harty, *An Historic Sketch of the Causes, Progress, Extent, and Mortality of the Contagious Fever Epidemic in Ireland during the Years 1817, 1818, and 1819: with Numerous Tables, Official Documents, and Private Communications, Illustrative of its General History and of the System of Management Adopted for its Suppression* (Dublin: Hodges and McArthur, 1820).

15 Barker and Cheyne, *Fever,* vol. 1, pp. 40–1, 309, 311, 319–320, 324, 328, 346–7, 392, 407, 420, vol. 2, pp. 36–7, 40–1, 68–71, 147, 152, 157.

16 *Ibid., Fever,* vol. 1, pp. 48–58, 139–141. See also, *First report of the General Board of Health* (Dublin, 1822), pp. 73–7.

17 Barker and Cheyne, *Fever,* vol. 1, pp. 178, 325–6, 332.

18 *First report of the General Board of Health,* pp. 72–3.

19 Harty, *An Historic Sketch of the ... Contagious Fever Epidemic in Ireland,* pp. 10–38.

20 K. H. Connell, *The Population of Ireland, 1750–1845* (Oxford: Clarendon Press, 1950), pp. 230–2.

21 Barker and Cheyne, *Fever,* 1, pp. 62, 94.

22 Cormac Ó Gráda, *Ireland. A New Economic History, 1780–1939* (Oxford: Clarendon Press, 1994), pp. 178–187.

23 *Dublin Quarterly Journal of Medical Science,* 4 (1847), pp. 130–4.

24 *Report of the Commissioners of Health, Ireland, on the Epidemics of 1846 to 1850* (Dublin, 1852), pp. 16–17.

25 'Report upon the recent epidemic fever in Ireland', *Dublin Quarterly Journal of Medical Science*, 7 (1849), pp. 64–126, 340–404, 8 (1849), pp. 1–86, 270–339.

26 Ó Gráda, *Ireland: A New Economic History*, p. 185.

27 *Dublin Medical Press*, 3 November 1847, p. 276.

28 *Report of the Commissioners of Health*, p. 16.

29 *Dublin Quarterly Journal of Medical Science*, 7 (1849), pp. 95–6. For the medical mortality, see Peter Froggatt, 'The response of the medical profession to the great famine', in Crawford, ed., *Famine*, pp. 134–156.

30 *Ibid.*, p. 90; *Dublin Medical Press*, 19 January 1848, pp. 33–5.

31 Daniel Donovan, 'Observations on the peculiar diseases to which the famine of last year gave origin, and on the morbid effects of insufficient nourishment', *Dublin Medical Press*, 2 February, 1 March, 3 May 1848, pp. 67–8, 129–132, 275–8. See also, *Ibid.*, 17 November 1847, pp. 306–7.

32 *Ibid.*, 9 February 1848, pp. 86–7. See also, *Ibid*, 17 November 1847, pp. 306–7, 19 January 1848, pp. 33–5; *Dublin Quarterly Journal of Medical Science*, 7 (1849), pp. 100–104, 368–9; *Report of the Commissioners of Health*, p. 13.

33 *Dublin Medical Press*, 19 January 1848, pp. 33–5.

34 *Report of the Commissioners of health*, pp. 21–2, 48–9.

35 *Dublin University Magazine*, 40 (1852), p. 658

36 *Dublin Medical Press*, 24 March 1847, pp. 186–7, 2 June 1847, p. 342, 2 February 1848, pp. 68–9.

37 See, for instance, Corrigan, *On Famine and Fever*, p. 26; *Poor Inquiry (Ireland), appendix B, part 2, supplement*, pp. 1–262; *Second report from the select Committee on the Contagious Fever in Ireland*, British Parliamentary Papers, 1818 (359) vii, pp. 15–16.

IDEOLOGY AND THE FAMINE

1 The focus of criticism has been *The Great Famine: Studies in Irish History* (Dublin, 1956), edited by R.D. Edwards and T.D. Williams. See Cormac Ó Gráda, 'Making History in the Ireland of the 1940s and 1950s: the saga of the Great Famine', *The Irish Review*, 12 (Spring/Summer 1992), pp. 87–107; James S. Donnelly, Jr, 'The Great Famine: its interpreters, old and new', *History Ireland*, I/3 (Autumn 1993), pp. 27–33.

2 Brendan Bradshaw, 'Nationalism and historical scholarship in modern Ireland', *Irish Historical Studies*, XXVI (1989), pp. 329–51.

3 See James S. Donnelly, 'The administration of relief, 1847–51', in W.E. Vaughan (ed.), *A New History of Ireland, V: Ireland Under the Union, I, 1801–70* (Oxford, 1989), pp. 316–31. This criticism has not yet trickled down into many survey texts, see, for example, D. George Boyce, *Nineteenth-century Ireland: the search for stability* (Dublin, 1990), chapter 4.

4 Cecil Woodham-Smith, *The Great Hunger: Ireland 1845–1849* (London, 1987 edn), pp. 58–61.

5 Ó Gráda's seminal work on the Irish famine is somewhat marred by a desire to add Nassau Senior and James Wilson to the list of demonised individuals, while seeing no way of measuring their influence. Close political analysis may serve as a suitable (if non-quantitative) method for doing so. See Cormac Ó Gráda, *Ireland: a New Economic History 1780–1939* (Oxford, 1994), pp. 191–4.

6 Clarendon to Russell, 10 August 1847, Clarendon Deposit Irish, Bodleian

Library, Oxford, letterbook I.

7 Charles Greville, *A Journal of the Reign of Queen Victoria, from 1837 to 1852* (3 vols, London, 1885), II, pp. 275–8 (29 March 1845).

8 D. P. O'Brien, *The Classical Economists* (Oxford, 1975), p. 48; G. Himmelfarb, *The Idea of Poverty: England in the early industrial age* (London, 1984), pp. 130–44.

9 For a concise statement of the classical position, see N. W. Senior, 'Ireland', *Edinburgh Review*, LXXIX (1844), pp. 189–266.

10 *Third Report of the Commission for Inquiring into the Condition of the Poorer Classes in Ireland*, British Parliamentary Papers 1836 [43], XXX, 1. For Whately's efforts to use state education to promote economic orthodoxy in Ireland, see Thomas A. Boylan and Timothy P. Foley, *Political Economy and Colonial Ireland: the Propagation and Ideological Function of Economic Discourse in the Nineteenth Century* (London, 1992), pp. 67–99.

11 Earl of Rosse, *Letters on the State of Ireland* (second edn, London, 1847), p. 10; Oliver MacDonagh, *States of Mind: a Study of Anglo-Irish Conflict 1780–1980* (London, 1983), p. 38.

12 N. W. Senior, *A Letter to Lord Howick on a Legal Provision for the Irish Poor* (London, 1831), pp. 11–54.

13 Senior's bitterness at his marginalisation is expressed in 'The relief of Irish distress in 1847 and 1848', *Edinburgh Review*, LXXXIX (1849), pp. 221–68.

14 W. D. Grampp, *The Manchester School of Economics* (Stanford, 1960), pp. 1–5.

15 See John Bright, in *Hansard*, third series, XCV, pp. 986–8 (13 December 1847).

16 See Thomas Campbell Foster, *Letters on the Condition of the People of Ireland* (London, 1846); Alexander Somerville, *Letters from Ireland during the Famine of 1847* (ed. K. D. M. Snell, Blackrock, 1994), pp. 181–2.

17 William Thomas Thornton, *Over-population and its Remedy* (London, 1846); Ann P. Robson and John M. Robson (eds), *John Stuart Mill, Collected Works, vol. XXIV: Newspaper writings, 1835–47* (London, 1986), pp. 879–1035; George Poulett Scrope, *How is Ireland to be Governed?* (second edn, London, 1846).

18 'Third report ... on the land question', *Report of the Parliamentary Committee of the Loyal National Repeal Association of Ireland* (2 vols, Dublin, 1845), II, pp. 319–27.

19 Peter Mandler, *Aristocratic Government in the Age of Reform: Whigs and Liberals, 1830–1852* (Oxford, 1990), pp. 13–22, 55–71. For a Foxite manifesto on Irish policy, see *The Government of Ireland: the Substance of a Speech ... by the Right Honourable Lord John Russell* (London, 1839)

20 *Hansard*, LXXXVIII, p. 346 (5 August 1846: Russell).

21 For a more detailed account of the role of Providentialism in the Famine, see Peter Gray, 'Potatoes and Providence: British Government's responses to the Great Famine', *Bullán: an Irish Studies Journal*, I/1 (Spring 1994), pp. 75–90.

22 Hugh McNeile, *The Famine a Rod of God; its provoking Cause, its Merciful Design* (Liverpool, 1847); John Poynder, *The late fast* (London, [1847]).

23 *Illustrated London News*, 20, 27 March 1847; John Travers Robinson, *A Sermon Preached ... in aid of the Famine Relief Fund for Ireland and Scotland* (Teignmouth, 1847); Charles Trevelyan, *The Irish Crisis* (London, 1848), pp. 115–29.

24 James Martineau, *Ireland and her Famine* (London [1847]); A. Peyton to Russell, 20 March 1847, Russell Papers, Public Record Office, London, 30/22/6B, fols 271–2; Greville, *Journal*, III, pp. 71 (23 March 1847).

25 Boyd Hilton, *The Age of Atonement: the Influence of Evangelicalism on Social and Economic Thought, 1795–1865* (Oxford, 1988), pp. 16–18.

26 See Gray, 'Potatoes and Providence', pp. 78–83; Boyd Hilton, 'Peel: a reappraisal', *Historical Journal*, XXII (1979), pp. 609–14.

27 See, for example, [Anon], *God's Laws Versus Corn Laws: a Letter ... From a Dignitary of the English Church* (London, 1846).

28 *The Times*, 8, 22 September 1846.

29 Trevelyan to Monteagle, 9 October 1846, Monteagle Papers MS 13,397/11, National Library of Ireland, Dublin.

30 See Robert Stewart, *The politics of Protection: Lord Derby and the Protectionist Party, 1841–52* (Cambridge, 1971), pp. 101–4. Unlike Peel and most other liberals, Russell was not unsympathetic to the principle of the bill, and defended a later grant of £620,000 to Irish railways as 'only an act of justice' to Ireland, *Hansard*, XC, pp. 65–8 (16 February 1847: Peel), LXXXIX, pp. 802–8 (4 February), XCIII, p. 989, (28 June: Russell).

31 [Archibald Alison], 'Lessons from the Famine', *Blackwood's Edinburgh Magazine*, LXI, no. 378 (April 1847), p. 524.

32 Dorothy Thompson, 'Ireland and the Irish in English Radicalism before 1850', in James Epstein and Dorothy Thompson (eds), *The Chartist Experience: Studies in Working-class Radicalism and Culture, 1830–1860* (London, 1982), pp. 120–51; David N. Buckley, *James Fintan Lalor: Radical* (Cork, 1990), p. 22.

33 'Ireland and the Irish. By a native', *Douglas Jerrold's Shilling Magazine*, IV, no. xix (July 1846), pp. 27–39, 'The moral of the potato rot', *ibid.*, V, no. xxvii (March 1847), pp. 213–21.

34 See Peter Gray, 'British politics and the Irish land question, 1843–1850' (unpublished Ph.D. dissertation, University of Cambridge, 1992), chapter 4.

35 Sir R. Routh to Trevelyan, 13 August 1846, Deputy Commissary-General Dobree to Trevelyan, 14 September 1846, *Correspondence, from July 1846 to January 1847, Relating to the Measures Adopted for the Relief of Distress in Ireland* (Commissariat series), British Parliamentary Papers 1847 [761], LI, pp. 7–8, 73–4

36 The best account of administrative thought in the Famine period is in R. J. Montague, 'Relief and reconstruction in Ireland 1845–9: a study of public policy during the Great Famine' (unpublished D.Phil. dissertation, University of Oxford, 1976).

37 Bessborough and Russell were aware that public works would prove futile if the market failed to provide food at prices in line with wages, but both failed to challenge the Treasury dogma that parliament could not regulate the price of grain, Bessborough to Russell, 13 September 1846, Wood to Russell, 25 September 1846, Russell Papers, Public Records Office, London 30/22/5C fols 144–8, 326–7; Russell to Bessborough, 15 October, G.P. Gooch (ed.), *The Later Correspondence of Lord John Russell, 1840–78* (2 vols, London, 1925), I, p. 154.

38 See James S. Donnelly, Jr., 'The administration of relief, 1846–7', in W. E. Vaughan (ed.), *A New History of Ireland, Vol. V* (Oxford, 1989), pp. 294–9.

39 Robert Collins, *Two Letters Addressed to the Rt. Hon. Henry Labouchere ... on the Extreme Destitution of the Poor* (Dublin, 1846).

40 [N. W. Senior], 'Proposals for extending the Irish poor law', *Edinburgh*

Review, LXXXIV (1846), pp. 267–314.

41 Russell to Wood, 15 October 1846, Hickleton Papers, A4/56/1; Russell memo on the state of Ireland, July 1847, Russell Papers, Public Records Office, London 30/22/6D, fols 84–7.

42 Diary of Earl Grey, 25 January 1847, Grey Papers, Durham University; Trevelyan, *Irish Crisis*, pp. 158–66, 183–91.

43 Russell to Bessborough, 2 October 1846, Bessborough to Russell, 4 October, Russell Papers, Public Records Office, London 30/22/5D, fols 38–41, 46–7; Wood to Grey, 30 September 1846, Hickleton Papers, A4/195/1.

44 Labouchere to Russell, 11, 16 December 1846, Russell Papers, Public Records Office, London 30/22/5F, fols 151–2, 195–6; *The Times*, 24 December 1846.

45 Larcom memo, January 1847, Larcom papers, National Library of Ireland, Dublin, MS 7745.

46 Bessborough to Russell, 2 January 1847, Russell to Bessborough, 5 January, Russell Papers, Public Records Office, London 30/22/6A, fols 19–20, 48–9. Russell had earlier expressed the view that pressure from British public opinion would render some extension of the Irish poor law inevitable in 1847, Russell to Lansdowne, 2 December 1846, Gooch, *Later Correspondence of Lord John Russell*, I, pp. 162–3.

47 *The Times*, 26 January 1847; *Morning Chronicle*, 26, 28 January 1847; [Anon], *Irish Improvidence Encouraged by English Bounty; Being a Remonstrance against the Government Projects for Irish Relief* (London, [1847]).

48 Clarendon to G. Grey, 22 March 1848, Clarendon Deposit Irish, letterbook II; *Hansard*, XC, pp. 1049–50 (8 March 1847).

49 See Gray, 'British politics', pp. 160–74.

50 Bessborough to Russell, 11 September, 8 December 1846, Russell Papers, Public Records Office, London 30/22/5C, fols 116–19, 5F, fols 98–9; Russell to Clarendon, 10 November 1847, Clarendon Deposit Irish box 43

51 Senior to (Whately), 20 April 1847, Monteagle Papers, MS 13,397/10.

52 Wood to Russell, 11 April, 1847, Russell Papers, Public Rrecords Office, London 30/22/6C, fols 68–70; Broughton Diary, 14 February 1847, British Library, London, Add. MSS 43,497, fols 109–10; G. Poulett Scrope, *Reply to the speech of the Archbishop of Dublin* (London, 1847).

53 This seems to have been Gregory's intention, see *Hansard*, XCI, pp. 585–7 (29 March 1847).

54 Russell to Bessborough, 1 March, Lansdowne to Russell [March 1847], Russell Papers, Public Records Office, London 30/22/6B, fols 172–3, 338–41.

55 *Copies of the Correspondence ... as to the Construction of the 10th Section of the Act 10 Vict. c. 31*, British Parliamentary Papers 1847–8 [442], LIII, pp. 519–23; Clarendon to Clanricarde, 7 June 1848, Clanricarde Papers, bundle 48, West Yorkshire Archive Service, Leeds.

56 John Prest, *Lord John Russell* (London, 1972), pp. 262–3.

57 Russell to Clarendon, 2 August 1847, Clarendon Deposit Irish box 43.

58 Wood to Clarendon, 15 August 1847, Hickleton Papers, A4/185/2; James Ward, *Remedies for Ireland* (London, 1847), pp. 5–7; *The Times*, 14, 24 August 1847.

59 Trevelyan to Wood, 28 July 1847, Hickleton Papers, A4/185/2

60 Russell to Clarendon, 17 November 1847, Clarendon Deposit Irish box 43.

61 Clarendon to Wood, 30 March 1848, *ibid*, letterbook II; Wood to Clarendon, 3 April, Hickleton Papers, A4/185/2.

62 Russell memo, 30 March 1848, Russell Papers, Public Records Office, London 30/22/7B, fols 158–61; Broughton Diary 1 April, Add. MSS 43,752, fol. 15.

63 See *The Times*, 22 September 1846, 2 December 1848.

64 *Ibid*, 11 December 1847; Greville, *Journal*, III, pp. 207–8 (21 July 1848).

65 *The Times*, 9 September, 4 October 1848.

66 Wood and Prince Albert initially regarded Clarendon as one of the 'Grey party', Prince Albert memo, 6 July 1846, A.C. Benson and Viscount Esher (eds), *Letters of Queen Victoria ... 1837–1861* (3 vols, London, 1907), II, p. 102; Wood to Clarendon 19 July 1847, Hickleton Papers, A4/185/2.

67 Clarendon to Russell, 10 November 1847, Clarendon Deposit Irish letter-book I.

68 Russell memo, 8 September 1848, *ibid*, box 43.

69 Russell to Clarendon, 5 February 1849, *ibid*.

70 Greville to Clarendon, 3 June 1848, Clarendon Papers, Bodleian Library, Oxford, c. 521.

71 Russell to Clarendon, 20 December 1848, 19 October 1849, Clarendon Deposit Irish box 26; *Hansard*, CVIII, pp. 823–33 (15 February 1850).

72 Clarendon to Russell, 6 January 1849, Clarendon Deposit Irish letterbook III. His specific objection was to Wood and Grey's insistence on 'letting things take their course' regardless of social consequences, and their dogmatic rejection of assisted emigration as expressed in Grey's memo 'Remarks on emigration, poor law and Ireland', 18 December 1848, Grey Papers.

73 *Hansard*, CIII, pp. 179–92 (5 March 1849), CIV, pp. 87–117 (30 March 1849); Gray, 'Potatoes and Providence', p. 87.

74 Montague, 'Relief and reconstruction', pp. 222–6, 229.

75 Wood to Bessborough, 16 September 1846, Hickleton Papers, A4/185/1. Even the most humanitarian Quaker observers agreed that this was the key to Irish regeneration, see [Jonathan Pim], *Observations on the Evils Resulting to Ireland from the Insecurity of Title and the Existing Laws of Real Property* (Dublin, 1847), pp. 5–17; William Bennett, *Narrative of a Recent Journey of Six Weeks in Ireland* (London, 1847), pp. 145–50.

76 Clarendon to Russell, 12 March 1849, Clarendon Deposit Irish letterbook IV. Both Clarendon and Russell sympathised and gave Twisleton's opinions 'great weight', Russell to Clarendon, 13 March, *ibid*, box 26.

77 S. Godolphin Osborne, *Gleanings in the West of Ireland* (London, 1850), pp. 254–6.

78 *Hansard*, LXXXVIII, pp. 777–8 (17 August 1846: Russell).

79 Anthony Trollope, *The Irish Famine: Six Letters to the Examiner 1849–50* (ed. L. O'Tingay, London, 1989), p. 29.

THE ROLE OF THE POOR LAW DURING THE
      FAMINE

1 T. R. Malthus, *An Essay on the Principle of Population* (first published 1798, reprinted, Cambridge 1992), Book III, p. 127, Book IV, p. 268, Appendix, p. 356 (although Malthus thought that Sweden rather than Ireland provided a better example of the dangers of population increase, see, for example, Note in answer to Mr Godwin in 1825 edition of *Principles*; Nassau Senior, *Proposals for Extending the Poor Law*, first printed in *Edinburgh Review*, reprinted in *Ireland. Journals, Conversations and Essays* (Longman, 1868), Vol. I, pp. 134–191.

2 *Third Report of His Majesty's Commissioners for Inquiry into the Condition of the Poorer Classes in Ireland 1836* (35), xxx.

3 George Nicholls, undertook a nine week tour in 1837, but returned for a further brief visit following the death of William IV. *Report by George Nicholls to his Majesty's Secretary of State for the Home Department*, 69, 1837, LI.

4 Letter from Nicholls to Lord John Russell, *Report by George Nicholls ... on Poor Laws, Ireland*, pp. 9–11.

5 1 and 2 Vic. c. 56. An Act for the more Effectual Relief of the Destitute Poor In Ireland (31 July 1838); M. E. Rose, *The Relief of Poverty, 1834–1914* (Second ed. 1986).

6 Senior, *Journals*, Vol. 1, p. 175.

7 N. C. Edsall, *The Anti-Poor Law Movement, 1834–44* (Manchester, 1974).

8 Poor Law Commissioners to D. Phelan, Assistant Poor Law Commissioner (APLC) (Letter Books of J. Burke, NAD) 18 October 1842; Minute Books of Dunfanaghy Workhouse, 1845; Eleventh and Twelfth Annual Reports of Poor Law Commissioners, 1845 and 1846.

9 George Nicholls, *A History of the English Poor Law* (London, 1898 edn).

10 George Nicholls, *A History of the Irish Poor Law* (London, 1856), pp. 309, 357.

11 Minute of Poor Law Commissioners, quoted in *Report of the Royal Commission on the Poor Laws and Relief of Distress – Report on Ireland*, 1909 (4630), xxxvii, p. 13

12 Report to Chief Secretary, Chief Secretary's Office Registered Papers, 73/4145 (Chief Secretary's Office, Registerial Papers, National Archive, Dublin) 7 January 1839; *Ibid.*, R. Hall, APLC, 1097, 20 June 1842; Nicholls, *Irish Poor Law*, p. 258; Minute of Poor Law Commissioners, *Commission on Poor Relief, 1909*, p. 13; Eighth Annual Report of Poor Law Commissioners, 1842, p. 50.

13 Circular of Poor Law Commissioners, Appendix to Twelfth Annual Report, 1846, 29 December 1845, p. 102; E. Twistleton to Graham, Public Records Office, London, Home Office 45, 1080, 16 December 1845.

14 Wendy Hinde, *Richard Cobden* (London, 1987), pp. 144–169.

15 Twelfth Annual Report of Poor Law Commissioners, 1846, pp. 37–41; Jonathan Sperber, *The European Revolutions, 1848-51* (1994), pp. 106-7.

16 Lord Heytesbury to Peel, Lord Mahon and E. Cardwell (eds) *Memoirs of the Right Honourable Sir Robert Peel*, p. 134; *Freemans Journal*, 19 December 1845.

17 Routh to Trevelyan, 14 February 1847, *Correspondence Explanatory of the Measures Adopted by Her Majesty's Government for the Relief of Distress arising from the Failure of the Potato Crop in Ireland*, 1847 (735), pp. 33-7.

18 C. Kinealy, 'The Irish Poor Law', 1838–62, unpublished Ph.D thesis (Trinity College, Dublin 1984), Chapter one.

19 Sir James Graham to Lord Lieutenant, Public Records Office, London, HO 45, 1080, box 1, 7 May 1846.

20 Act 6 & 7 Vic. c. 92 (24 August 1843); Graham to Lord Lieutenant, 7 May 1846, Public Records Office, London, Home Office, 45, 7 May 1846.

21 Summary of weekly returns of paupers in the workhouses in Ireland, Appendix to Twelfth Annual Report, p. 168.

22 Minute Books of Lowtherstown (Irvinestown) Guardians, 29 October 1845, 12 November 1845, 7 January 1846.

23 Minute Book of Inishowen union, 16 November 1845; Minute Book of Belfast union, 11 November 1845; Twelfth Annual Report, 1846, p. 51.

24 Circular to all Boards of Guardians in Ireland, 10 September 1846.

25 Poor Law Commissioners to Labouchere, Chief Secretary's Office, Registerial Papers (National Archive, Dublin) 0.18344, 17 October 1846; *Roscommon and Leitrim Gazette*, 27 March 1847; Appendix to Thirteenth Annual Report, 1847.

26 Twistleton to Sir George Grey, *Copies of Extracts of Correspondence Relating to Union Workhouses in Ireland* (first series), 1847 (766) lv, p. 13.

27 C. Kinealy, *This Great Calamity; The Irish Famine, 1845–52* (Dublin 1994), Chapter 3.

28 Minute Book of Galway union, 30 September 1846.

29 Grey to Twistleton, 21 December 1846, *Correspondence Relating to Union Workhouse*, pp. 12–13.

30 This idea had been forcefully argued by Edmund Burke in *Thoughts on Scarcity* (London 1795). This pamphlet, which was written during a subsistence crisis in England, was admired by leading members of the Whig administration. Charles Trevelyan, the Secretary at the Treasury, sent copies of this to relief officials in Ireland during the Famine.

31 *The Times*, 4 January, 7 January 1847.

32 *Dublin Evening Mail*, 7 April 1847.

33 Act 10 Vic. cap. 7.

34 Not all of this money was spent. Only £1,724,631–17–3 of the £2,255,000 voted by parliament was spent. Of this amount, £953,355–17–4 had to be repaid by the local unions.

35 Nassau W. Senior, *Ireland. Journals, Conversations and Essays* (London 1868), vol. 1, p. 209.

36 Kevin B. Nowlan 'The Political Background' in R. Dudley Edwards and T. Desmond Williams *The Great Famine. Studies in Irish History* (New York 1957), pp. 160–163.

37 C. Trevelyan, *The Irish Crisis* (London 1848), pp. 116–19

38 Twistleton to Trevelyan, Public Records Office, London, T.64 370 c/4, 27 February 1848.

39 An Act to Make Further Provision for the Relief of the destitute Poor in Ireland, 10 Vic. cap. 31 (8 June 1847).

40 *Ibid.*, Section 10.

41 An Act for the Further Amendment of an Act for the more effectual Relief of the Destitute Poor in Ireland, 24 August 1843.

42 *Copies of Correspondence upon which the Commissioners of the Poor Laws in Ireland took Legal Advice as to the Construction of the Tenth Section of the Act 10 Vic. c. 31; and of the Case Submitted by them to Counsel; and of the Circular Letter of the Commissioners Issued thereon*, British Parliamentary Papers, 1847–48, liii, 519.

43 Home Secretary to Poor Law Commissioners, Chief Secretary's Office, Registered Papers 0.8186, 30 June 1848.

44 Memorial of Lord Palmerston to John Russell, 31 March 1848, G.P. Gooch, *The Later Correspondence of Lord John Russell* (London 1925), p. 225.

45 Twistleton to Trevelyan, Public Records Office, London, T.64. 370 B/1, 13 September 1848.

46 Various Annual Reports of Poor Law Commissioners.

47 First, Second, Third and Eleventh Annual Reports of Poor Law Commissioners.

48 Trevelyan, *Irish Crisis*.

49 *Return of all Sums of Money either Granted or Advanced from the Exchequer of*

the *United Kingdom, on Account of the Distress and Famine, or in Aid of the Administration of the Poor Law in Ireland, during the Famine Years 1846, 1847 and 1848, with the Amount of Repayments,* British Parliamentary Papers,1849 (352), p. 48.
50 Twistleton to Home Secretary, Public Records Office, London, Home Office. 45. 2521, 12 February 1849, 19 February 1849.
51 12 and 13 Vic. c. 24.
52 *Hansard's* Parliamentary Debates, col. 62, 1 March 1849.
53 Second Annual Report of Poor Law Commissioners for Ireland.
54 Twistleton to Trevelyan, Public Records Office, London, T.64. 366.A., 24 March 1849.
55 Evidence of Twistleton, *Select Committee on the Irish Poor Law*, British Parliamentary Papers 1849 (209), xv, p. 717.
56 Nicholls, *The Irish Poor Law*, pp. 309, 357.

THE OPERATIONS OF FAMINE RELIEF, 1845–47

1 James S. Donnelly, 'The administration of relief, 1847–51' , in W. E. Vaughan (ed.), *A New History of Ireland*, V: *Ireland under the Union* I, *1801–70* (Oxford 1989), pp. 316–331.
2 John D. Post, *The Last Great Subsistence Crisis in the Western World* (Baltimore and London 1977), p. 114–5.
3 Timothy P. O'Neill, 'The state, poverty and distress in Ireland, 1815–45', Ph.D. thesis, University College, Dublin 1971, pp. 8–45.
4 Amartya Sen, *Poverty and Famines, an Essay on Entitlements and Deprivation* (Oxford 1981); Amartya Sen and Jean Dietz, *Hunger and Public Action* (Oxford 1989).
5 Mary E. Daly, *The famine in Ireland* (Dublin 1986), pp. 33–41.
6 O'Neill, 'The state, poverty and distress'.
7 Desmond Bowen, *The Protestant Crusade in Ireland, 1800–70* (Dublin 1978), p. 83; Desmond Bowen, *Souperism: Myth or Reality?*(Cork 1970), p. 154.
8 The most extreme versions of the above is found in Sir Charles Trevelyan, *The Irish crisis* (London 1850); for others see R. D. Collison Black, *Economic thought and the Irish question, 1817–70* (Cambridge 1960).
9 Cormac Ó Gráda, *Ireland: a New Economic History 1780–1939* (Oxford 1994), pp. 67–104.
10 Boyd Hilton, *The Age of Atonement. The Influence of Envangelicalism on Social and Economic Thought, 1785–1865;* Peter Gray, 'Potatoes and Providence', *Bullán,* 1994.
11 P. M. A. Bourke, 'The extent of the potato crop in Ireland at the time of the famine', in *Statistical and Social Inquiry Society of Ireland Journal*, xx, part 3 (1959–60) pp. 1–35.
12 Austin Bourke, 'The Irish grain trade 1839–48' in Jacqueline Hill and Cormac Ó Gráda (eds), *'The Visitation of God'? The Potato and the Great Irish Famine* (Dublin 1993), pp. 159–169.
13 Thomas P. O'Neill, 'The organisation and administration of relief, 1845–52', in R. D. Edwards, and T. D. Williams (eds), *The Great Famine* (Dublin 1956), pp. 209–222.
14 Cited in O'Neill, 'relief', p. 222.
15 Kevin B. Nowlan, 'The political background', in Edwards and Williams, pp. 141–3.
16 For details see 'Correspondence explanatory of the measures adopted by

her majesty's government for the relief of distress arising from the failure of the potato crop in Ireland', House of Commons 1846 xxxvii; Daly, *Famine in Ireland*, pp. 71–75.

17 Donal A. Kerr, *'A nation of beggars'? Priests, People and Politics in Famine Ireland 1846–1852* (Oxford 1994), p. 31.

18 Daly, *Famine*, pp. 71–2; O'Neill, 'relief', pp. 223–5.

19 Daly, *Famine*, pp. 71–2; O'Neill, 'relief', pp. 223–5; Peter Solar, 'The Great Famine was no Ordinary Subsistence Crisis', in E. M. Crawford, (ed.), *Famine: the Irish experience, 900–1900* (Edinburgh), p. 123.

20 Bourke 'Irish grain trade'; Solar, 'The Great Famine was no ordinary subsistence crisis'.

21 Daly, *Famine* , pp. 77–87; Kerr, *'Nation of Beggars'*, pp. 30–68; Patrick Hickey, 'Famine, mortality and emigration: a profile of six parishes in the Poor Law union of Skibbereen, 1846–7', in Patrick O'Flanagan and Cornelius Buttimer, (eds), *Cork: History and Society: Interdisciplinary Essays on the History of an Irish County*, (Dublin 1993), pp. 873–918; *Transactions of the Central Relief Committee of the Society of Friends During the Famine in Ireland in 1846 and 1847* (Dublin 1852), p. 440.

22 *Irish crisis*, p. 4; A. R. G. Griffiths, 'The Irish Board of Works in the famine years', *Historical journal*, xiii, 4 (1970), p. 63.

23 O'Neill, 'relief', p. 232–5.

24 Donnelly, 'The soup kitchens'; 'The administration of relief', in Vaughan, *New History* , pp. 294–329; O'Neill, 'relief', pp. 235–244.

25 Nowlan, 'political background', in Edwards and Williams, pp. 154–69.

THE STIGMA OF SOUPERISM

1 Desmond Bowen, *The Protestant Crusade in Ireland, 1800–70. A Study of Protestant-Catholic Relations Between the Act of Union and Disestablishment* (Dublin and Montreal: 1978), pp. 186–9.

2 For an example of a model study of the intellectual origins and evolution of European racism since the eighteenth century see George A. Mosse, *Towards the Final Solution. A History of European Racism* (Madison, Wisconsin, 1978).

3 Linda Colley, *Britons. Forging the Nation, 1707–1837* (Yale and London, 1992), pp. 12–54.

4 Brian Stanley, *The Bible and the Flag. Protestant Missions and British Imperialism in the Nineteenth and Twentieth Centuries* (Leicester, England, 1990), pp. 55–84.

5 Irene Whelan, 'Evangelical Religion and the Polarisation of Protestant-Catholic Relations in Ireland, 1780–1840', Ph.D. dissertation, University of Wisconsin-Madison, 1994.

6 Fergus O'Farrell, *Catholic Emancipation. Daniel O'Connell and the Birth of Irish Democracy, 1820–30* (Dublin and New York, 1985), pp. 234–57.

7 S. J. Connolly, *Priests and People in Pre-Famine Ireland, 1780–1845* (Dublin and New York, 1982), p. 86.

8 David Hempton and Myrtle Hill, *Evangelical Protestantism in Ulster Society, 1740–1890* (London and New York, 1992), pp. 91–2.

9 J. G. MacWalter, *The Irish Reformation Movement in its Religious, Social and Political Aspects* (Dublin, 1852), p. 170.

10 The most thorough contemporary account of the Dingle Colony is to be found in Mrs D. P. Thompson, *A Brief Account of the Change in Religious Opinion Now Taking Place in Dingle and the West of the County Kerry* (Dublin,

1846). For the career of Thomas Chute Goodman see 'Seamus Goodman (1828–96), Bailitheoir Ceoil' [James Goodman (1828–96), Music Collector], *Journal of the Kerry Archaeological and Historical Society*, vi (1973), pp. 152–71.

11 For a complete account of the Achill Mission see Irene Whelan, 'Edward Nangle and the Achill Mission, 1834–52,' in R. Gillespie and G. Moran, eds., *'A Various Country': Essays in Mayo History, 1500–1900* (Westport, Co. Mayo, 1987), pp. 113–134.

12 According to the evidence of Sean Mhic Chonmhara, a native of Achill who was interviewed by the *Connaught Tribune* in 1934 at the age of eighty-seven, the land purchased by the Rev. Nangle's colony at Dugort was among the best in western Mayo. Existing tenants were evicted if they did not attend Protestant service and their land given to converts; over forty families were said to have been put out in this manner. *Connaught Tribune*, 13 October, 1934.

13 George Ensor, *The New Reformation: Letters Showing the Inutility and Exhibiting the Absurdity of What is Rather Fantastically Termed 'The New Reformation'* Dublin, 1828).

14 At the time of the Rev. Edward Nangle's first visit to Achill in August of 1831, for example, there was a furious controversy raging in Ballina, the consequence of attempts by local Catholic priests to prevent the Protestant-dominated relief committee from entrusting funds to the Baptist Society which had a proselytising mission in the locality. See Whelan, 'Nangle and the Achill mission', p. 121.

15 Thompson, *Dingle Mission*, p. 28. The following comprehensive description of what constituted a 'souper' was provided by Fr Patrick Lavelle of Partry, Co. Mayo: ' ... a person who trafficks in religion by inducing starving creatures to abandon a creed which they believe for one which in their hearts they reprobate, and this for some temporal consideration, be that meal, or money, or soup, or possession of a house and land', *The Report of the Galway Libel case: Lavelle vs. Bole* (Galway, 1860), p. 56.

16 A classic example of the type was Henry Blake who settled in Renvyle in 1811 and wrote an account of his experiences in the area in his *Letters from the Irish Highland of Connemara* in 1825.

17 *Dublin Evening Post*, 29 April 1824.

18 For an account of Bishop Plunket's evangelical sympathies and his record during the famine years and after see Desmond Bowen, *Souperism: Myth or Reality. A Study in Souperism* (Cork, 1970), pp. 160–179.

19 An outline of the proposed colony appeared in a printed circular entitled: 'Connemara Mission and Asylum Under the Approval and Sanction of His Grace the Archbishop of Tuam', (Trinity College Dublin, Rev. Francis Kinkead Papers, Ms. 3207, Item No. 32).

20 MacWalter, *Irish Reformation Movement*, p. 232. The Society for the Conversion of the Jews was the most popular philanthropy among those who subscribed to pre-millenialism. The fact that the Rev. Thomas was secretary of its Irish branch for thirteen years suggests that the Connemara evangelicals did not have to wait to be introduced to apocalyptic prophecy until the Rev. Dallas arrived among them.

21 The most comprehensive account of the anti-Catholic dimensions of evangelicalism in the nineteenth century, and the social and political background against which it evolved is John Wolffe, *The Protestant Crusade in Great Britain, 1829–60* (Oxford, 1991), pp. 1-144.

22 *Ibid.*, pp. 113-4.

23 *Ibid.*, p. 122.

24 William Marrable, *The Rise and Progress of the Irish Church Missions* (Dublin, 1850), pp. 10–11; Bowen, *Protestant Crusade*, pp. 215–9.

25 *Ibid.*, p. 37.

26 John Forbes, *Memorandums Made in Ireland in the Autumn of 1852* (London, 1853), p. 251; Marrable, *Irish Church Missions*, p. 27.

27 Rev. Edward Bickersteth to the Duchess of Manchester, 31 March 1848 (Public Record Office of Northern Ireland, Manchester Papers, D. 1208/0/11).

28 James S. Donnelly, Jr, 'The Administration of Relief, 1847–51', in W. E. Vaughan, ed. *A New History of Ireland* (Vol. V): *Ireland Under the Union, I, 1801-70* (Oxford, 1989), p. 327.

29 Bowen, *Protestant Crusade*, p. 218.

30 Fr Peter Ward, Aughagower, Co. Mayo to Fr Synnott, Archbishop's House, Dublin. 4 April 1848. (Dublin Diocesan Archives, Archbishop's House, Drumcondra, Murray Papers).

31 Fr Timlin P.P., Ballisakenny, Ballina to Fr Synnott, Archbishop's House, Dublin, 26 January 1848; Fr Edward Waldron, P.P. Kilmolara, Kilmaine, Co. Mayo to Fr Synnott, Archbishop's House, Dublin. 31 December 1848.

32 Fr Flannelly, Ballinakill, Clifden to Archbishop Murray, 6 April 1849.

33 Fr Michael Gallagher, Achill, to Fr Synnott, Archbishop's House, Dublin, 28 January 1848.

34 Fr Martin Hart, P.P., Ballycastle to Fr Synnott, Archbishop's House, Dublin, 25 January 1848.

35 Stephen Gwynn, *A Holiday in Connemara* (New York, 1909), pp. 103.

36 Sr (unclear signature), Presentation Convent, Galway to Archbishop Murray, 21 March 1848 (D.D.A. Murray Papers).

37 Edward Dill, *Ireland's Mysteries: The Grand Cause and Cure* (Edinburgh, 1852), p. 23.

38 Fr Michael Enwright, Castletownbere to Fr Synnott, Archbishop's House Dublin, 13 March 1849 (D.D.A. Murray Papers).

39 Forbes, *Memorandums of a Tour*, pp. 252-3.

40 Patrick Hickey, 'A Study of Four Peninsular Parishes in West Cork, 1796–1851,' M.A. thesis, Univesity College, Cork, 1980, p. 543.

41 Henry Wilberforce, *Proselytism in Ireland. The Catholic Defence Association versus the Irish Church Missions on the Charge of Bribery and Corruption. A Correspondence between the Rev. A.R.C. Dallas and the Rev. Henry Wilberforce* (2nd ed., London, 1852), p. 41.

42 *Ibid.*, pp. 17–22.

43 *Freeman's Journal*, 8 July 1851.

44 *Freeman's Journal*, 24 October 1851.

45 Emmet Larkin, 'The Parish Mission Movement in Ireland, 1850–75', paper read at the annual meeting of the American Historical Association, Chicago, Ill., 30 December 1991.

46 *Freeman's Journal*, 12 May 1854.

47 Interview with Mrs Mary A. Henry (nee McGrath) b. 1898, of River Edge, New Jersey, formerly of Ballyconree, Connemara, 11 December 1994.

48 Alannah Heather, *Errislannon. Scenes from a Painter's Life* (Mullingar, 1993).

49 Gwynn, *Holiday in Connemara*, p. 106.

50 Tullycross I.C.A., *Portrait of a Parish. Ballinakill, Connemara* (Renvyle, Co. Galway, 1985) pp. 97–9; Erin Gibbons, ed. *Conomara Faoi Ceilt (Hidden*

Connemara), (Connemara West Press, 1991) pp. 51–2.

MASS EVICTION AND THE GREAT FAMINE

1 For these sharply contrasting views, see James S. Donnelly, Jr, 'The Great Famine: Its Interpreters, Old and New', in *History Ireland*, i, no. 3 (Autumn 1993), pp. 27–33.

2 For an extended discussion of these aspects of the clearances, see my chapter on landlords and tenants during the Great Famine in W. E. Vaughan, ed., *A New History of Ireland*, vol. v, *Ireland under the Union*, part 1, *1801–70* (Oxford, 1989), pp. 332–49.

3 Dr John O'Neill to Valentine Barry, 24 August 1847, Falkiner Papers (in the possession of P. W. Bass and Co., Solicitors, 9 South Mall, Cork).

4 O'Neill to Barry, 13 June 1850 *(ibid.)*.

5 O'Neill to Barry, 5 January 1851 *(ibid.)*.

6 Quoted in *Nation*, 1 January 1848.

7 James S. Donnelly, Jr, ed., 'The Journals of Sir John Benn-Walsh Relating to the Management of His Irish Estates, 1823–64', in *Journal of the Cork Historical and Archaeological Society*, lxxx, no. 230 (July–December 1974), p. 117.

8 *Cork Constitution*, 2 June 1866.

9 Quoted in Donald E. Jordan, Jr, *Land and Popular Politics in Ireland: County Mayo from the Plantation to the Land War* (Cambridge, 1994), p. 111.

10 Quoted *ibid.*, pp. 111–12.

11 *Ibid.*, pp. 112–13. See also *Nation*, 10, 17, 24 June, 1 July 1848.

12 *Nation*, 29 July 1848.

13 See his entry in the *Dictionary of National Biography*.

14 Poor Relief (Ireland) Act, 8 June 1847 (10 Vict., c. 31).

15 Objecting strenuously to the Gregory clause in the House of Commons, the English M.P. George Poulett Scrope declared, 'Its consequence would be a complete clearance of the small farmers in Ireland – a change which would amount to a perfect social revolution in the state of things in that country. Such a change might be desirable if effected by degrees; but to introduce it at once would have the effect of turning great masses of pauperism adrift on the community – a catastrophe which would undoubtedly not be without its effects in this country.' See *Hansard's Parliamentary Debates*, third series, xci, cols. 588–9.

16 *Ibid.*, col. 590.

17 *Ibid.*, cols. 592–3.

18 Canon John O'Rourke, *The Great Irish Famine* (Veritas Publications ed., Dublin, 1989), p. 171.

19 Minute Book, Bandon Board of Guardians, 1847–8, 24 July 1847, p. 308 (in the possession of the Cork Archives Council, Cork); see also James S. Donnelly, Jr, *The Land and the People of Nineteenth-Century Cork: The Rural Economy and the Land Question* (London and Boston, 1975), p. 99.

20 Donnelly, *Cork*, pp. 99–100.

21 *Nation*, 4 March 1848.

22 *Nation*, 29 January, 5 February, 4 March, 3 June, 1 July 1848.

23 For the destruction of tenants' houses on the Blake estate and the ensuing parliamentary controversy, see *Nation*, 26 February, 4, 25 March, 1 April 1848.

24 *Nation*, 25 March 1848.

25 *Nation*, 1 April 1848.

26 *Nation*, 15 April 1848.
27 Quoted in Peter H. Gray, 'British Politics and the Irish Land Question, 1843–1850' (Ph.D. dissertation, Cambridge University, 1992), p. 204.
28 Quoted *ibid.*, p. 205.
29 *Ibid*.
30 *Ibid*.
31 *Nation*, 8 April 1848.
32 Gray, 'British Politics', pp. 205–6.
33 11 & 12 Vict., c. 47.
34 Gray, 'British Politics', pp. 223, 241–2, 326–8.
35 Quoted in *Nation*, 3 June 1848.
36 *Nation*, 10 June 1848.
37 Quoted in *Nation*, 24 June 1848.
38 Quoted in *Nation*, 1 July 1848.
39 Quoted in *Nation*, 8 July 1848.
40 Quoted in *Nation*, 22 July 1848.
41 Quoted in *Nation*, 1 September 1849.
42 *Nation*, 22 April 1848.
43 Quoted in *Nation*, 29 April 1848.
44 *Nation*, 29 July 1848.
45 *Nation*, 1 September 1849.
46 For an account of this notorious case, see Stephen J. Campbell, *The Great Irish Famine: Words and Images from the Famine Museum, Strokestown Park, County Roscommon* (Strokestown, 1994), pp. 39–50.
47 *Nation*, 6 May 1848.
48 Oliver MacDonagh, 'Irish Emigration to the United States of America and the British Colonies during the Famine', in R. D. Edwards and T. D. Williams, eds., *The Great Famine: Studies in Irish History, 1845–52* (New York, 1957), pp. 336–7.
49 *Nation*, 19 February 1848.
50 *Nation*, 8 January 1848.
51 *Nation*, 29 January 1848.
52 Gray, 'British Politics', pp. 269–90.
53 Charles E. Trevelyan, *The Irish Crisis* (London, 1848), p. 201.
54 Hugh McNeile, *The Famine a Rod of God: Its Provoking Cause, Its Merciful Design. A Sermon Preached in St. Jude's Church, Liverpool, on Sunday, February 28, 1847* (London, 1847); see also T. D. Sullivan, *Recollections of Troubled Times in Irish Politics* (Dublin, 1905), p. 4.
55 Sullivan, *Recollections*, pp. 3–4.
56 Katharine Tynan Hinckson, ed., *The Cabinet of Irish Literature: Selections from the Works of the Chief Poets, Orators, and Prose Writers of Ireland* (new ed., 3 vols., London, 1902), iii, pp. 92–4.
57 *Nation*, 8 January 1848.
58 *Ibid*.
59 *Nation*, 1 April 1848.
60 John Mitchel, *The Last Conquest of Ireland (Perhaps)* (Glasgow, n.d.), p. 219.
61 Considered 'the most widely read of Mitchel's works' next to his *Jail Journal*, *The Last Conquest of Ireland (Perhaps)* appeared first as a series of letters published in 1858 in the *Southern Citizen*, a newspaper which he conducted in Knoxville, Tennessee, and later in Washington, D.C., from 1857 to 1859. The letters were 'collected and republished in book form' in the United States in 1860 and in Dublin a year later. See William Dillon, *Life of John*

Mitchel (2 vols, London, 1888), ii, 101, 118. The views which Mitchel expressed in *The Last Conquest* about British government responsibility for mass death during the Great Famine were repeated in his later work, *The History of Ireland from the Treaty of Limerick to the Present Time*, first published in the autumn of 1867 and later reprinted many times on both sides of the Atlantic (*ibid.*, pp. 253–4).

FLIGHT FROM FAMINE

1 Thomas Burke (Drummullen, Catholic parish of Aughrim, Co. Roscommon) to his wife's sister Catherine Burke (Sydney), 27 April 1846. Copies of the Burke letters were kindly supplied by Mr Russell Campbell of Griffith, New South Wales. For analysis of other sequences of Irish-Australian letters, see David Fitzpatrick, *Oceans of Consolation: Personal Accounts of Irish Migration to Australia* (Ithaca, New York, 1995).

2 Thomas Burke to Catherine Burke, 29 May 1847.

3 John Nowlan to Patrick Nowlan, 30 September 1847, in Public Archives of Canada, MG 24 I 22. Part of this passage appears in Kerby Miller, *Emigrants and Exiles: Ireland and the Irish Exodus to North America* (New York, 1985), p. 285.

4 Letters from A. Kelly (Meath), 12 July 1850; J. Phelan, 24 March 1850 [?]; J. Johnston (Antrim), 11 April 1849; Mrs Nolan (King's County), October 1850 [?]; Michael and Mary Rush (Sligo), 6 September 1846. With the exception of the last letter, a copy of which was kindly supplied by Professor Miller, the extracts appear in Miller, *Emigrants and Exiles*, pp. 295, 300, 286, 285.

5 Edward Senior to Select Committee on Poor Removal, *Minutes of Evidence*, Q 2921, in House of Commons Papers, 1854–55 (308), xiii. For more detailed analysis of the structures of emigration, see David Fitzpatrick, *Irish Emigration, 1801–1921* (Dublin, 1984); and 'Emigration, 1801–70', in W. E. Vaughan (ed.), *A New History of Ireland*, vol. v (Oxford, 1989), pp. 562–622.

6 Edward Senior to Select Committee of the House of Lords Appointed to Inquire into the Operation of the Irish Poor Law, *Minutes of Evidence*, Q 1847, in House of Commons Papers, 1849 (192), xvi.

7 Nassau William Senior, *Journals, Conversations and Essays relating to Ireland* (London, 1868), i, p. 284.

8 T. W. C. Murdoch, *ibid.*, Q 9592.

9 J. and E. Taylor, 6 June 1847; Mrs. Nolan (King's County), October 1850 [?]: in Miller, *Emigrants and Exiles*, pp. 299, 293; Michael and Mary Rush (Sligo), 6 September 1846.

10 Mary Burke to Catherine Burke, 30 January 1849 (see note 1).

11 Stephen de Vere, Diary, 16 June 1847, in Trinity College Dublin, MS 5061.

12 Wyly (Adelaide), 2 July 1856.

13 Normile (Maitland), 28 April 1854, 18 April 1862, 3 August 1856. The Normile and Wyly letters are among those analysed in Fitzpatrick, *Oceans*.

14 Copy of broadside in Clarke Collection, National Library of Australia, Canberra (punctuation amended); a version also appears in Georges-Denis Zimmermann, *Songs of the Irish Rebellion* (Dublin, 1967), p. 237. See, however, Miller, *Emigrants and Exiles*, p. 311: 'from 1848 onward, "Poor Pat *Must* Emigrate", as, almost without exception, ballad composers ignored the ambiguities of late-nineteenth-century emigration and portrayed the departed as sorrowing, dutiful, and vengeful exiles'.

1 Patrick Hickey, 'Famine, mortality and emigration' *Cork: History and Society* (eds) P. O'Flanagan and C. G. Buttimer (Dublin, 1993), pp. 873-6.

2 *Famine, Ireland,* Irish University Press series of *British Parliamentary Papers* (Shannon, 1970), vol. 1, p. 72.

3 *Famine, Ireland,* Irish University Press series of *British Parliamentary Papers* (Shannon, 1970), vol. 5, p. 843: *ibid.,* vol. 1, p. 45.

4 Hickey, 'Mortality', pp. 874–9.

5 *Cork Constitution,* 9 January 1847.

6 *Famine, Ireland, Irish University Press series of British Parliamentary Papers* (Shannon, 1970), vol. 5, p. 899.

7 *Ibid.,* vol. 7, p. 398.

8 *Statement of the present condition of the Skibbereen Poor Law Union District,* Skibbereen, 1 February 1847. (Relief Commission Papers.)

9 *Famine, Ireland,* Irish University Press series of *British Parliamentary Papers* (Shannon 1970), vol. 7, p. 416.

10 C. Woodham-Smith, *The Great Hunger: Ireland 1845–9* (London, 1962), p. 165.

11 Patrick Hickey, 'The visit of the artist, James Mahoney, to west Cork in 1847', *O'Mahony Journal,* vol. 12 (Summer 1982), p. 26.

12 Hickey, 'Mortality', pp. 882–3

13 *Famine, Ireland,* Irish University Press series of *British Parliamentary Papers* (Shannon, 1970), vol. 7, p. 515.

14 Hickey, 'Mortality', pp. 883–6.

15 *Famine, Ireland,* Irish University Press series of *British Parliamentary Papers* (Shannon, 1970), vol. 1, p. 115.

16 *Narrative of the Journey from Oxford to Skibbereen During the Year of the Irish Famine by Lord Dufferin and the Hon. G. F. Boyle,* (Oxford, 1847).

17 *Cork Constitution,* 3 April, 1847.

18 J. O'Rourke, *The Great Irish Famine* (Dublin, 1989), p. 271.

19 Hickey, 'Mortality', pp. 889–894.

20 *Ibid.,* p. 911

21 *Cork Examiner,* 4 July 1849.

22 *Famine, Ireland,* Irish University Press series of *British Parliamentary Papers* Shannon, 1970), vol. 3, p. 530.

23 Patrick Hickey, 'A study of four peninsular parishes in west Cork 1796–1855', MA thesis, University College, Cork, (1980), p. 499.

24 Hickey, 'Mortality', p. 873.

25 Cited, *Cork Constitution,* 1 June 1847.

26 Hickey, 'Four Parishes', pp. 500–555.

27 D. Bowen, *Souperism: Myth or Reality?* (Cork, 1980); Traill's letter in *Cork Constitution,* 15 February 1847.

28 Hickey, 'Mortality', pp. 896-903.

29 *Ibid.,* pp. 903–5.

30 *Cork Examiner,* 21 October 1846; 14 December 1847.

31 *Cork Examiner,* 22 January 1847; 26 March 1847.

32 *Southern Reporter,* 30 November 1847.

33 *Cork Examiner,* 19 November 1847.

34 Hickey, 'Four Parishes', pp. 601–4, 570, 607, 584.

35 B. Ó Conchúir, 'Thomas Swanton, réamhchonraitheoir in Iar-Chairbre', *Journal of the Cork Historical and Archaeological Society,* vol. 98 (1993), p. 54.

36 Hickey, 'Four Parishes', p. 539.
37 Patrick Hickey, 'Some famine letters of Dr Traill, Rector of Schull (1830–47)' in *Mizen Journal*, 1994. A daughter of his, Kathleen, married a John Synge and became the mother of J. M. Synge, the playwright.
38 Hickey, 'Mortality', p. 911.
39 Hickey, 'Four Parishes', p. 626.
40 *Cork Examiner*, 8 March 1847; *Cork Constitution*, 3 June 1847.
41 Hickey, 'Four Parishes', pp. 619–21.
42 Hickey, 'Mortality', p. 911.

THE PERSISTENCE OF FAMINE IN IRELAND

1 National Archives, D/T, S1693, S4278A; See also Tim P. O'Neill, 'Minor famines in Galway, 1815–1925' in Ray Gillespie and Gerard Moran, *Galway; a county history* (Geographical publications, Dublin, forthcoming.)
2 *Ibid*.
3 In spite of this a special commissioner of *The Irish Times* said there was need for a fund of £500,000 to supplement the government relief plan in 1925; *Irish Truth*, 14 February 1925, p. 103.
4 Tim P. O'Neill, 'The state, poverty and distress in Ireland, 1815–45', unpublished Ph.D. thesis, University College Dublin, 1971.
5 Hill to Peel, 8 October 1816. (British Library, Add. Mss 40212 f. 168.)
6 H. Robinson, *Memories wise and otherwise* (London, n.d.), p. 112.
7 Larcom Papers, National Library of Ireland, Mss. 7784.
8 *Galway; a county history*.
9 Lavelle to Gerard Balfour, 8 and 23 November 1897. (National Archives, Registered Papers, 1897.)
10 *Freeman's Journal*, 3 August 1859.
11 Carter to Carlisle, 16 May 1860. (National Library of Ireland, Larcom Papers, Mss. 7783.)
12 James S. Donnelly, Jr, 'The agricultural depression of 1859–64' in *Irish Economic and Social History*, 111, 1976, pp. 33–54.
13 Larcom Papers, National Library of Ireland, Mss 7723, 7784 and 7785.
14 *Galway; a county history*.
15 *Ibid*.
16 Report of the Mansion House Relief Committee (Dublin, 1862).
17 James S. Donnelly Jr, *op. cit*, p. 48.
18 W. A. Day, *The Famine in the west* (Dublin, 1862), *passim*; H. Coulter, *The West of Ireland* (London, 1862), *passim*.
19 James S. Donnely Jr, *op. cit.*, p. 49.
20 See for example; T.W. Russell, M.P., *Distressed Ireland: a Tour of Inquiry; with Pen, Pencil and Camera* (London, 1890); *The Daily Express*, 'Mr. Balfour's tour of Connemara and Donegal' (Dublin, 1890).
21 *Galway; a County History*.
22 Gerard Moran, 'Famine and the Land War: relief of distress in Mayo, 1879–81' in *Cathair na Mart: Journal of the Westport Historical Society*, vols 5 and 6, 1985–6, pp. 111–28, 54–67; Catherine Jennings, '1880: a most distressful year in Connemara' in *Journal of the Clifden and Connemara Heritage Group*, vol. 1, no. 1, pp. 37–47.
23 Report of the Local Government Board for Ireland, 1880 British Parliamentary Papers, 1880, XXVII, 1.
24 *Hansard*, June 1879.
25 *Galway; a County History*.

26 Edward Fry, *James Hack Tuke: a memoir* (London, 1899).

27 *Ibid.; The Irish Crisis of 1879–80: Proceedings of the Dublin Mansion House Relief Committee*, 1880.

28 *Galway; a county history*.

29 Records in the Muniments Room, City Hall.

30 *The Irish Crisis of 1879–80: Proceedings of the Dublin Mansion House Relief Committee*, 1880, p. 20–21.

31 Jean Dreze, *Famine prevention in India* (Helsinki, 1988), pp. 23–5.

32 Relief abroad file. National Archives, S13373. Includes Dáil debates on the proposal which was opposed by some T.D.s.

33 *The Irish Crisis of 1879–80: Proceedings of the Dublin Mansion House Relief Committee*, 1880, p. 73.

34 Tim P. O'Neill, 'The food crisis of the 1890s' in Margaret Crawford (ed.) *Famine the Irish experience, 900–1900* (Edinburgh, 1989), p.180.

35 'Relief of distress in Ireland, 1890–1' (National Archives, Mss reports for the Commission on Congestion); See Tim P. O'Neill, 'The food crisis of the 1890s' in Margaret Crawford (ed.) *Famine the Irish Experience, 900–1900* (Edin-burgh, 1989), pp. 176–97.

36 *Galway; a county history; Expenditure on relief of distress, 1879 and 1890.* (National Archives, Registered Papers 1891, 17944.); Mansion House, 1880, pp. 44–7.

37 *The Irish Crisis of 1879–80: Proceedings of the Dublin Mansion House Relief Committee*, 1880, p. 73.

38 The charities firmly backed radical land reform in 1880. *The Irish Crisis of 1879–80: Proceedings of the Dublin Mansion House Relief Committee*, 1880, p. 76. In contrast in 1852 the charities had a more conservative approach to land reform. *Transactions of the Central Committee of the Society of Friends during the Famine in Ireland in 1846 and 1847* (Dublin, 1852), pp. 128a–128c.

39 *The Irish Crisis of 1879–80: Proceedings of the Dublin Mansion House Relief Committee*, 1880, p. 73.

40 Tim P. O'Neill, 'The food crisis of the 1890s' in Margaret Crawford, (ed.), *Famine: the Irish Experience, 900–1900* (Edinburgh, 1989).

41 M. L. Micks, *A history of the Congested Districts Board* (Dublin, 1925); Tim P. O'Neill, 'The food crisis of the 1890s' in Margaret Crawford, *Famine: the Irish Experience, 900–1900* (Edinburgh, 1989), footnote 119.

42 *Relief works*, Ireland, 1890–91, p. 68.

43 James Connolly, 'Famine in Ireland' in *The People*, New York, 28 May 1898. My thanks to Paul Dillon, University College Dublin, for a copy of this newspaper report.

44 Aodh de Blacam, *From a Gaelic Outpost* (Dublin, 1921), *passim*. My thanks to Dr P. Maume, University College Dublin, for bringing this reference to my attention.

45 *Galway; a County History*.

FOLK MEMORY AND THE FAMINE

1 I thank the Head of the Department of Irish Folklore in University College Dublin for his permission to quote from the manuscript collection in this article. RBE (Roinn Bhéaloideas Éireann.)

2 RBÉ 1075: 142–152.

3 RBÉ 1069:182–190.

4 RBÉ 1174:464–468.

5 RBÉ 1075:663–660.

6 RBÉ 1071:77–154.
7 RBÉ 1075:142–152.
8 RBÉ 1072:185–230.
9 RBÉ 1075:179–180.
10 RBÉ 1395:218–230.
11 RBÉ 1069:26–32.
12 RBÉ 1071:1a–73.
13 RBÉ 1071:233–241.
14 RBÉ 1075:67–129.
15 RBÉ 1075:621–627.
16 RBÉ 1075:663–660.
17 RBÉ 1075:200–222.
18 RBÉ 1069:351–378.
19 RBÉ 1074:441–454.
20 RBÉ 1071:77–154.
21 RBÉ 1136:284–288.
22 RBÉ 1072:237–309
23 For a fuller treatment of this material, see Cathal Póirtéir, *Famine Echoes*, (Dublin, Gill and Macmillan, 1995 [forthcoming]), and Cathal Póirtéir, *Glórtha ón Ghorta*, (Baile Átha Cliath, Coiscéim, 1995 [forthcoming]).
24 See also Cormac Ó Gráda, *An Drochshaol, Béaloideas agus Amhráin* Coiscéim, Baile Átha Cliath, 1994 and Roger J. McHugh, The Famine in Irish Oral Tradition in *The Great Famine, Studies in Irish History*, Edwards and Williams (ed.), (Dublin, 1957).

IRISH FAMINE IN LITERATURE

1 William Carleton, *The Black Prophet* [1847], Shannon: Irish University Press, 1972, p. 344.
2 George Steiner, *Literature and Silence: Essays 1958–1966* [1966], new edition: London and Boston: Faber and Faber, 1985, p. 146.
3 Laurence Langer, *The Holocaust and the Literary Imagination*, New Haven: Yale, 1975, p. 8.
4 Paul Ricoeur, *Time and Narrative*, Vol. 3. Translated by Kathleen McLaughlin and David Pellauer, London and Chicago: Chicago University Press, 1988, p. 188.
5 Anthony Trollope, *Castle Richmond* [1860], Oxford: University Press, 1989.
6 *The Saturday Review*, 19 May 1860, pp. 643–4.
7 Mary Anne Hoare, *Shamrock Leaves*, Dublin: McGlashan; London: Partridge & Oakey, 1851, p. 206.
8 Mary Anne Sadlier, *New Lights*, New York: Sadlier, 1853; Elizabeth Hely Walshe, *Golden Hills*, London: Religious Tract Society, 1865, p. 6.
9 Annie Keary, *Castle Daly: The Story of an Irish Home Thirty Years Ago*, London: Macmillan, 1875; reprinted New York: Garland, 1879.
10 Emily Fox ('Toler King'), *Rose O'Connor*, Chicago: Sumner, 1880. Rosa Mulholland, 'The Hungry Death' in W. B. Yeats (ed.) *Representative Irish Tales*, New York and London: Putnam, 1891; reprinted with a foreword by Mary Helen Thuente, Gerrards Cross: Colin Smythe, 1979.
11 Margaret Brew, *The Chronicles of Castle Cloyne*, London: Chapman and Hall, 1884; 1885 edition reprinted New York: Garland, 1979.
12 Louisa Field, *Denis*, London: Macmillan, 1896.
13 *The Saturday Review*, 40 (1875) pp. 470–1.
14 cf. review of *Castle Daly* in *The Graphic* (21 August 1875) and Stanley

Lane-Poole 'Annie Keary' in *Macmillan's Magazine* 42 (1880), p. 263.

15 *The Examiner*, 6 April 1850, p. 217.

16 Chris Morash, *The Hungry Voice: Poetry of the Irish Famine*, Dublin: Irish Academic Press, 1989. The nineteenth-century poems referred to in this text are available in this anthology.

17 Daniel Connolly, *The Household Library of Ireland's Poets*, New York; privately published, 1887.

18 *Gill's Irish Reciter*, edited by J. J. O'Kelly, Dublin: Gill, 1907.

19 Mangan's death has been attributed both to cholera and to starvation; in *Nationalism and Minor Literature: James Clarence Mangan and the Emergence of Irish Cultural Nationalism* (California: University of Press, 1987), David Lloyd notes that Mangan's death took place in the cholera sheds of the Meath Hospital but was diagnosed as due to starvation.

20 Mildred Darby ('Andrew Merry'), *The Hunger: Being Realities of the Famine Years in Ireland, 1845 to 1848*, London: Melrose, 1910, p. 1.

21 Paul Ricoeur, 'Narrative Time', *Critical Inquiry* (1980), p. 179.

22 Liam O'Flaherty, *Famine* [1937], Dublin: Wolfhound, 1979.

23 Seán O'Faolain, review of *Famine, Ireland Today* II. 2 (February 1937), pp. 81–2

24 M. L., review of *Famine, Irish Book Lover* 25 (January–February 1937), pp. 22–3.

25 John O'Rourke, *The History of the Great Irish Famine of 1847 with Notices of Earlier Irish Famines*, 1874. Abridged edition, London: Veritas, 1989, p. 98.

26 M. L., review of *Famine, Irish Book Lover* 25 (January–February 1937), pp. 22–3.

27 Edith Somerville and Martin Ross, *The Big House of Inver*, 1925, London: Quartet Books, 1978, p. 18.

28 John Hewitt, *Out of My Time*, Belfast: Blackstaff, 1974.

29 William Trevor, *Fools of Fortune*, New York: Viking Press, 1983.

30 William Trevor, 'The News from Ireland' from *The News from Ireland and Other Stories* [1986], London: Penguin, 1987, p. 24.

31 William Trevor, *Silence in the Garden*, London: Bodley Head, 1986, p. 118.

32 *cf.* Cormac Ó Gráda, *The Great Irish Famine*, London: Macmillan, 1989, p. 11.

33 Seamus Heaney, *Death of a Naturalist*, London: Faber, 1966.

34 Patrick Kavanagh, *Lough Derg*, The Curragh: Goldsmith, 1978. My warm thanks to John Devitt for this reference.

35 Tom Murphy, *Famine*, Dublin: Gallery Press, 1977.

36 Introduction to *Murphy: Plays One*, London: Methuen, 1992.

37 John Banville, *Birchwood* [1973], London: Paladin, 1987.

38 Eavan Boland, *Outside History*, Manchester: Carcanet, 1990.

39 'That the Science of Cartography is Limited' from Eavan Boland, *In a Time of Violence*, Manchester: Carcanet, 1994.

THE GREAT FAMINE AND TODAY'S FAMINES

1 Edmund M. Hogan, *The Irish Missionary Movement: A Historical Survey 1830–1980* (Dublin, 1990). Note also the remarks of Conor Cruise O'Brien in *To Katanga and Back* (London, 1965), p. 170.

2 Marcel Lachiver, *Les Années de Misère: la Famine au Temps du Grand Roi* (Paris, 1991).

3 Amartya Sen, *Poverty and Famines: An Essay on Entitlement and Deprivation*

(Oxford, 1981), pp. 86, 116, 134, 195–216; S. G. Wheatcroft and R. W. Davies, 'Population', in R. W. Davies, M. Harrison and S. G. Wheatcroft (eds.), *The Economic Transformation of the Soviet Union, 1913–1945* (Cambridge, 1994), pp. 67–77; B. Ashton, K. Hill, A. Piazza and R. Zeitz, 'Famine in China, 1958–61', *Population and Development Review*, Vol. 10 (4) (December 1984), pp. 613–46.

4 Sen, *Poverty and Famines*, pp. 93–6; Stephen Devereux, *Theories of Famine* (London, 1993), pp. 95–7; W. Dando, *The Geography of Famine* (London, 1980), pp. 101–2.

5 The issue is discussed further in my own *Ireland Before and After the Famine* (Manchester, 1993), ch. 3, and *Ireland: A New Economic History 1780–1939* (Oxford, 1994), ch. 8. See also Peter Gray, 'Punch and the Great Famine', *History Ireland*, Vol. 1 (2) (1993), pp. 26–33; R.D. Edwards, *The Pursuit of Reason: 'The Economist' 1843–1993* (London, 1993), ch. 4.

6 See M. Bergman, 'The potato blight in the Netherlands and its social consequences (1845–1847)', *International Review of Social History*, vol. 17 (3), (1967), pp. 391–431.

7 Devereux, *Theories of Famine*, pp. 133–147; information from Trócaire.

8 Sen, *Poverty and Famines*, chs. 6–7. See also Jean Drèze and Amartya Sen, *The Political Economy of Hunger*, 3 vols (Oxford, 1991).

9 For discussion and references, see Devereux, *Theories of Famine*, pp. 76–81.

10 For an overview of the potato's importance and the shortfalls in 1845 and 1846 see Austin Bourke, *The Visitation of God? The Potato and the Irish Famine* (Dublin, 1993), chs. 4–8.

11 On emigration the best source remains Oliver MacDonagh, 'Irish emigration to the United States of America and the British colonies during the famine', in R. D. Edwards and T. D. Williams (eds), *The Great Famine: Studies in Irish History 1845–52* (new edition, Dublin, 1994), pp. 319–390.

12 Stephen J. Campbell, *The Great Irish Famine: Words and Images from the Famine Museum Strokestown Park, County Roscommon* (Strokestown, 1994), pp. 40–2.

13 Sen, *Poverty and Famines*, p. 215.

14 Peter Solar, 'The Great Famine was no ordinary subsistence crisis', in E. M. Crawford (ed.), *Famine: The Irish Experience* (Edinburgh, 1989), p. 118.

15 For an overview see Cormac Ó Gráda, *An Drochshaol: Béaloideas agus Amhráin* (Dublin, 1994).

MORE MERCIER BESTSELLERS

Robert Whyte's 1847 Famine Ship Diary
The Journey of an Irish Coffin Ship

Edited by James J. Mangan

Early on the morning of 20 May 1847, the *Ajax* weighed anchor in Dublin harbour with 258 passengers on board facing a six-week crossing of the North Atlantic to what they hoped would be a land of promise somewhere in Canada. Within a year after landing in Canada one of the passengers of the *Ajax* published a diary that gives remarkable details about the voyage from Dublin to Grosse Île, the Canadian quarantine station. The passenger signed his name as Robert Whyte.

Whyte was a protestant gentleman of education and position as well as a professional writer who intended to publish his diary. The diary appeared in print in 1848. It is signed in the author's own handwriting and features vivid descriptions of the spectacular scenery along the St Lawrence River and striking delineations of the passengers, including the captain and his wife, the crew and the suffering travellers.

Vessels constituting what has aptly been called the coffin fleet transported over 100,000 immigrants in panic flight from famine, fever and conditions involving deprivation of all human rights. Greedy captains and shipping agents were responsible for the crowding which resulted in much suffering and enormous loss of life on the ocean.

The Course of Irish History

Edited by T.W. Moody and F. X. Martin

Though many specialist books on Irish history have appeared in the past fifty years, there have been few general works broadly narrating and interpreting the course of Irish history as a whole, in the light of new research. That is what this book set out to do; and it is a measure of its success that it is still in demand.

The first of its kind in its field, the book provides a rapid short survey, with geographical introduction, of the whole course of Ireland's history. Based on the series of television programmes first transmitted by Radio Telefis Éireann from January to June 1966, it is designed to be both popular and authoritative, concise but comprehensive, highly selective but balanced and fair-minded, critical but constructive and sympathetic. A distinctive feature is its wealth of illustrations.

The present edition is a revised and enlarged version of the original book. New material has been added, bringing the narrative to the I.R.A. ceasefire of 31 August 1994; the bibliography, chronology and index have been augmented accordingly.

The Diary of an Irish Countryman 1827-1835

A Translation of Cín Lae Amhlaoibh by Tomás de Bhaldraithe

This diary is, at one and the same time, both a fascinating social history and the self-portrait of a most sensitive man.

It was written in Irish between 1827 and 1835 by Humphrey O'Sullivan, while living in Callan, Co. Kilkenny. He followed his father's calling when he became a hedgeschool master but later went on to become a prosperous businessman and philanthropist.

No aspect of life escaped his attention, from the dire poverty and degradation of the peasantry to the flora and fauna of the region.

An Introduction to Irish High Crosses

Hilary Richardson and John Scarry

The Irish high crosses are the most original and
interesting of all the monuments which stud the
Irish landscape. They are of international importance in early medieval art. For their period there is
little to equal them in the sculpture of Western
Europe as a whole.

This book gives basic information about the
crosses. A general survey is followed by an inven-
tory to accompany the large collection of photographs which illustrate their variety and richness.
In this way readers will readily have at their dis-
posal an extensive range of the images created in
stone by sculptors working in Ireland over a
thousand years ago.

In the composition of this book the text and
drawings have been the responsibility of Hilary
richardson and John Scarry has been responbsible
for the photographs from the Photographic Collection of the Office of Public Works, Ireland, which
make up the major bulk of the illustrations.

h

t

Things Irish provides the reader with an entertaining and informative view of Ireland, seen through the practices, beliefs and everyday objects that seem to belong specifically to this country. Discarding the usual format of lengthy chapters on a variety of themes, the book uses short descriptive passages on anything from whiskey to standing stones, from May Day to hurling, in order to create a distinctive image of Irish life. The reader is free to roam from topic to topic, from passage to passage, discovering a wealth of new and surprising facts and having a number of misguided beliefs put right.